Straight to the Point

Microsoft Excel 2010

Straight to the Point

Microsoft Excel 2010

Dinesh Maidasani
B.A., Dip. Comp. Sc.

FIREWALL MEDIA
(An Imprint of Laxmi Publications Pvt. Ltd.)

BANGALORE • CHENNAI • COCHIN • GUWAHATI • HYDERABAD
JALANDHAR • KOLKATA • LUCKNOW • MUMBAI • RANCHI
NEW DELHI • BOSTON, USA

Published by :

FIREWALL MEDIA

(An Imprint of Laxmi Publications Pvt. Ltd.)
113, Golden House, Daryaganj,
New Delhi-110002

Phone : 011-43 53 25 00
Fax : 011-43 53 25 28

www.laxmipublications.com
info@laxmipublications.com

First Edition : 2013

OFFICES

✆ **Bangalore**	080-26 75 69 30	✆ **Chennai**	044-24 34 47 26
✆ **Cochin**	0484-237 70 04, 405 13 03	✆ **Guwahati**	0361-251 36 69, 251 38 81
✆ **Hyderabad**	040-24 65 23 33	✆ **Jalandhar**	0181-222 12 72
✆ **Kolkata**	033-22 27 43 84	✆ **Lucknow**	0522-220 99 16
✆ **Mumbai**	022-24 91 54 15, 24 92 78 69	✆ **Ranchi**	0651-221 47 64

FST-3106-150-STTP_MS EXCEL 2010-BAN C—

Typeset at : Kalyani Computer Services, New Delhi. *Printed at* :

Contents

1

Introduction to Microsoft Office 2010

WHAT IS MICROSOFT OFFICE?

There are software and software. But, when you come to using the computer and a single software which can do everything for you, the choice mostly is Microsoft Office. This is not a software but a combination of software which can perform various aspects of your office routines. It can be writing letters, maintaining accounts, keeping databases, making a presentation, etc. This Microsoft Office has a solution for everything.

Office 2010 contains a number of new features, the most notable of which is the entirely new graphical user interface called the Fluent User Interface, replacing the menus and toolbars that have been the cornerstone of Office since its inception with a tabbed toolbar, known as the Ribbon. Office 2010 requires Windows XP with Service Pack 2 or 3, Windows Server 2003 with Service Pack 1 or higher, or Windows Vista.

The 'Ribbon User Interface' is a task-orientated Graphical User Interface (GUI). It features a central menu button, widely known as the 'Office Button'. The Ribbon Interface has been rumoured to be introduced into Microsoft Office 14.

Microsoft FrontPage has been removed from the Office suite entirely. It has been replaced by Microsoft Office SharePoint Designer, which is aimed towards development of SharePoint portals. Its designer-oriented counterpart Microsoft Expression Web is targeted for general web development. However, neither application is included in any of the Office suites.

Speech recognition and handwriting recognition are now part of Windows Vista. Speech and ink components have been removed from Office 2010. Handwriting and speech recognition work with Office 2010 only on Windows Vista or Windows XP Tablet PC Edition. However, XP users can use an earlier version of Office to use speech recognition.

Let us take a look at the various constituents which are there in Microsoft Office 2010.

Microsoft Office Word 2010

A word processing software which allows you to write letters, edit them and print them after formatting it according to your needs. It has all the possible options of a word processor in the

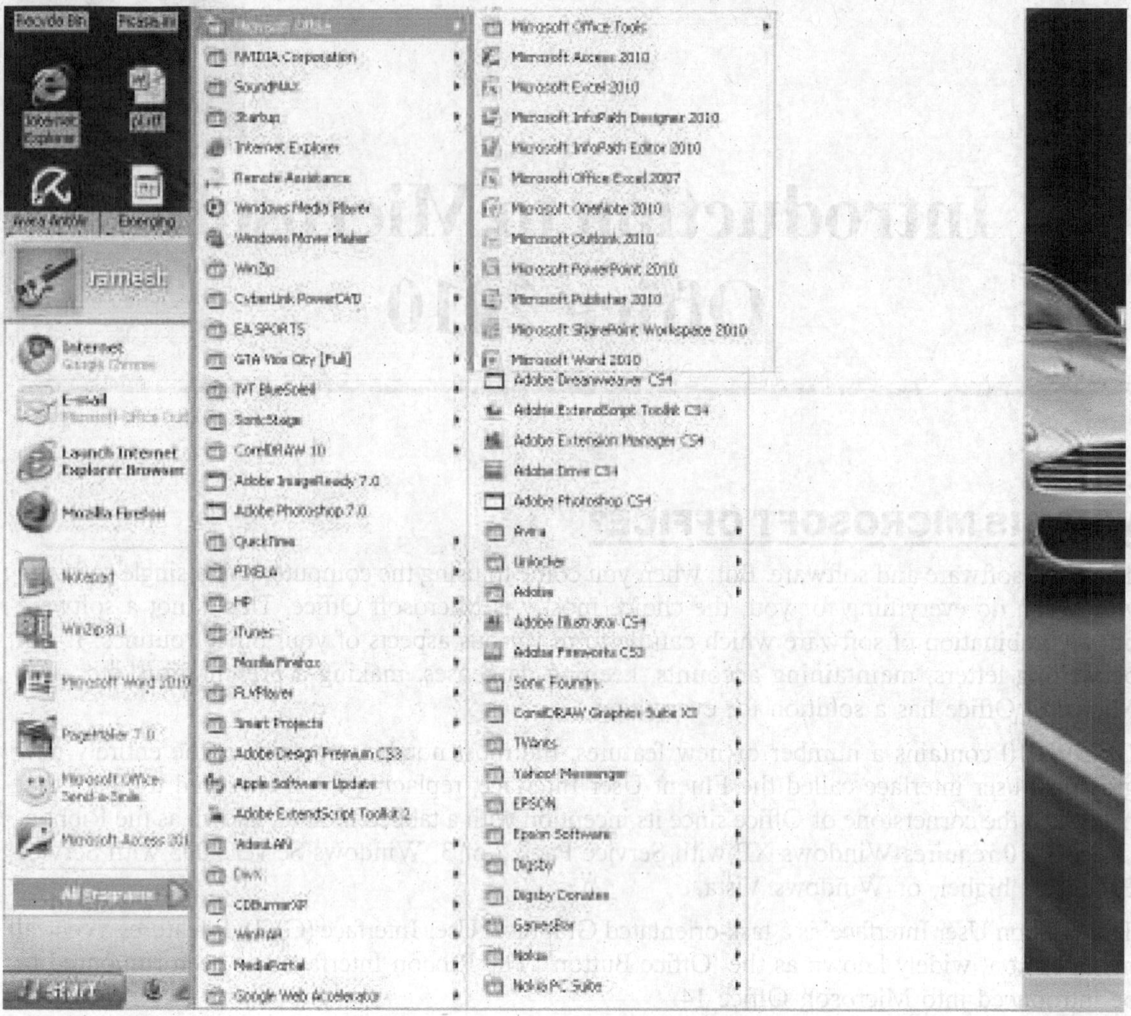

Constituents of Microsoft Office 2010

form of font style and size; indents; line spacing; margins; spell checking and grammar checkers to name a few.

Microsoft Office Excel 2010

This spreadsheet program allows you to manipulate and present your data in almost any way you choose. It allows you to work on a tabular pad consisting of columns and rows where you can perform all your mathematical, financial and statistical calculations. These calculations can be as simple as totalling a row or column of values or as complex as figuring the rate of return on an investment under varying circumstances. It also allows you to make a graphical representation of all your data in the form of 2-dimensional or 3-dimensional graph or pie chart.

Microsoft Office Access 2010

A software to take care of most of your database requirements. It allows you to store and organize information in sets of tables, which can be displayed in the form of columns and rows to look like a table or an index card. What's more it allows you to perform calculations and find for you simple statistics like totals and averages. It allows you to sort the data in any form and extract the required information based on the key given by you.

Microsoft Office PowerPoint 2010

Want to make a presentation in a hurry! This is an ideal program of the same. Make sophisticated slide shows and professional looking electronic presentations. It also allows you to add charts, tables and pictures for make the presentation look alive.

Microsoft Office Outlook 2010

It is an electronic tool for managing appointments, addresses, e-mail, and notes. With lots of stress being given to the e-mail these days, it is an ideal software for sending and receiving e-mail.

Microsoft Office Publisher 2010

It is Microsoft's answer to the various other publishing software available in the market like PageMaker. It allows you to create invitations, design business-cards, and letter-heads, make your own calenders, produce newsletter, etc.

Microsoft Office OneNote 2010

It is used to gather information during meetings, brainstorming sessions, interviews, and more. The notes you create can include text, drawings, images, and audio recordings. OneNote uses a freeform page layout, so you can place and move information wherever you want.

Microsoft Office InfoPath 2010

It is helps you collect and work with data by using dynamic, online forms that have a familiar Office interface. Based on the Extensible Markup Language (XML), InfoPath makes it easy to create and use robust forms to more effectively gather and share information throughout your organization.

Microsoft Office Groove 2010

Microsoft Office Groove 2010 is Internet software for making direct connections with the people who are important to you. With Office Groove 2010, you can bring together team members from both inside and outside your company, with no IT assistance required and no need to waste time thinking about firewalls, servers, security, or network access. Additionally, you can enjoy the efficiency of always knowing each other's virtual location, or online presence, thus allowing for organic and quick conversation and collaboration.

STARTING ABOVE SOFTWARE

You can start any of the above mentioned software by one of the following methods:

From Start Button

Click at Start button to access the various commands. Click on Programs to get the various programs. From here click at the program called Microsoft Office 2010 group and then the required program

From Icon of Word

You can choose to have an icon of the software on your desktop. This icon can be created by using the feature of Creating Shortcut.

WORKING WITH VARIOUS CONSTITUENTS OF MICROSOFT OFFICE 2010

Let me give you here the tips for working under various constituents of Office 2010.

Microsoft Word 2010

As you know that Word is used for creating a document. So in simple terms, follow the following procedure to create a document.

1. Open Word 2010.
2. Click at New from the Office button.
3. A new blank slate for writing would be opened for you.
4. Type the text as you would otherwise too.

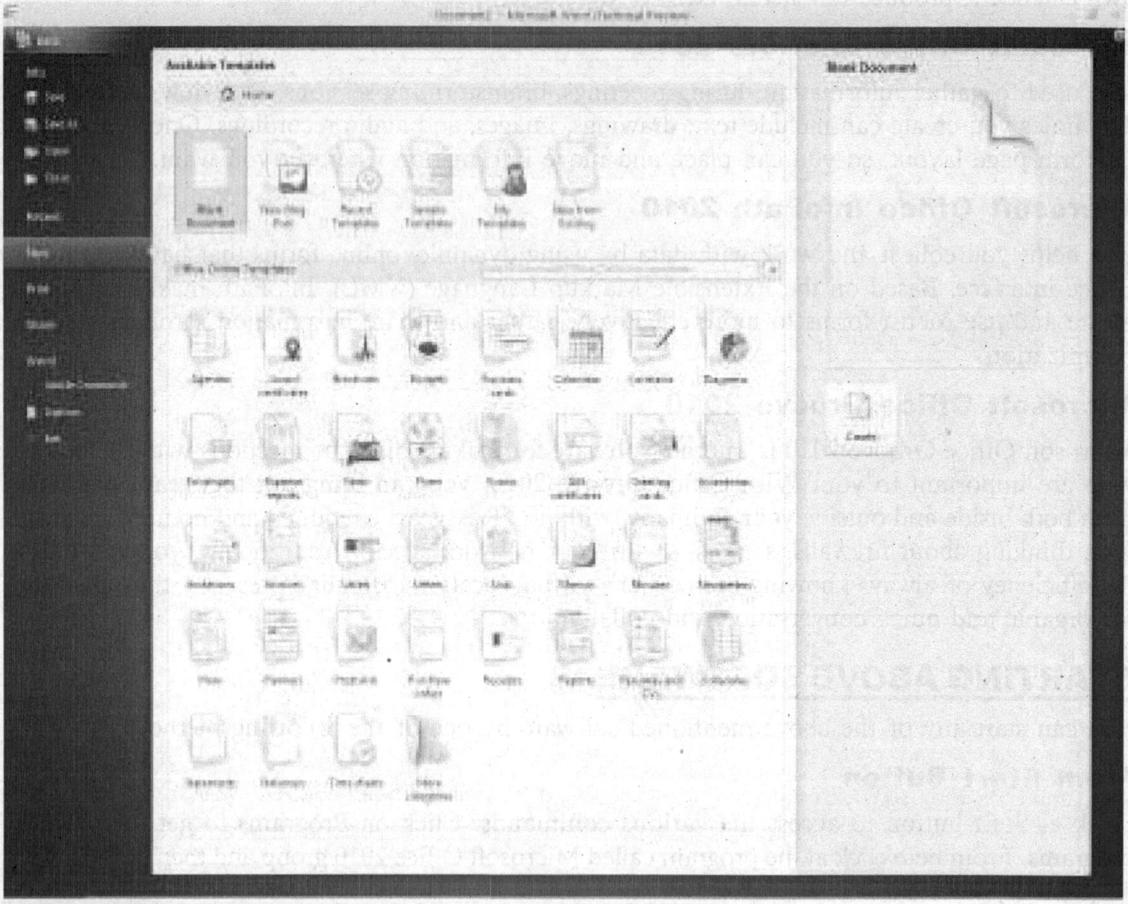

5. Do not bother about any formatting or spelling.
6. Save the document at this stage to avoid loosing the text, if the lights go out.
7. Now format the text of the document according to your needs, i.e., Bold, Italics, etc.
8. If required, change the alignment of the text or part of it.
9. Save again.
10. Close the document from Office button.
11. Now open the same document again.
12. Spell check the whole document, correcting the wrong words.
13. Your document is ready.
14. Print it on the attached printer.
15. See the result of your effort.

If you follow these steps for creating a document in Word 2010, I am sure that you would never fail.

Microsoft Excel 2010

As you know that Excel is used for creating a spreadsheet. So in simple terms, follow the following procedure to create a spreadsheet.

1. Open Excel 2010.
2. Click at New from the Office button.
3. A new blank spreadsheet would be opened for you.
4. Type the number, text, formula, as the case may be.
5. Do not bother about any formatting at this stage.
6. Save the document at this stage to avoid loosing the typing, if the lights go out.
7. Now format the spreadsheet according to your needs, i.e., Bold, Italics, etc.
8. If required, change the alignment of the cells.
9. Save again.
10. Close the spreadsheet from Office button.
11. Now open the same spreadsheet again.
12. Spell check the whole spreadsheet, correcting the wrong words.
13. Your spreadsheet is ready.
14. Print it on the attached printer.
15. See the result of your effort.

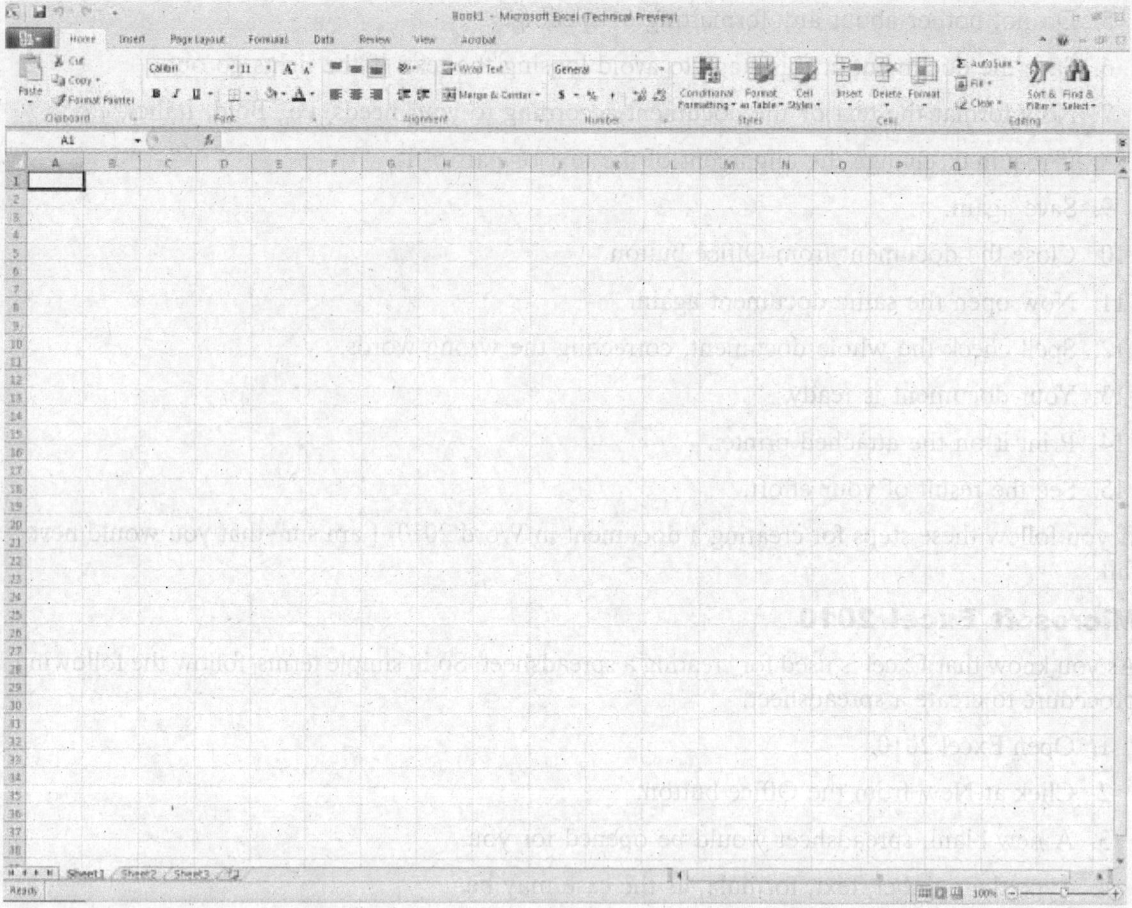

Microsoft PowerPoint 2010

As you know that PowerPoint is used for creating a presentation. So in simple terms, follow the following procedure to create a presentation.

1. Open PowerPoint 2010.
2. Click at New from the Office button.
3. A new blank presentation would be opened for you.
4. Select the type of slide you want to create.
5. Type the text and other details, as the case may be.
6. Save the slide/presentation.
7. Now format the slide according to your needs, i.e., Bold, Italics, etc.
8. If required, change the alignment of the text within presentation.
9. Save again.

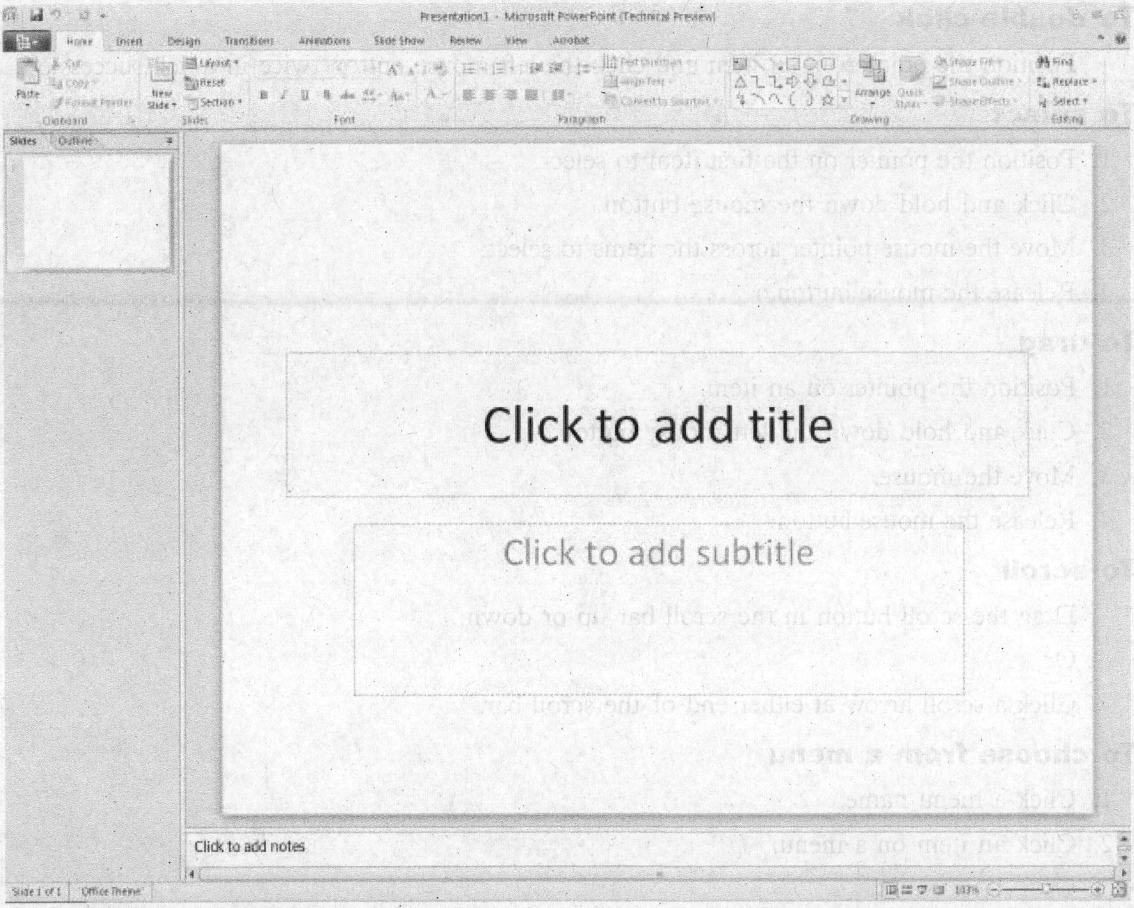

10. Add a new slide, if the need be.
11. Close the slide from Office button.
12. Now open the same presentation again.
13. Create a slide show of the slides.
14. Run the slide show to see the effect.

In similar way, you can run the other software of Microsoft Office 2010.

USING THE MOUSE

Since most of the activities in Microsoft Office are done using the mouse, it is very important to have the complete knowledge of working of mouse while using the constituents of Microsoft Office.

To click

Position the pointer on a menu, a button, or an icon and click the left mouse once.

To double-click

Position the pointer on an item and click the left mouse button twice in quick succession.

To select

1. Position the pointer on the first item to select.
2. Click and hold down the mouse button.
3. Move the mouse pointer across the items to select.
4. Release the mouse button.

To drag

1. Position the pointer on an item.
2. Click and hold down the left mouse button.
3. Move the mouse.
4. Release the mouse button.

To scroll

Drag the scroll button in the scroll bar up or down.

Or

Click a scroll arrow at either end of the scroll bar.

To choose from a menu

1. Click a menu name.
2. Click an item on a menu.

   Or

   If the item is followed by an arrow, position the mouse pointer on the item to open the submenu and then click an item on the submenu.

To move a window

Position the pointer on the window's title bar and press and hold the mouse button as your drag the window.

To resize a window

Position the pointer on the window's corner and, when you see the diagonal pointer, drag to resize the window.

To minimize a window

Click the Minimize button.

To restore a minimized window

Click the button for the window on the taskbar.

To maximize a window

Click the Maximize button.

To switch windows

Click any visible part of the window

Or

Click the button for the window on the taskbar.

To close a window

1. Click the Close button on the window

   Or

   Right click the button for the window on the taskbar and choose Close from the shortcut menu.

Remember

1. Menus in Office programs might be collapsed to show only frequently used items. To view the complete menu, click the More icon at the bottom of the menu or pause with the pointer on any menu option.
2. Menu items that are grayed out are not currently available.
3. To display a tooltip, which is a description of a toolbar button, position the pointer on the button and pause for a moment without clicking.
4. To minimize all windows, you can rightclick the taskbar and then click Minimize All Windows from the shortcut menu.
5. If one window fills the screen, you might have to click its Restore button to return it to a partial-screen window. You will then be able to see and click other windows.

COMMON KEYBOARD COMMANDS

Ctrl + N	Open a new document
Ctrl + O	Opens a existing document
Ctrl + S	Saves the current document
Ctrl + W	Close the current document
Ctrl + P	Prints the current document
Ctrl + C	Copies the highlighted matter to store it in clipboard
Ctrl + X	Cuts the highlighted matter to store it in clipboard
Ctrl + V	Pastes the matter available on the clipboard
F1	Call for help
Shift + F1	Use the What's This? Button

Ctrl + F6	Switch between open documents
Ctrl + Z	Undo an action
Ctrl + Y	Redo an action

Review Questions

1. Name the other popular constituents of Microsoft Office 2010.
2. Describe the various ways of starting Microsoft Office 2010 and its constituents.
3. Describe the working of following:

   Microsoft Word 2010

   Microsoft Excel 2010

   Microsoft PowerPoint 2010
4. How is mouse used for various operatings of Microsoft Office?
5. List out the various common keyboard commands of various Microsoft Office constituents.

2

What's New in Microsoft Excel 2010

INTRODUCTION

Before we go into the study of Microsoft Excel 2010, let us see what is new in the newer version of ever popular spreadsheet program called Microsoft Excel.

WHAT'S NEW IN MICROSOFT EXCEL 2010

Results-oriented user interface

The new results-oriented user interface makes it easy for you to work in Microsoft Office Excel. Commands and features that were often buried in complex menus and toolbars are now easier to find on task-oriented tabs that contain logical groups of commands and features. Many dialog boxes are replaced with drop-down galleries that display the available options, and descriptive tooltips or sample previews are provided to help you choose the right option.

No matter what activity you are performing in the new user interface—whether it's formatting or analyzing data—Excel presents the tools that are most useful to successfully complete that task.

More rows and columns, and other new limits

To enable you to explore massive amounts of data in worksheets, Office Excel 2010 supports up to 1 million rows and 16 thousand columns per worksheet. Specifically, the Office Excel 2010 grid is 1,048,576 rows by 16,384 columns, which provides you with 1,500% more rows and 6,300% more columns than you had available in Microsoft Office Excel 2003. For those of you who are curious, columns now end at XFD instead of IV.

Instead of 4 thousand types of formatting, you can now use an unlimited number in the same workbook, and the number of cell references per cell are increased from 8 thousand to limited by available memory.

To improve the performance of Excel, memory management has been increased from 1 GB of memory in Microsoft Office Excel 2003 to 2 GB in Office Excel 2010.

You will also experience faster calculations in large, formula-intensive worksheets because Office Excel 2010 supports dual-processors and multithreaded chipsets.

Office Excel 2010 also supports up to 16 million colors.

Office themes and Excel styles

In Office Excel 2010, you can quickly format the data in your worksheet by applying a theme and by using a specific style. Themes can be shared across other 2010 Office release programs, such as Microsoft Office Word and Microsoft Office PowerPoint, while styles are designed to change the format of Excel-specific items, such as Excel tables, charts, PivotTables, shapes, or diagrams.

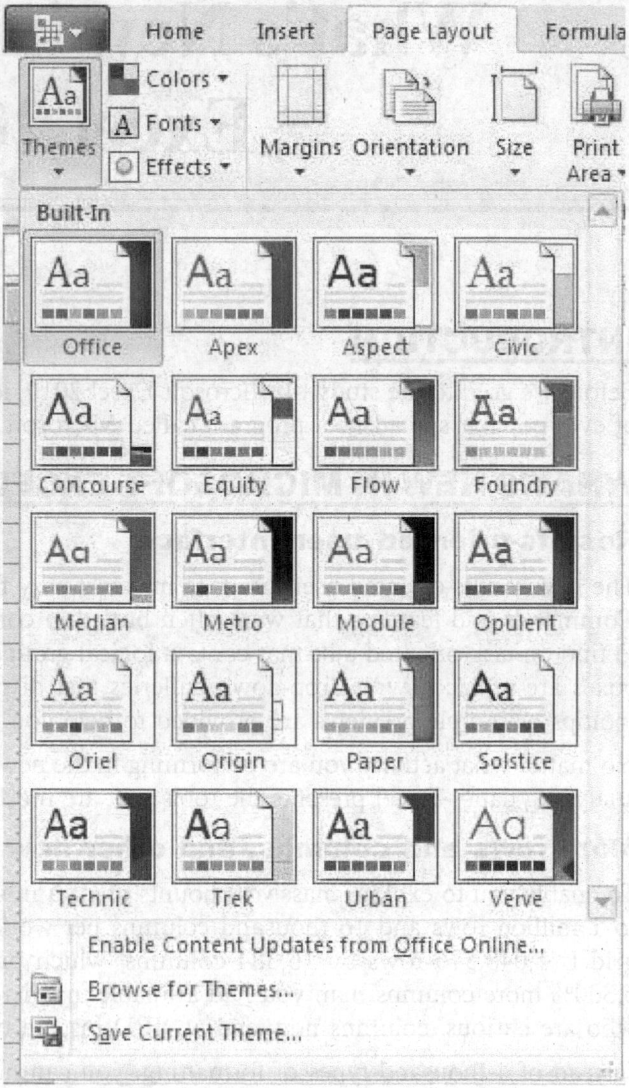

Applying a theme

A theme is a predefined set of colors, fonts, lines, and fill effects that can be applied to your entire workbook or to specific items, such as charts or tables. They can help you create great-looking documents. Your company may be providing a corporate theme that you can use, or you can choose from the predefined themes that are available in Excel. It's also easy to create your own theme for a uniform, professional look that can be applied to all of your Excel workbooks and other 2010 Office release documents. When you create a theme, the color, font, and fill effects can be changed individually so that you can make changes to any or all of these options.

Using styles

A style is a predefined theme-based format that you can apply to change the look of Excel tables, charts, PivotTables, shapes, or diagrams. If built-in predefined styles don't meet your needs, you can customize a style. For charts, you can choose from many predefined styles, but you cannot create your own chart styles.

As in Excel 2003, cell styles are used to format selected cells, but you can now quickly apply a predefined cell style. Most cell styles are not based on the theme that is applied to your workbook, and you can easily create your own.

Rich conditional formatting

In 2010 Office release, you can use conditional formatting to visually annotate your data for both analytical and presentation purposes. To easily find exceptions and to spot important trends in your data, you can implement and manage multiple conditional formatting rules that apply rich visual formatting in the form of gradient colors, data bars, and icon sets to data that meets those rules. Conditional formats are also easy to apply—in just a few clicks, you can see relationships in your data that you can use for your analysis purposes.

Easy Formula Writing

The following improvements make formula writing much easier in Office Excel 2010.

Resizable formula bar

The formula bar automatically resizes to accommodate long, complex formulas, which prevents the formulas from covering other data in your worksheet. You can also write longer formulas with more levels of nesting than you could in earlier versions of Excel.

Function AutoComplete

With Function AutoComplete, you can quickly write the proper formula syntax. From easily detecting the functions that you want to use to getting help completing the formula arguments, you will be able to get formulas right the first time and every time. Structured references In addition to cell references, such as A1 and R1C1, Office Excel 2010 provides structured references that reference named ranges and tables in a formula.

Easy access to named ranges

By using the Office Excel 2010 name manager, you can organize, update, and manage multiple named ranges in a central location, which helps anyone who needs to work on your worksheet interpret its formulas and data.

New OLAP formulas and cube functions

When you work with multidimensional databases (such as SQL Server Analysis Services) in Office Excel 2010, you can use OLAP formulas to build complex, free form, OLAP data bound reports. New cube functions are used to extract OLAP data (sets and values) from Analysis Services and display it in a cell. OLAP formulas can be generated when you convert PivotTable formulas to cell formulas or when you use AutoComplete for cube function arguments when you type formulas.

Improved Sorting and Filtering

In Office Excel 2010, you can quickly arrange your worksheet data to find the answers that you need by using enhanced filtering and sorting. For example, you can now sort data by color and by more than 3 (and up to 64) levels. You can also filter data by color or by dates, display more than 1000 items in the AutoFilter drop-down list, select multiple items to filter, and filter data in PivotTables.

Excel table enhancements

In Office Excel 2010, you can use the new user interface to quickly create, format, and expand an Excel table (known as an Excel list in Excel 2003) to organize the data on your worksheet so that it's much easier to work with. New or improved functionality for tables includes the following features.

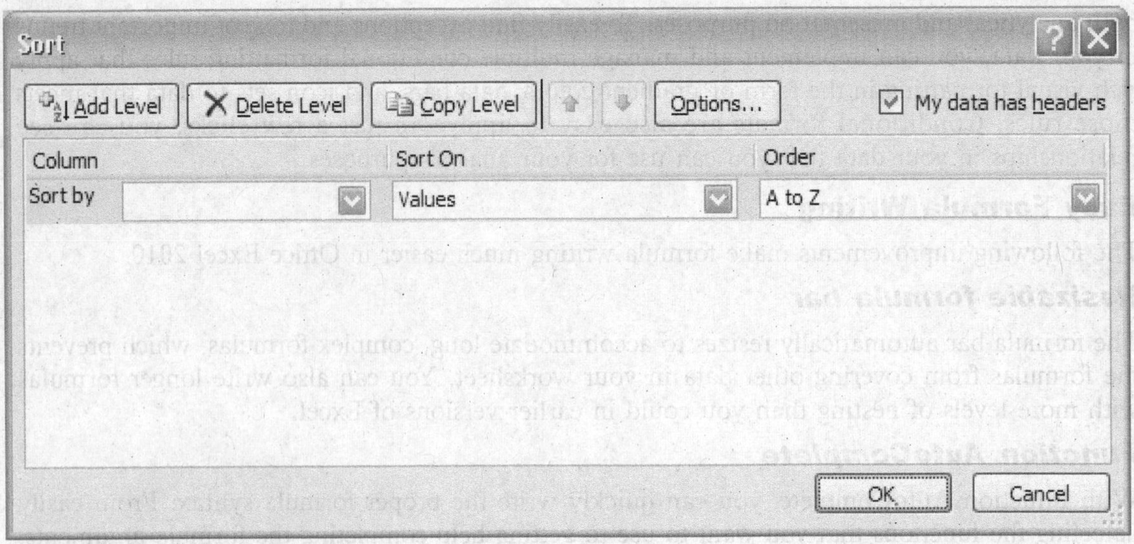

Table header rows

Table header rows can be turned on or off. When table headers are displayed, they stay visible with the data in the table columns by replacing the worksheet headers when you move around in a long table.

Calculated columns

A calculated column uses a single formula that adjusts for each row. It automatically expands to include additional rows so that the formula is immediately extended to those rows. All that you have to do is enter a formula once—you don't need to use the Fill or Copy commands.

Automatic AutoFiltering

AutoFilter is turned on by default in a table to enable powerful sorting and filtering of table data.

Structured references

This type of reference allows you to use table column header names in formulas instead of cell references, such as A1 or R1C1.

Total rows

In a total row, you can now use custom formulas and text entries.

Table styles

You can apply a table style to quickly add designer-quality, professional formatting to tables. If an alternate-row style is enabled on a table, Excel will maintain the alternating style rule through actions that would have traditionally disrupted this layout, such as filtering, hiding rows, or manual rearranging of rows and columns.

New look for charts

In Office Excel 2010, you can use new charting tools to easily create professional-looking charts that communicate information effectively. Based on the theme that is applied to your workbook,

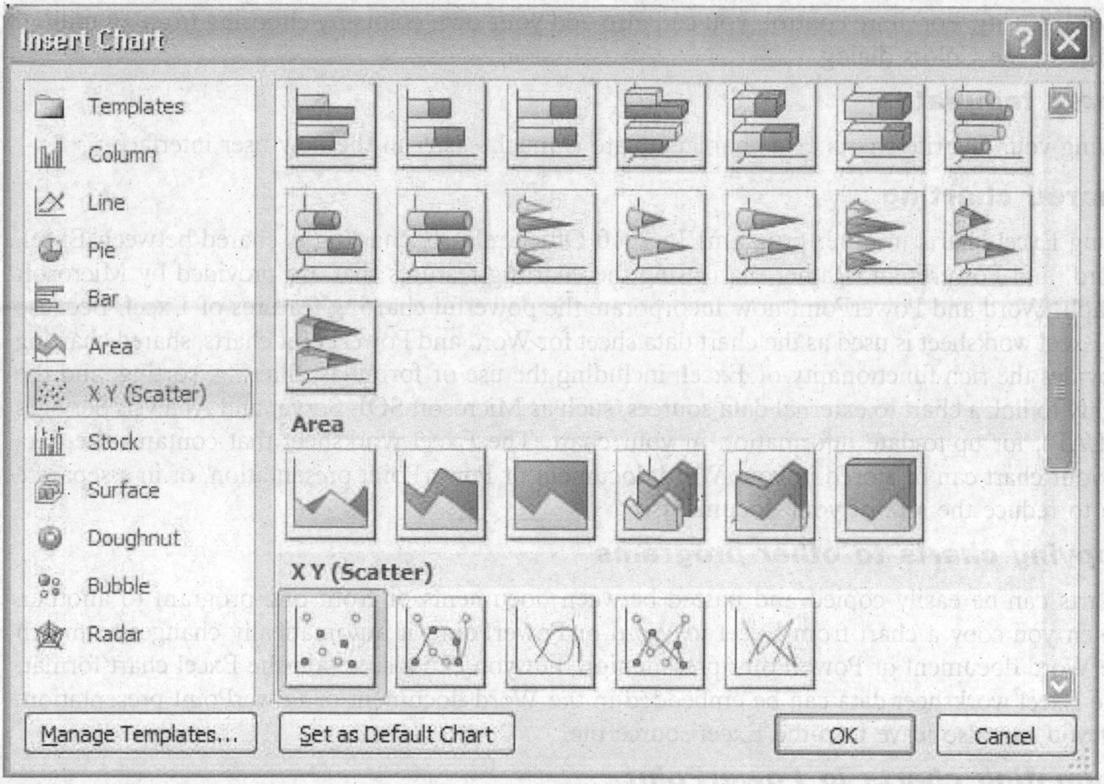

the new, up-to-date look for charts includes special effects, such as 3-D, transparency, and soft shadows.

The new user interface makes it easy to explore the available chart types so that you can create the right chart for your data. Numerous predefined chart styles and layouts are provided so that you can quickly apply a good-looking format and include the details that you want in your chart.

Visual chart element pickers

Besides the quick layouts and quick formats, you can now use the new user interface to quickly change every element of the chart to best present your data. In a few clicks, you can add or remove titles, legends, data labels, trendlines, and other chart elements.

A modern look with OfficeArt

Because charts in Office Excel 2010 are drawn with OfficeArt, almost anything you can do to an OfficeArt shape can also be done to a chart and its elements. For example, you can add a soft shadow or bevel effect to make an element stand out or use transparency to make elements visible that are partially obscured in a chart layout. You can also use realistic 3-D effects.

Clear lines and fonts

Lines in charts appear less jagged, and ClearType fonts are used for text to improve readability. More colors than ever You can easily choose from the predefined theme colors and vary their color intensity. For more control, you can also add your own colors by choosing from 16 million colors in the Colors dialog.

Chart templates

Saving your favorite charts as a chart template is much easier in the new user interface.

Shared charting

Using Excel charts in other programs In 2010 Office release, charting is shared between Excel, Word, and PowerPoint. Rather than using the charting features that are provided by Microsoft Graph, Word and PowerPoint now incorporate the powerful charting features of Excel. Because an Excel worksheet is used as the chart data sheet for Word and PowerPoint charts, shared charting provides the rich functionality of Excel, including the use of formulas, filtering, sorting, and the ability to link a chart to external data sources, such as Microsoft SQL Server and Analysis Services (OLAP), for up-to-date information in your chart. The Excel worksheet that contains the data of your chart can be stored in your Word document or PowerPoint presentation, or in a separate file to reduce the size of your documents.

Copying charts to other programs

Charts can be easily copied and pasted between documents or from one program to another. When you copy a chart from Excel to Word or PowerPoint, it automatically changes to match the Word document or PowerPoint presentation, but you can also retain the Excel chart format. The Excel worksheet data can be embedded in the Word document or PowerPoint presentation, but you can also leave it in the Excel source file.

Animating charts in PowerPoint

In PowerPoint, you can more easily use animation to emphasize data in an Excel-based chart. You can animate the entire chart or the legend entry and axis labels. In a column chart, you can even animate individual columns to better illustrate a specific point. Animation features are easier to find and you have a lot more control. For example, you can make changes to individual animation steps, and use more animation effects.

Easy-to-use PivotTables

In Office Excel 2010, PivotTables are much easier to use than in earlier versions of Excel. By using the new PivotTable user interface, the information that you want to view about your data is just a few clicks away—you no longer have to drag data to drop zones that aren't always an easy target. Instead, you can simply select the fields that you want to see in a new PivotTable field list.

And after you create a PivotTable, you can take advantage of many other new or improved features to summarize, analyze, and format your PivotTable data.

Using Undo in PivotTables

You can now undo most actions that you take to create or rearrange a PivotTable.

Plus and minus drill-down indicators

These indicators are used to indicate whether you can expand or collapse parts of the PivotTable to see more or less information.

Sorting and filtering

Sorting is now as simple as selecting an item in the column that you want to sort and using sort buttons. You can filter data by using PivotTable filters, such as Greater than, Equals, or Contains.

Conditional formatting

You can apply conditional formatting to an Office Excel 2010 Pivot Table by cell or by intersection of cells.

PivotTable style and layout

Just like you can for Excel tables and charts, you can quickly apply a predefined or custom style to a PivotTable. And changing the layout of a PivotTable is also much easier to do in the new user interface.

PivotCharts

Like PivotTables, PivotCharts are much easier to create in the new user interface. All of the filtering improvements are also available for PivotCharts. When you create a PivotChart, specific PivotChart tools and context menus are available so that you can analyze the data in the chart. You can also change the layout, style, and format of the chart or its elements the same way that you can for a regular chart. In Office Excel 2010, the chart formatting that you apply is preserved when you make changes to the PivotChart, which is an improvement over the way it worked in earlier versions of Excel.

Quick connections to external data

In Office Excel 2010, you no longer need to know the server or database names of corporate data sources. Instead, you can use Quicklaunch to select from a list of data sources that your administrator or workgroup expert has made available for you. A connection manager in Excel allows you to view all connections in a workbook and makes it easier to reuse a connection or to substitute a connection with another one.

New file formats

XML-based file format In 2010 Microsoft Office system, Microsoft is introducing new file formats for Word, Excel, and PowerPoint, known as the Office Open XML formats. These new file formats facilitate integration with external data sources, and also offer reduced file sizes and improved data recovery. In Office Excel 2010, the default format for an Excel workbook is the Office Excel 2010 XML-based file format (.xlsx). Other available XML-based formats are the Office Excel 2010 XML-based and macro-enabled file format (.xlsm), the Office Excel 2010 file format for an Excel template (.xltx), and the Office Excel 2010 macro-enabled file format for an Excel template (.xltm). Office Excel 2010 binary file format In addition to the new XML-based file formats, Office Excel 2010 also introduces a binary version of the segmented compressed file format for large or complex workbooks. This file format, the Office Excel 2010 Binary (or BIFF12) file format (.xls), can be used for optimal performance and backward compatibility.

Compatibility with earlier versions of Excel

You can check an Office Excel 2010 workbook to see if it contains features or formatting that are not compatible with an earlier version of Excel so that you can make the necessary changes for better backward compatibility. In earlier versions of Excel, you can install updates and converters that help you open an Office Excel 2010 workbook so that you can edit it, save it, and open it again in Office Excel 2010 without losing any Office Excel 2010-specific functionality or features.

Better printing experience

Page Layout View In addition to the Normal view and Page Break Preview view, Office Excel 2010 provides a Page Layout View. You can use this view to create a worksheet while keeping an eye on how it will look in printed format. In this view, you can work with page headers, footers, and margin settings right in the worksheet, and place objects, such as charts or shapes, exactly where you want them. You also have easy access to all page setup options on the Page Layout tab in the new user interface so that you can quickly specify options, such as page orientation. It's easy to see what will be printed on every page, which will help you avoid multiple printing attempts and truncated data in printouts.

Saving to PDF and XPS format You can save as a PDF or XPS file from a 2010 Microsoft Office system program only after you install an add-in.

New ways to share your work

Using Excel Services to share your work If you have access to Excel Services, you can use it to share your Office Excel 2010 worksheet data with other people, such as executives and other stakeholders in your organization. In Office Excel 2010, you can save a workbook to Excel Services and specify the worksheet data that you want other people to see. In a browser, they can then use Microsoft Office Excel Web Access to view, analyze, print, and extract this worksheet data. They can also create a static snapshot of the data at regular intervals or on demand. Office Excel Web Access makes it easy to perform activities, such as scrolling, filtering, sorting, viewing charts, and using drill-down in PivotTables. You can also connect the Excel Web Access Web Part to other Web Parts to display data in alternative ways. And with the right permissions, Excel Web Access users can open a workbook in Office Excel 2010 so that they can use the full power of Excel to analyze and work with the data on their own computers if they have Excel installed.

Using this method to share your work ensures that other people have access to one version of the data in one location, which you can keep current with the latest details. If you need other people, such as team members, to supply you with comments and updated information, you may want to share a workbook the same way that you did in earlier versions of Excel to collect the information you need before you save it to Excel Services.

Using Document Management Server

Excel Services can be integrated with Document Management Server to create a validation process around new Excel reports and workbook calculation workflow actions, such as a cell-based notification or a workflow process based on a complex Excel calculation. You can also use Document Management Server to schedule nightly recalculation of a complex workbook model.

Review Questions

1. Describe the various new commands of Microsoft Office Excel 2010.
2. Describe the new OLAP formulas and cube functions.
3. Describe the vairous new file formats supported by Microsoft Office Excel 2010.
4. What is meant by Shared Charting?

3

Spreadsheet Basics

INTRODUCTION

Before we go into understanding the various commands of Excel 2010, let us first understand the working of a spreadsheet.

WHAT IS A SPREADSHEET?

A spreadsheet as the name suggests is a sheet which is spread in such a way that it divides itself into the various horizontal rows and vertical columns. Rows are numbered from 1 onwards and Columns are numbered from A onwards. Graphically they can be represented as shown on the next page.

When we take this to the computer and see it electronically using our software Microsoft Office Excel 2010, this becomes Electronic Spreadsheet, also called Worksheet. So the main features of the worksheet are:

Rows These are the horizontal cells which can contain any information.

Columns These are vertical cells which can also contain information.

Cells It is the intersection of a row with a column. Each cell is identified with its position.

NAMING CONVENTION

It is not I have named rows from 1 onwards and columns A onwards on my own but they are so numbered by the software itself. These are the standard way of expressing these columns and rows. If we have to name a large number of cells or columns, for that too we have the convention which asks us to call them with starting cell address and last cell address with colon in between. For example, see the addressed cells next.

Another convention is of the sheets in the worksheet.

SHEETS

These are like pages in a book. Initially there are 16 worksheets in a file. But, you can add more.

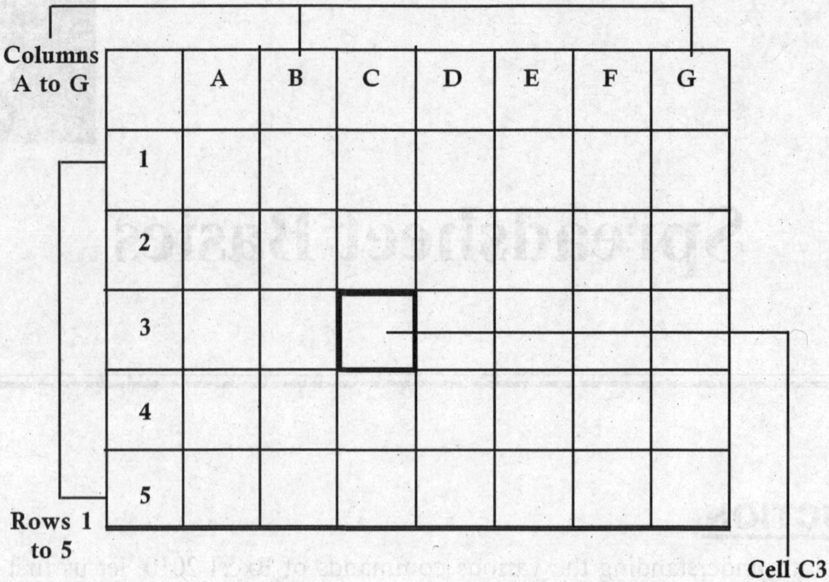

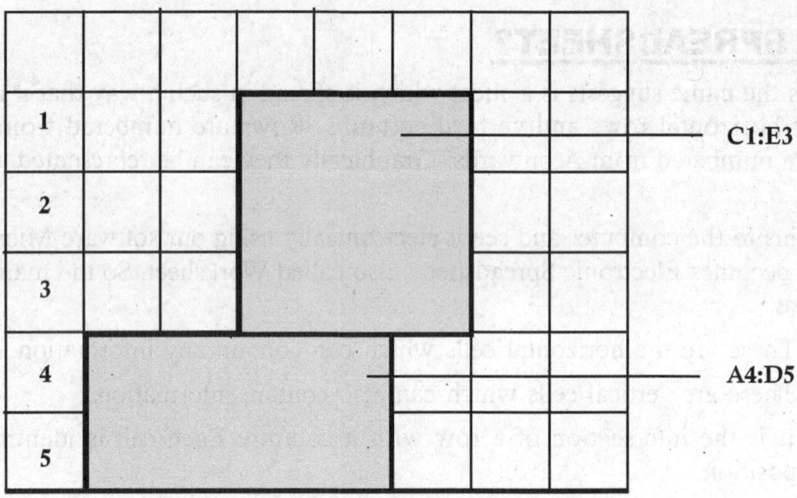

However, there may be only 6 of them visible on the screen. These sheets are independent but you can transfer data from one sheet to another.

These sheets are very helpful. For example, for a salary spreadsheet, one sheet may belong to one month and there may be a sheet for the total of the year.

MOVING WITHIN A SHEET

To enter data in a cell, you must first move to that particular cell.

To Move to a Cell

1. Click in the cell.

Or

Press the arrow keys to move the cell pointer to the cell.

Or

Select the current cell address in the **Name** box and replace it with the address of the cell to which you want to move.

Remember

1. The cell surrounded by the cell pointer is called the active cell.
2. You can use the scroll bars to scroll through the document without changing the active cell.
3. To move within the worksheet, you can use the keyboard shortcuts, given below:

Keyboard Shortcuts for Moving Around the Worksheet

Keyboard Shortcut	*Result*
Arrow key	Moves to the adjacent cell (Up, Down, Left or Right)
Ctrl+Arrow Key	Moves to the edge of the current data region (Up, Down, Left or Right)
Tab	Moves right one cell
Shift + Tab	Moves left one cell
Enter	Moves down one cell
Shift + Enter	Moves up one cell
Home	Moves to the first cell of the row
Ctrl + Home	Moves to cell A1
Ctrl + End	Moves to last cell of last row with data
Page Down	Moves down one screen
Page Up	Moves up one screen
Alt + Page Down	Moves one screen to the right
Alt + Page Up	Moves one screen to the left
Ctrl + Page Down	Moves to the next sheet in the workbook
Ctrl + Page Up	Moves to the previous sheet in the workbook

ENTERING DATA

You can enter text, a number, or a formula into each cell in a worksheet. You enter text to create a label, such as a column heading. You can enter a number to provide information with which you can do calculations.

To Type Data in a Cell

1. Select the cell.

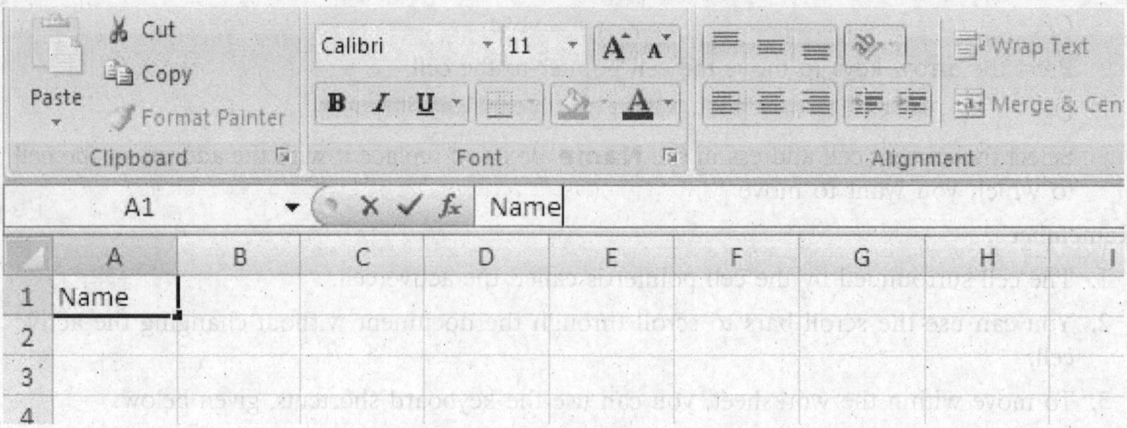

2. Type text, a number, or a formula. A flashing insertion point will appear at the end of whatever you type. You will notice that whatever you type will appear not only in the active cell but also in the Formula bar.
3. Press Enter key to move to the next cell. The cell below will become the new active cell.

Remember

1. You don't have to press Enter after you type the contents of a cell. You can simply press right arrow key to move to the next cell.
2. Excel right aligns the numbers in the cell but left aligns the text.

EDITING THE DATA

The easiest way to change the text or number in a cell is to click the cell and then type right over the contents. But if you have a formula or extensive text in the cell, you might prefer to edit the existing contents to avoid retyping the whole entry.

To Edit Data in a Cell

1. Click the cell and then type over its contents

   Or

   Double click the cell to position an insertion point with the cell contents.
2. Edit the contents as though you were editing text in Word.
3. Press Enter to enter the revised text in the cell.

This is if you have just one cell to edit, But, if you have more than one cell to edit. Then you need to select the various cells.

SELECTING CELLS

You can select a number of consecutive cells called a range by one of the following methods:

1. Click and drag over the selection.
2. Click in one cell, and then hold down the Shift key and click in the opposite corner of the selection.

3. Click on the Select All button, the gray rectangle where the column and row heading meet, to select the entire worksheet.
4. Click in a column or row heading to select the whole column or row.

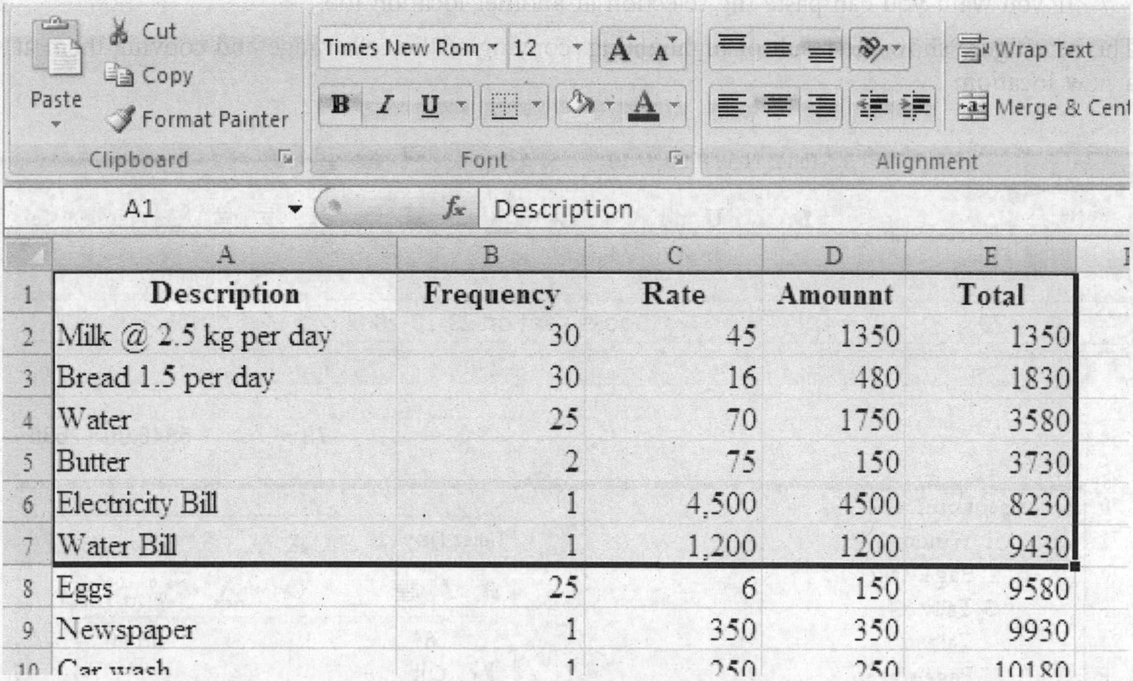

MOVING DATA

1. Select a range of cells. The cells will be highlighted.
2. Click on the Cut button. Moving dashes (called a marquee) will appear around your selection.
3. In this case the data does not disappear like text does in a word processor.
4. Click in the cell that will be upper left corner of the new location of the range. The cell will be selected.
5. Click on the Paste button. The data will be pasted in the new location.

COPYING DATA

Copying puts selected data in a new location. Unlike moved data, copied data also remains in the original location.

1. Select a range of cell. The cells will be highlighted.
2. Click the Copy button.
3. A marquee (running dashes) will appear around your selection.

4. Click in the cell at the top left of the range where you want to place a copy.
5. Click on Paste button.
6. The selected range will appear in both the original location and new location.
7. If you want you can paste the selection at another location too.

The next figure show the result of highlighting, copying of the cells range and copying them at a new location.

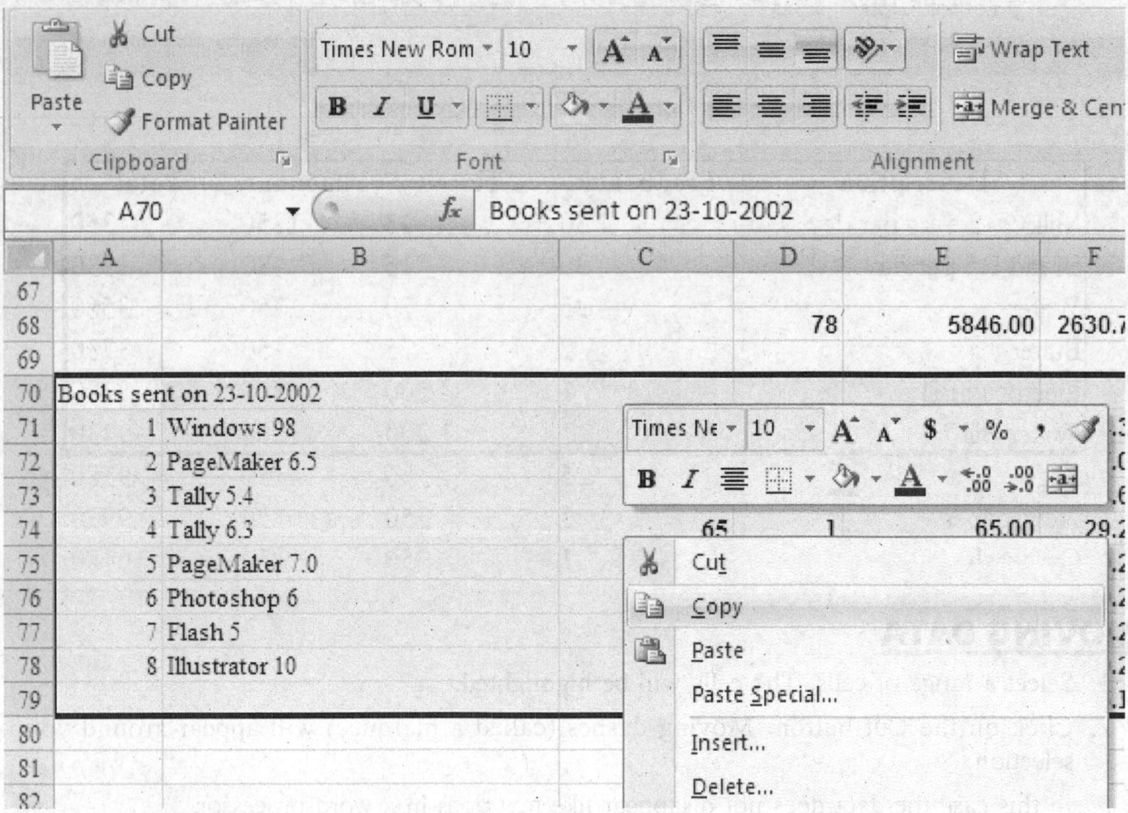

DRAG AND DROP METHOD

This method makes the best use of mouse. You can move and copy using the mouse in a shorter way.

1. Select the cells you want to move or copy. The cells will be highlighted.
2. Hold down the Ctrl key if you want to copy. If you just want to move then do not hold the Ctrl key.
3. Position the mouse pointer over the border of the selected area. The mouse pointer will become an arrow.
4. Press and hold mouse button as you drag the cells to a new location. The cell location you are dragging over will appear in a box below the mouse arrow.

5. Release the mouse button.
6. The cells will be dropped in the new location. This is much quicker than using buttons or menus.

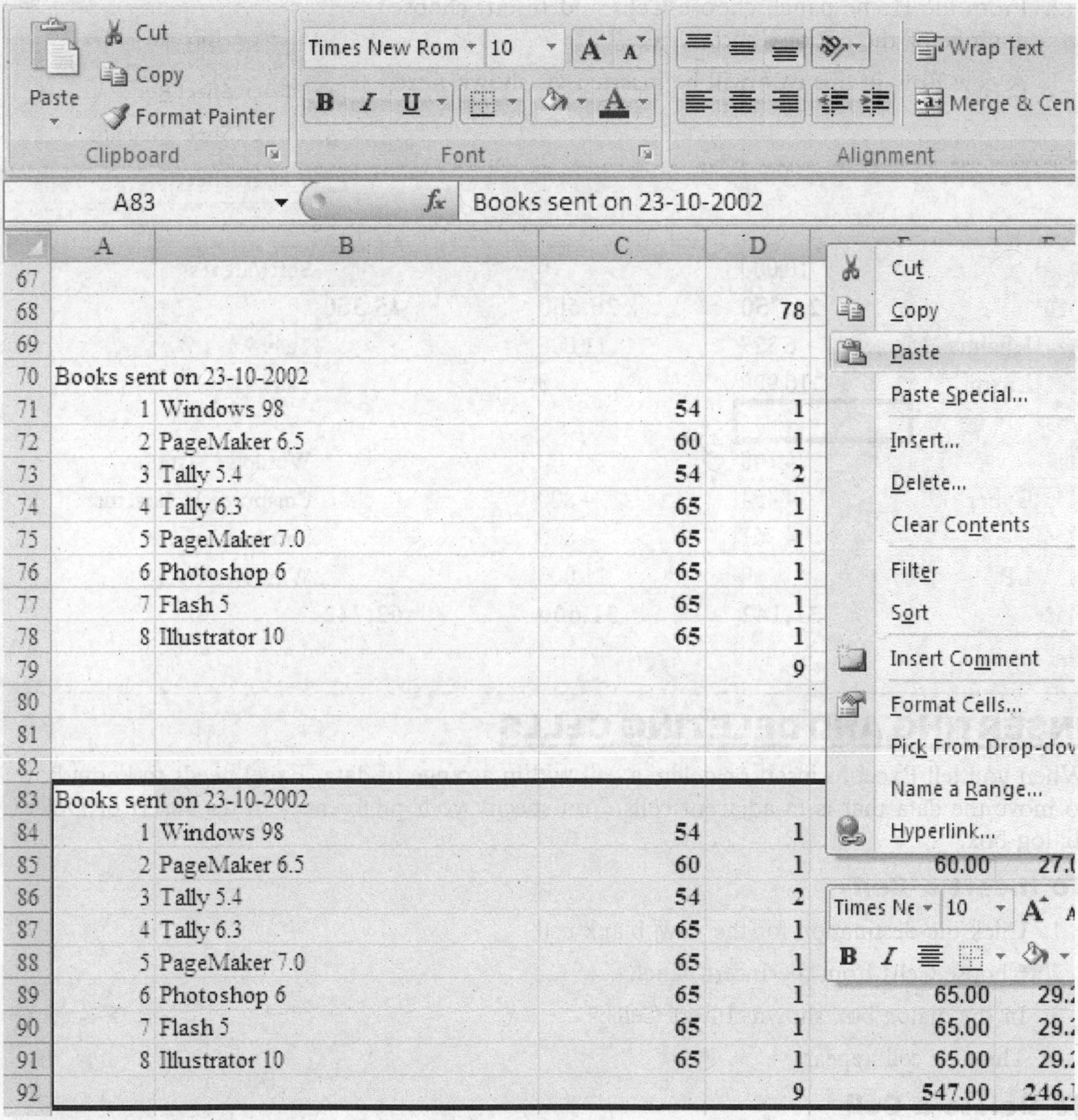

INSERTING ROWS AND COLUMNS

You can insert rows and columns at any time, and Excel adjusts all formulas to accommodate the new rows or columns. If you insert a row, it will appear **above** the selected cell; if you insert a column, it will appear to the **left** of the selected cell.

To Insert a Row or a Column

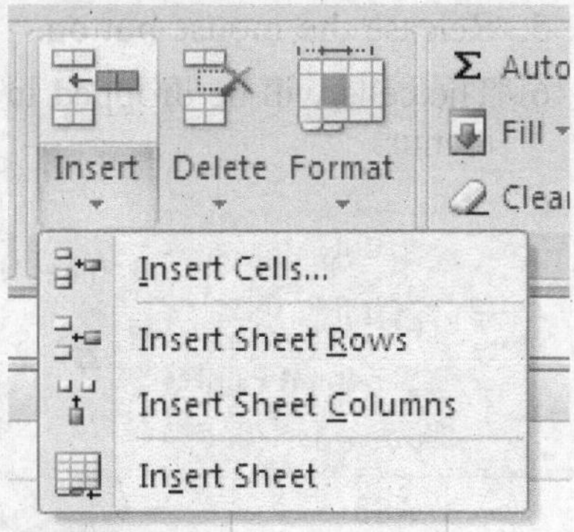

1. Click any cell of the row or column in which you had like to insert the new blank row or column.
2. From the Home panel, choose Cells and Insert, choose any one of the options, shown here.
3. A new Row in this case will be inserted, as shown next.

149		10,000	0		Software test
150		**24,750**	**20,600**	**45,350**	
151	Khanna	6,327	11,000		Tally 9.0
152	Laxmi	10,900	0		Tally 9.0
153					
154		4,700	0		Windows Vista
155	Cyber	4,454	4,800		Computer Architecture
156		4,761	4,800		Software Testing
157	LP	0	11,000		Windows Vista
158		**31,142**	**31,600**	**62,742**	
159					

INSERTING AND DELETING CELLS

When you tell Excel to insert or delete a cell within a range of data, Excel needs to know how to move the data that is in adjacent cells. You specify your preferences in the Insert or Delete dialog box.

To Insert a Cell

1. Click the destination for the new, blank cell.
2. Choose Cells from the Insert panel.
3. In the dialog box shown, Insert Cells.
4. The new cell appears.

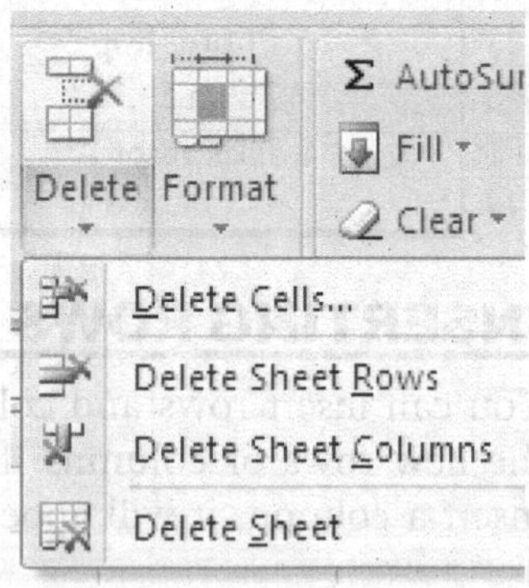

To Delete a Cell

1. Click the cell you want to delete.
2. Choose Cells from the Home panel and then Delete.
3. In the Delete dialog box, as shown here, select the option which you want to apply.
4. The cell or row will be deleted.

CHANGING WIDTH OF A COLUMN

1. Position the mouse pointer on the right edge of the gray column heading button for the column you want to widen.
2. When the mouse pointer changes to a double arrow, drag right or left. While you are dragging, you will see the new width of the column in a ToolTip measured in pixels.
3. You can also select Column Width from the Cell, Format from Home panel. In this case, you can specify the exact setting.

CHANGING HEIGHT OF A ROW

1. Position the mouse pointer on the bottom edge of the gray row heading button for the row whose height you want to change.
2. When the mouse pointer changes to a double arrows, drag up and down.
3. You can also select Row Height from the Cell, Format from Home panel to open the Row Height dialog box. In this case, you can specify the exact setting.

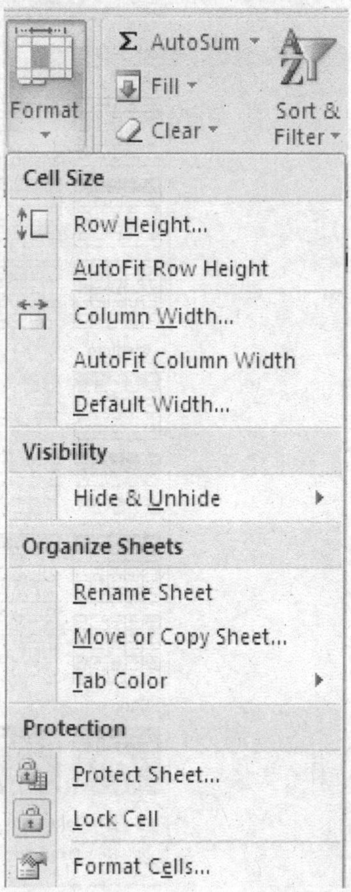

FORMATTING TEXT

You can use formatting to improve the appearance of your worksheet and to make it easier to locate the information you need.

To format selected text

1. Select the cell or cells containing the text to format.
2. Choose Format Cells from Cell, Format in the Home panel.

AUTOFORMAT

The fastest and easiest way to make a worksheet presentable is to give an AutoFormat command. **AutoFormat** supplies a complete look for a range of data by changing the font, text alignment, number formatting, borders, patterns, colours, column widths, and row heights. Excel provides a selection of AutoFormats, each with a unique look.

To choose an AutoFormat

1. Click any cell in the range to format.

   Or

   Select the range to format.

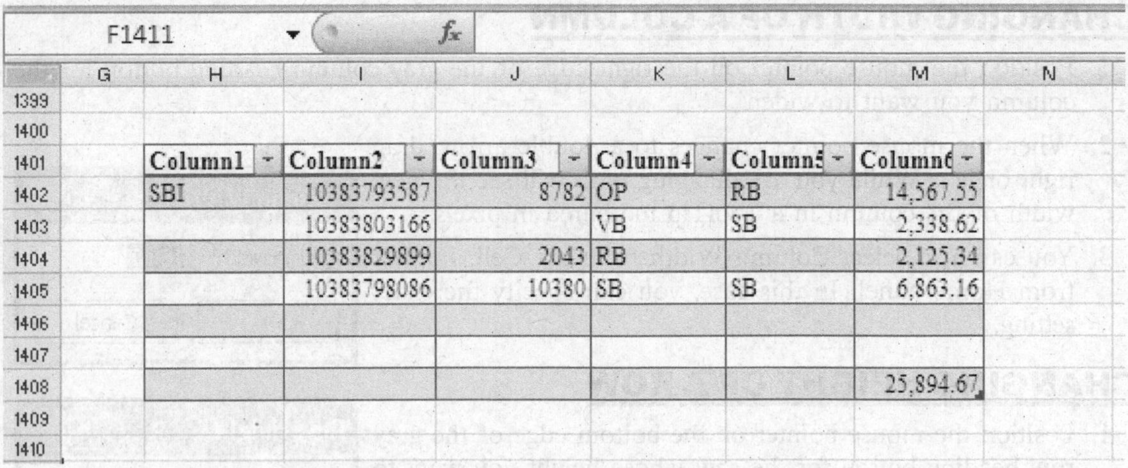
F1411
Column1
Column2
Column3
Column4
Column5
Column6
SBI
10383793587
8782
OP
RB
14,567.55
10383803166
VB
SB
2,338.62
10383829899
2043
RB
2,125.34
10383798086
10380
SB
SB
6,863.16
25,894.67

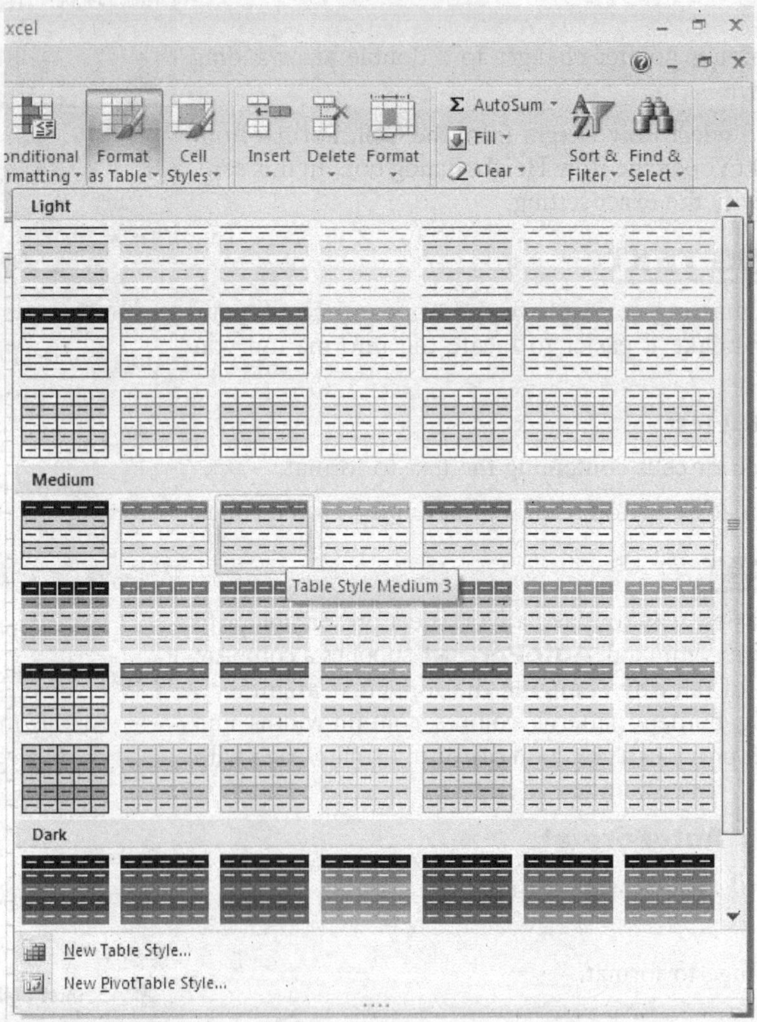
Format as Table
Cell Styles
Insert
Delete
Format
AutoSum
Fill
Clear
Sort & Filter
Find & Select
Light
Medium
Table Style Medium 3
Dark
New Table Style...
New PivotTable Style...

2. From the Format as Table in Style on the Home panel.
3. You will get a complete range of styles to choose from.
4. Click at the one which you want and click Ok.
5. The style will be applied to the selected range of cells.

FORMATTING NUMBERS

Excel makes available to you a variety of number formatting options, some from the Formatting toolbar and others from the Format Cells dialog box.

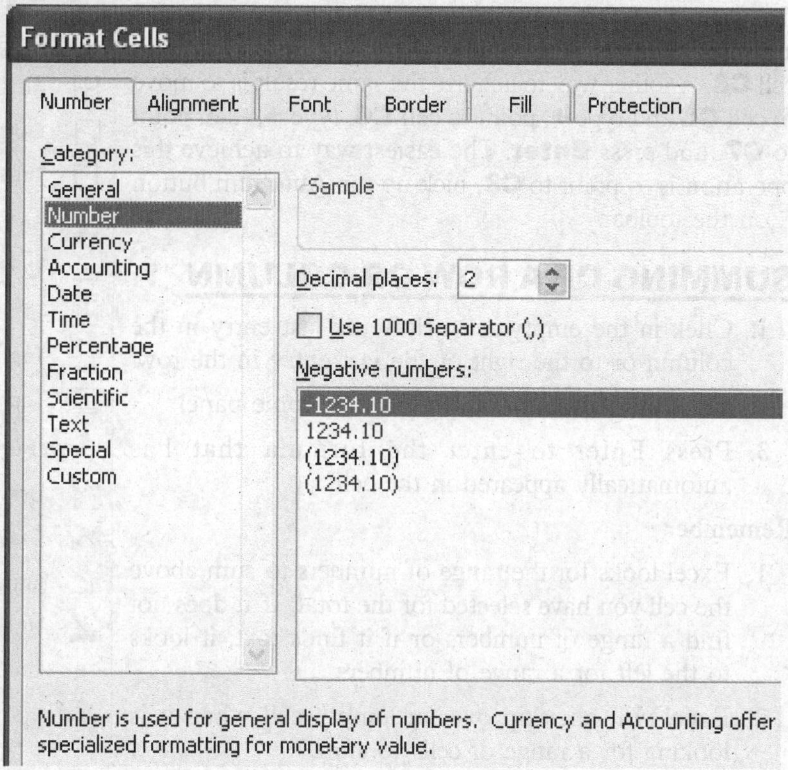

To format numbers

1. Select the numbers to format.
2. Click the Number button on the Cells of the Home panel, to get the Format Cells dialog box.
3. Click at Number panel in the dialog box.
4. Select the option required by you, which includes the number of decimal places, 1000 separator and negative number formatting.
5. Once chosen, you can click at Ok.

ADDING BORDER TO A RANGE

A border is a line at the edge of a cell. You can use borders to divide the information on the sheet into logical regions. Borders appear on the screen and will print when you print the sheet.

To add a border to a cell

1. Select the range to which you want to apply a border.
2. Click the arrow button next to the Borders button to see the full range of border you want for the range

   Or

1. Select the range to which you want to apply a border.
2. From the Border button, choose More Border from the list.

3. On the Border tab of the Format Cells dialog box, choose a border, a border style, and a colour.
4. Click Ok and the border is added to the range.

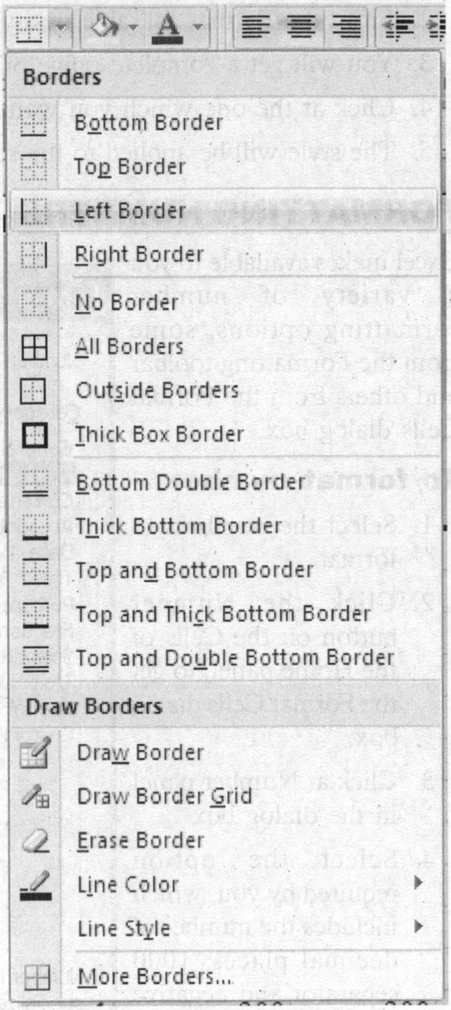

FORMULAE

They establish relationships between two or more cells. If you want to add the values in cells **C6** and **C7** and put the result in cell **C8**, move to the cell **C8** and type **=C6+C7** and press **Enter**. The result is displayed immediately in cell **C8**. Another way to achieve the same result is to move to cell **C8** and type **+**, point to cell **C6**, type **+**, then point to **C7**, and press **Enter**. The easiest way to achieve this operation is to point to **C8**, pick up the AutoSum button Σ on the toolbar.

SUMMING OF A ROW OR COLUMN

1. Click in the empty cell below the last entry in the column or to the right of the last entry in the row.
2. Click the AutoSum button on the Home panel.
3. Press Enter to enter the formula that has automatically appeared in the cell.

Remember

1. Excel looks for the range of numbers to sum above the cell you have selected for the total. If it does not find a range of numbers or if it finds text, it looks to the left for a range of numbers.
2. Excel will not skip over an empty cell when it is looking for a range of cells to sum.
3. To quickly enter sums below multiple adjacent columns, select the empty cells at the bottoms of all the columns before clicking the AutoSum button. Excel will insert a sum in each selected cell.

SUM FUNCTION

The **Sum** function is perhaps the most commonly used of the Excel functions that carry out mathematical, statistical, financial, date, time, and other calculations.

1. Click the destination cell for the formula.
2. Type an equal sign to start the formula and then type the word SUM and a left parenthesis.
3. Drag down the column of numbers to sum.
4. Press Enter.

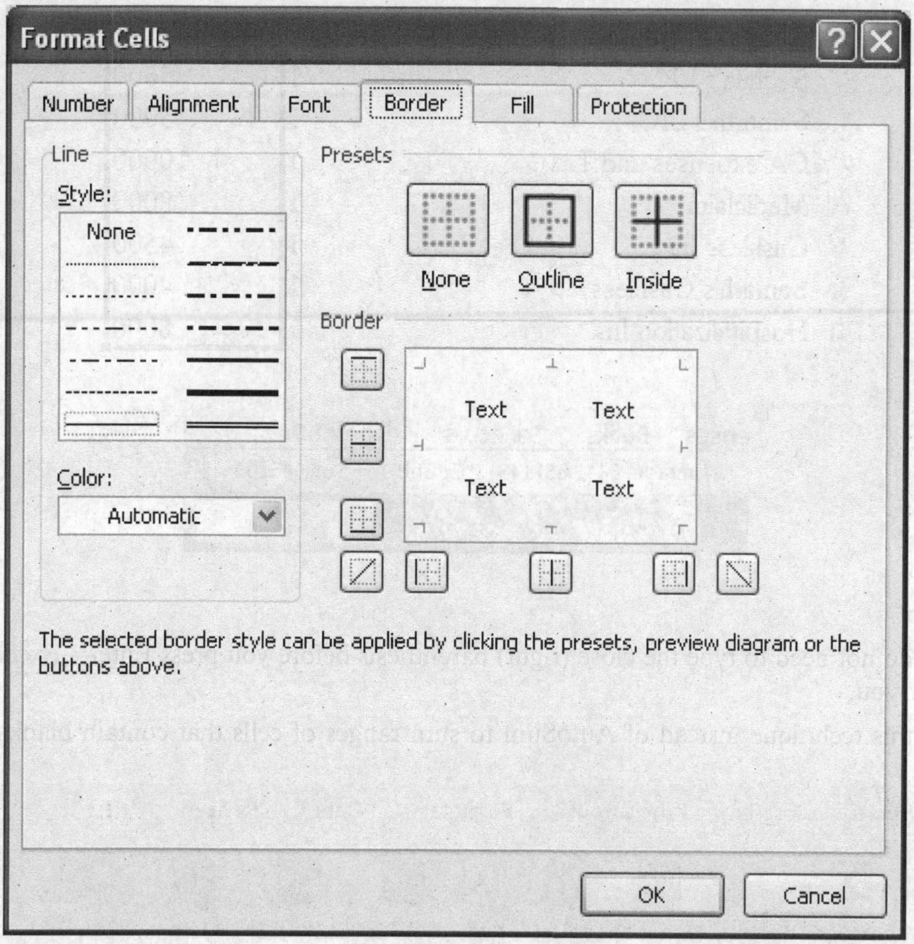
Format Cells
Number
Alignment
Font
Border
Fill
Protection
Line
Style:
None
Color:
Automatic
Presets
None
Outline
Inside
Border
Text
Text
Text
Text
The selected border style can be applied by clicking the presets, preview diagram or the buttons above.
OK
Cancel

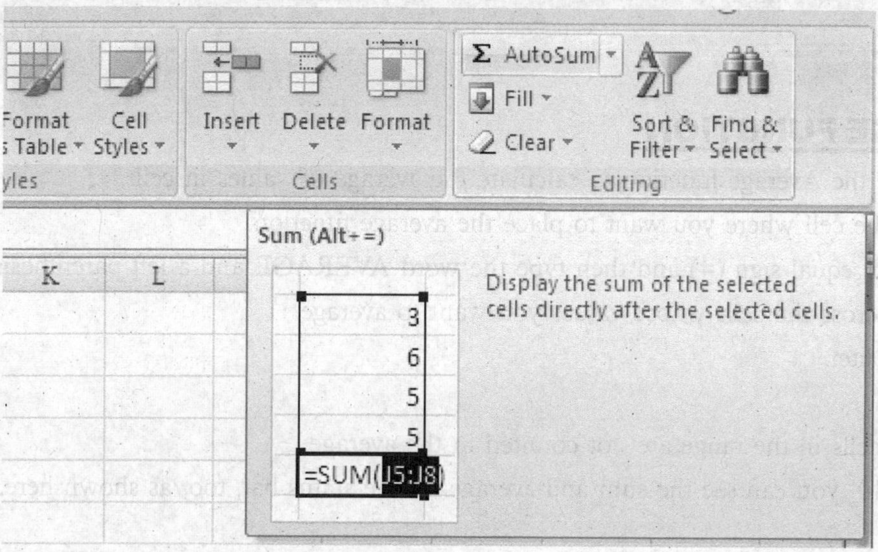
Format as Table
Cell Styles
Insert
Delete
Format
Cells
AutoSum
Fill
Clear
Sort & Filter
Find & Select
Editing
Sum (Alt+=)
Display the sum of the selected cells directly after the selected cells.
K
L
3
6
5
5
=SUM(J5:J8)

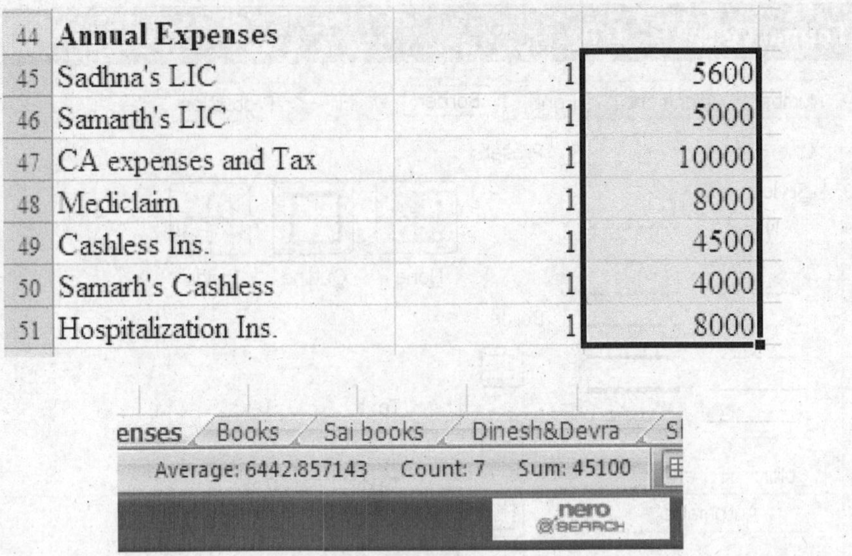

Remember

1. You do not need to type the close (right) parenthesis before you press Enter—Excel will do it for you.
2. Use this technique instead of AutoSum to sum ranges of cells that contain blanks.

AVERAGE FUNCTION

You can use the Average function to calculate the average of values in cells.

1. Click the cell where you want to place the average function.
2. Type an equal sign (=) and then type the word AVERAGE and a left parenthesis.
3. Drag across the cells whose values you want to average.
4. Press Enter.

Remember

1. Blank cells in the range are not counted in the average.

In Excel 2010, you can see the sum and average on the status bar, too, as shown here.

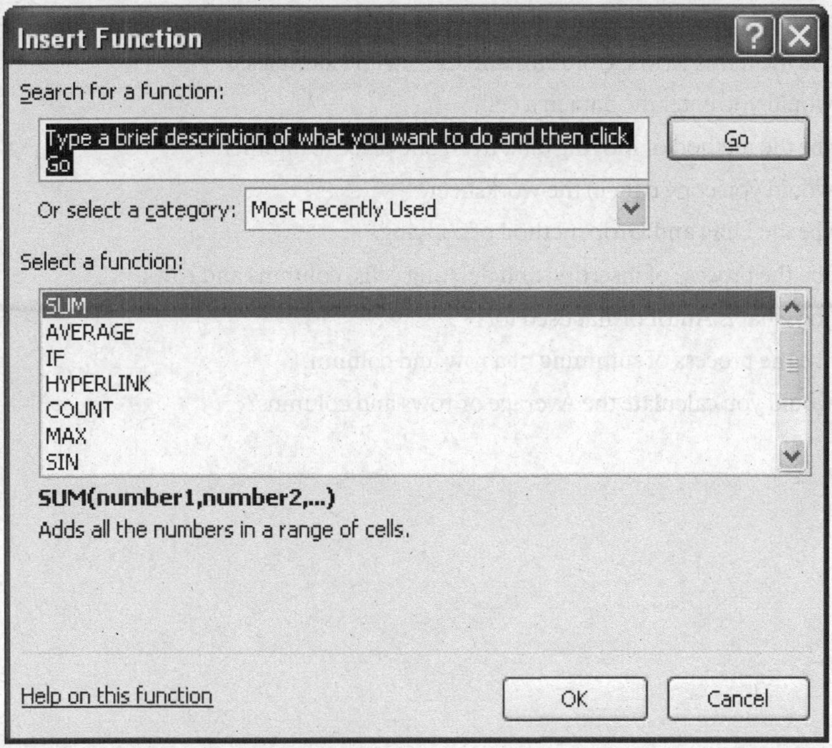

USING FUNCTION WIZARD

Sum and Average are just two of the most commonly used functions whereas there are lots of them in Excel 2010. You can use them to get the desired results in a flash. To get them click the **Insert Function** button on the Formulas panel as your are building the formula. The Paste Function wizard takes you through the steps of building a formula.

1. Click the destination cell for the formula.
2. Click the Paste Function button on the Standard toolbar.
3. In the Paste Function dialog box, select the category and then the function.
4. Click Ok.
5. Use the Paste Function Wizard to guide you in completing the formula.
6. Click Ok when you have finished.

Common Functions

In a later chapter you will read about the various functions.

Review Questions

1. Describe the terms Rows, Columns and Cells with examples.
2. How would you enter the data in a cell?
3. Describe the method of moving data from one place to another.
4. How would you copy data in the worksheet?
5. Describe the Drag and Drop method of copying.
6. Describe the process of inserting and deleting cells, columns and rows.
7. Describe what is AutoFormat used for?
8. Describe the process of summing of a row and column.
9. How would you calculate the Average of rows and columns?

4

Creating a Worksheet in Microsoft Excel 2010

INTRODUCTION

We have learnt quite a number of commands and naturally would like to use them in a worksheet. So let us create a worksheet and use these commands side-by-side to see how they work out.

CREATING A WORKSHEET IN EXCEL 2010

Supposing we have the financial highlights of a company as given below:

Year	Total Income (A)	Interest Paid (B)	Profit (C)	Tax (D)	Profit After Tax (E)
1999	4,500	To be	To be	To be	To be
2000	5,500	Calculated	Calculated	Calculated	Calculated
2001	7,000	as 15%	as Income	as 12% of	as Profit
2002	8,000	of the	minus	the Profit	minus Tax
2003	9,000	Total	Interest		(C) - (D)
2004	12,000	Income	(A) - (B)		
2005	15,000				
2006	20,000				

As you can see that there are quite a number of fields which have to be calculated. This will act as a good exercise for you to do. Let us start from the very beginning, i.e., start the software Microsoft Excel 2010. You will end up with a blank worksheet, ready for you to take action, with the first cell **A1**, totally at your command to do something, as shown in the figure next.

So what we have to do here. We have to type "Year". So just type the word Year and press **Enter**. You will see the word being shown in the formula bar too. This will also take you to the cell **A2**. But, for typing the next heading, you have to go to the cell **B1**. So use the arrow keys right and up to reach **B1**.

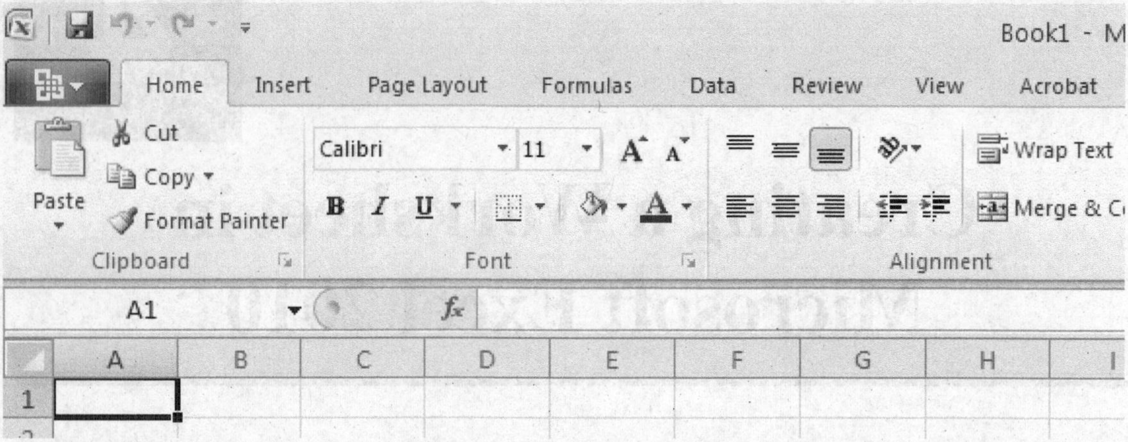

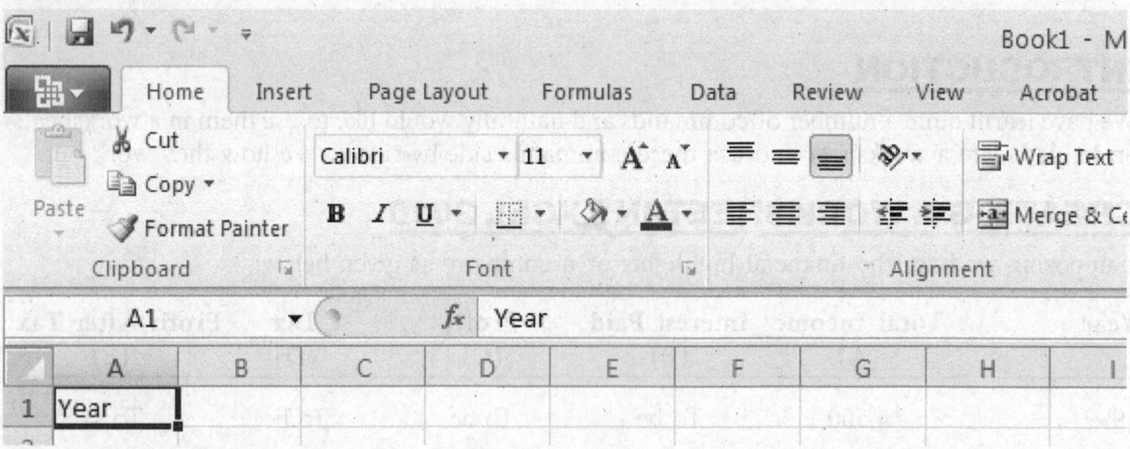

Next we have to type "Total Income". (Please note that for the sake of convenience I had shown this heading in 2 lines, but, if permitted we will type it in one line. Also (A), (B), etc., in the table are just symbolic and are not to be typed).

So for type the next heading, "Total Income" in the cell **B1**, as shown next.

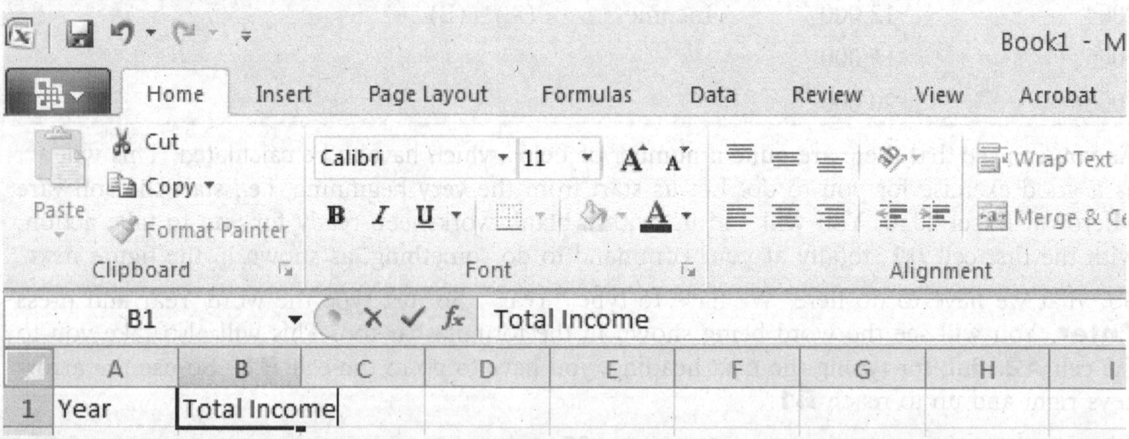

Did you notice anything wrong here? Well, the cell is not big enough to carry your heading. So what will we do? We will increase the width of the column **B**, by using one of the methods mentioned earlier in the chapter, i.e., by using the Cells command under Tools.

This way now we will type the complete headings, i.e., all of them, as shown next.

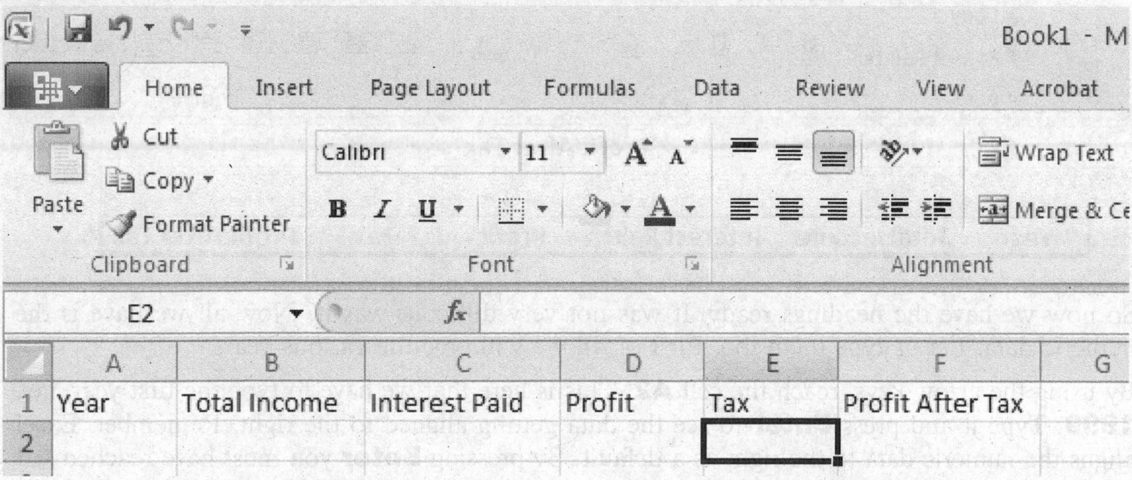

But, since these are headings, and are to be highlighted. We will make them **Bold** and put them in the centre of the cells. This way they will look good.

Highlight all the cells by just clicking at cell **A1** and then while pressing **Shift** key click mouse in the cell **F1**, the whole row gets highlighted.

Now click at B in the formatting bar to make the whole text as Bold.

With the text in the cells remaining highlighted, click at  in the alignment panel of Home menu. This will make the text in the cells centralized in all the cells. This is shown in the figure shown next.

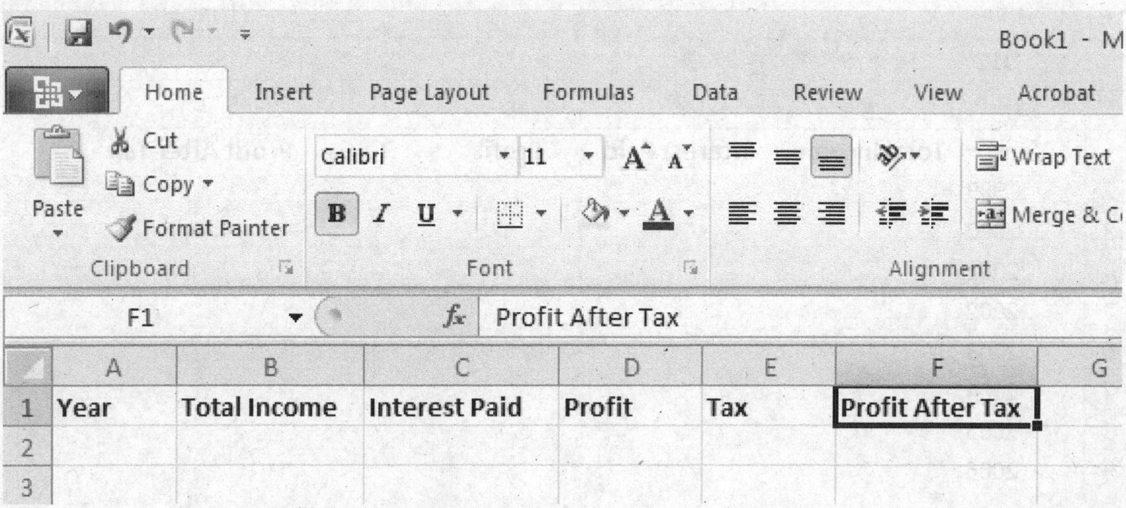

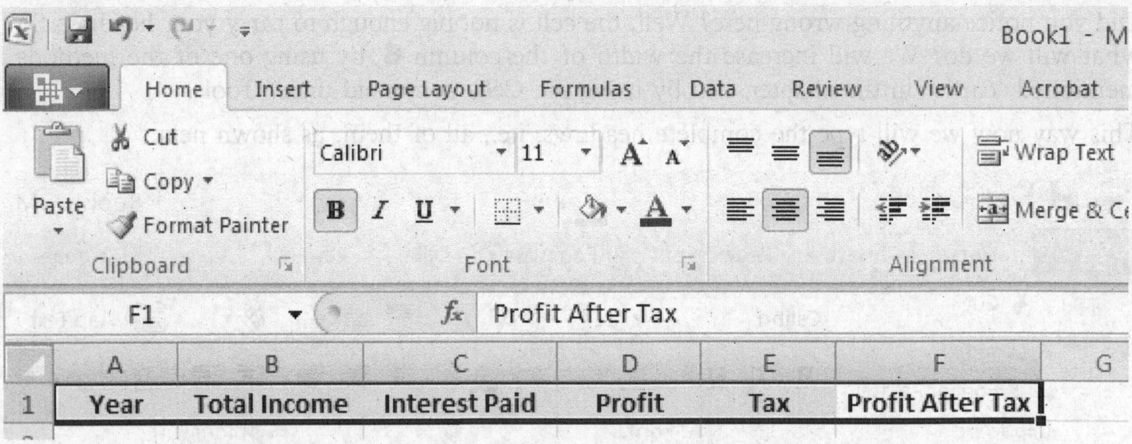

So now we have the headings ready. It was not very difficult, was it? Now all we have is the numeric data. Let us type them too. First of all we will type the various years.

By using the arrow keys, reach the cell **A2**. This is here that we have to type the first year, i.e., **1999**. Type it and press **Enter** to see the data getting aligned to the right. Remember, Excel aligns the numeric data to the right as a default. By pressing **Enter** you must have reached **A3** and this is where you wanted to be for typing the next year, i.e., **2000**.

So now type one year and press **Enter** to reach the next cell for typing the next year, till you reach the last year, i.e., **2006**. At this stage your worksheet will look like the one shown next.

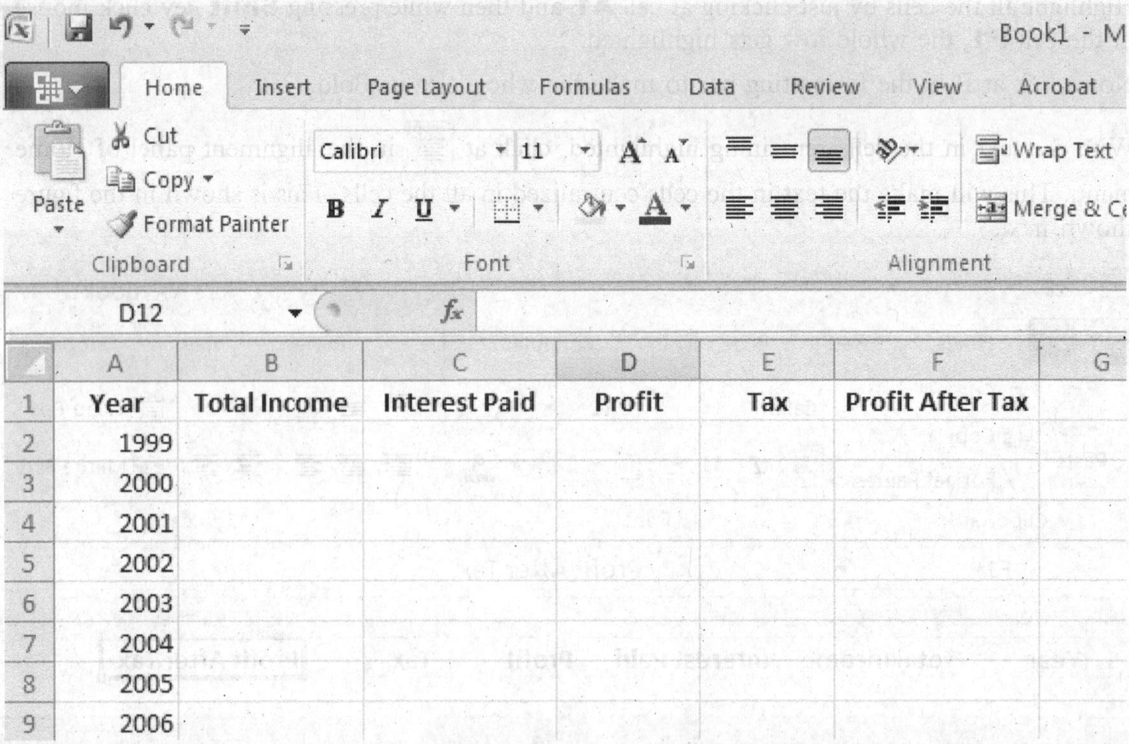

Next step is also easy. You have to just type the numbers in the cells **B2** to **B9**. All these figures are available with you. Just type one figure and press **Enter** to reach the next cell and so on till you reach the last cell in the column. After doing this your worksheet will look like the one shown next.

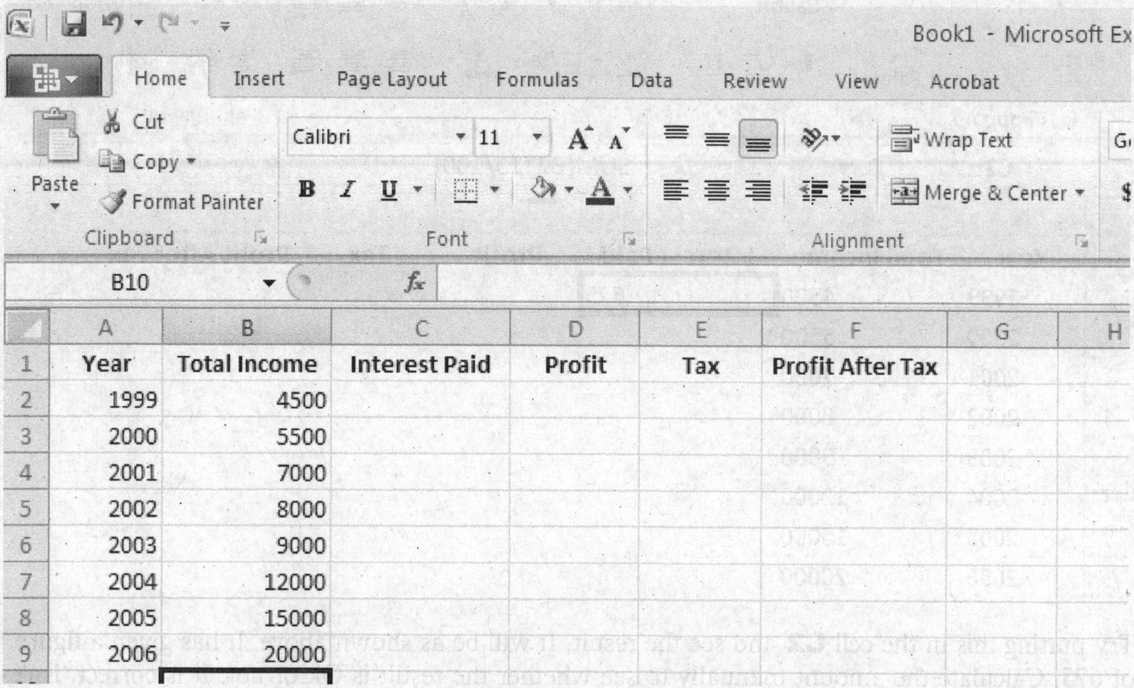

	A	B	C	D	E	F	G	H
1	Year	Total Income	Interest Paid	Profit	Tax	Profit After Tax		
2	1999	4500						
3	2000	5500						
4	2001	7000						
5	2002	8000						
6	2003	9000						
7	2004	12000						
8	2005	15000						
9	2006	20000						

It would not be a bad idea to save this worksheet at this stage. For god forbid, if something happens, like power cut or so. So just press **Ctrl+S** to give the save command, as you would give in any other software. Now all you have to do it to give it a name and decide where you want to save this worksheet. Let us give the name **Finance** to it.

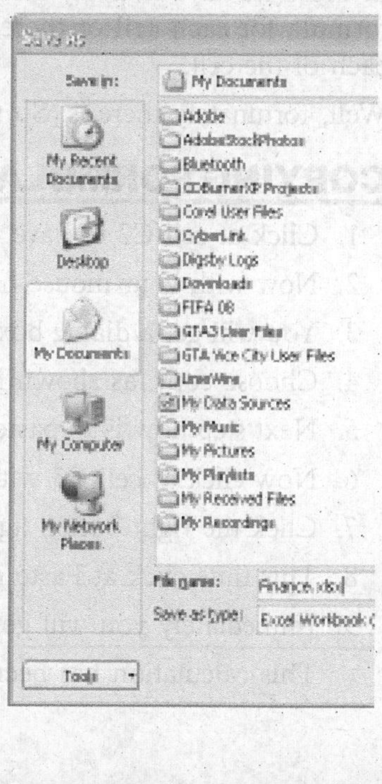

Now we come to the interesting part of this worksheet. So far we have typed whatever was available. Now we have to generate the figures. The column **C** is of Interest Paid which is to be calculated by using the formula.

$$\text{Interest Paid} = \frac{\text{Total Income} \times 15}{100}$$

Transformed to the computer language it will become:

Interest Paid = (Total Income x 15)/100

If we put this in Cell **C2**, it will become:

C2 = SUM(B2*15/100)

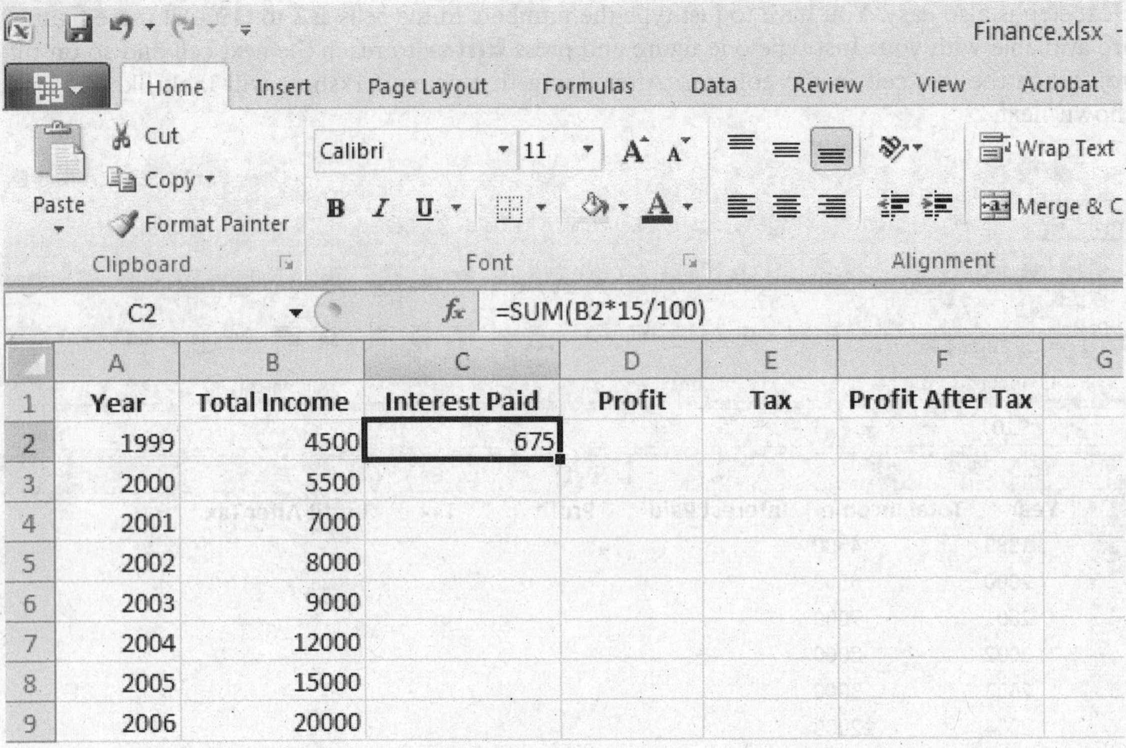

Try putting this in the cell **C2** and see the result. It will be as shown above. It has given a figure of 675. Calculate the amount manually to see whether the result is Ok or not. It is correct, isn't it? Now we have to apply this formula to all the cells from **C3** to **C9**. Do you have to put the formula for each cell or there is a method in Excel which allows you to copy the formula in each of the cell.

Well, fortunately there is. So this is how you will do it.

COPYING FORMULA

1. Click at cell C2 to have the formula displayed in the formula bar.
2. Now with your mouse having clicked at cell C2, press the right button of the mouse.
3. You will get a dialog box, as shown below, which has various commands at your disposal.
4. Choose copy, as shown here, to copy the formula.
5. Next step now is to paste the formula in their respective cells.
6. Now click at cell C3 with the mouse (left button).
7. Click the right button again to get the dialog box.
8. This time click at Paste instead, as shown next.
9. Immediately you will get the figure in cell C3.

   This calculation has been based on B3 (see the formula bar) and not B2 which had been

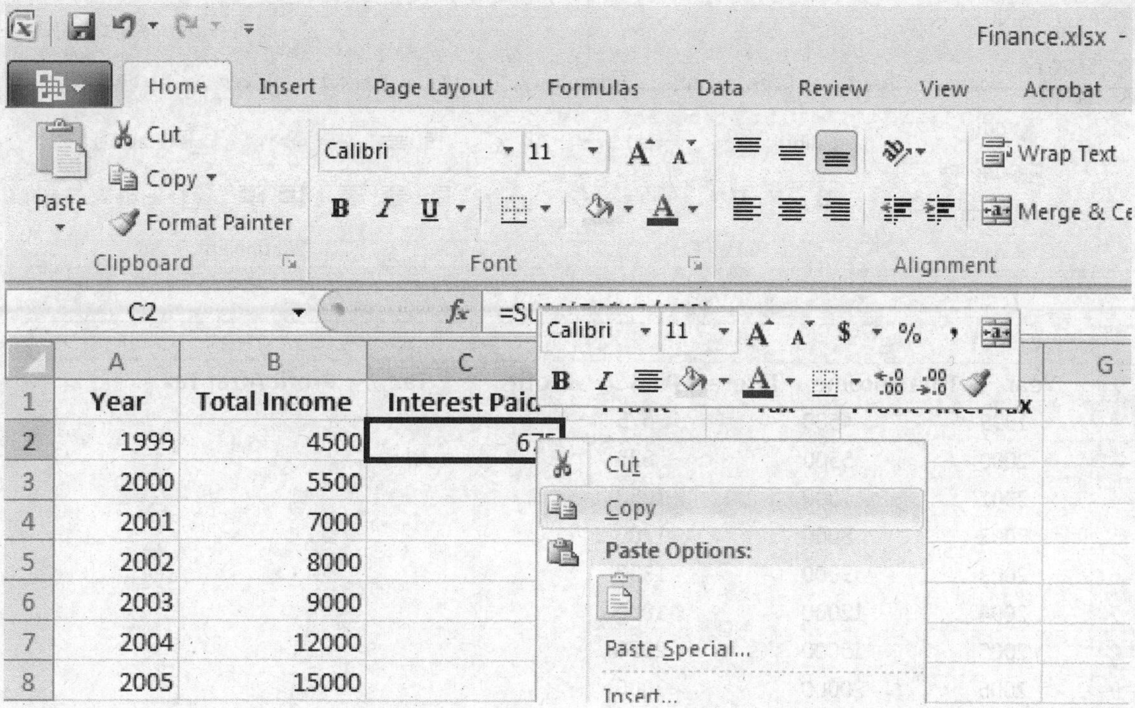
Finance.xlsx -
Home
Insert
Page Layout
Formulas
Data
Review
View
Acrobat
Cut
Copy
Paste
Format Painter
Clipboard
Calibri
11
Font
Wrap Text
Merge & Ce
Alignment
C2
=SU
Year
Total Income
Interest Paid
1999 4500 675
2000 5500
2001 7000
2002 8000
2003 9000
2004 12000
2005 15000
Cut
Copy
Paste Options:
Paste Special...
Insert...

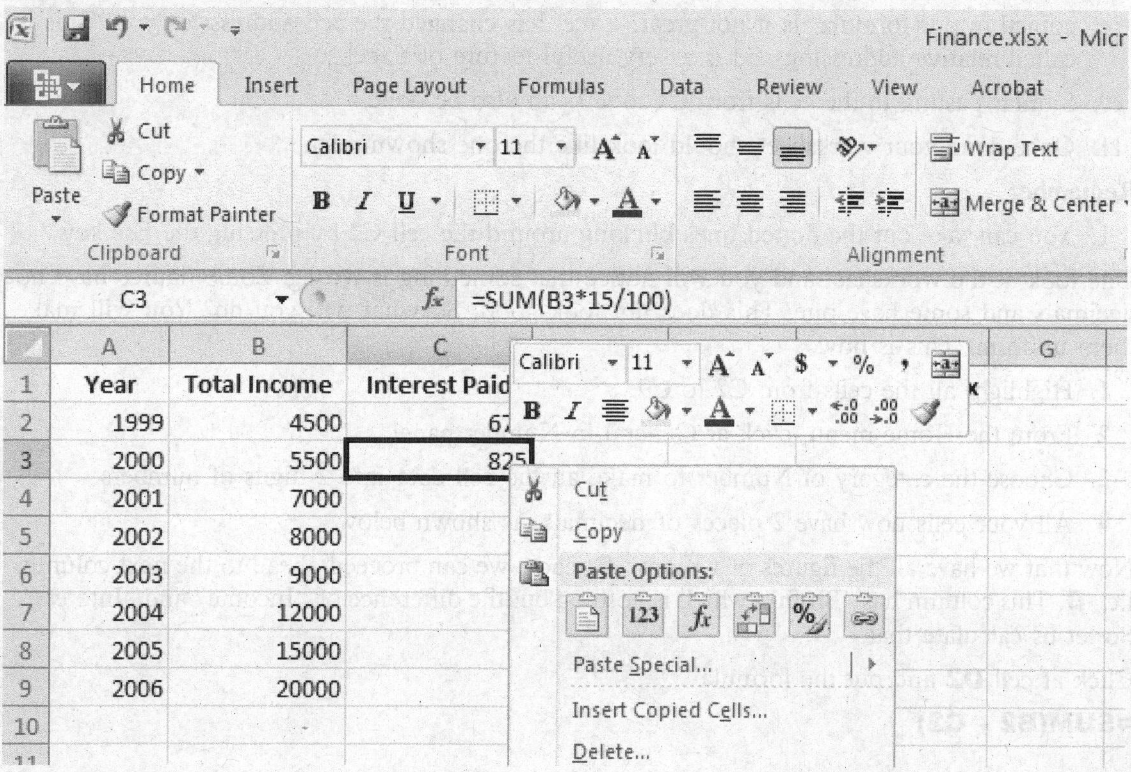
Finance.xlsx - Micr
Home
Insert
Page Layout
Formulas
Data
Review
View
Acrobat
Cut
Copy
Paste
Format Painter
Clipboard
Calibri
11
Font
Wrap Text
Merge & Center
Alignment
C3
=SUM(B3*15/100)
Year
Total Income
Interest Paid
1999 4500 67
2000 5500 825
2001 7000
2002 8000
2003 9000
2004 12000
2005 15000
2006 20000
Cut
Copy
Paste Options:
Paste Special...
Insert Copied Cells...
Delete...

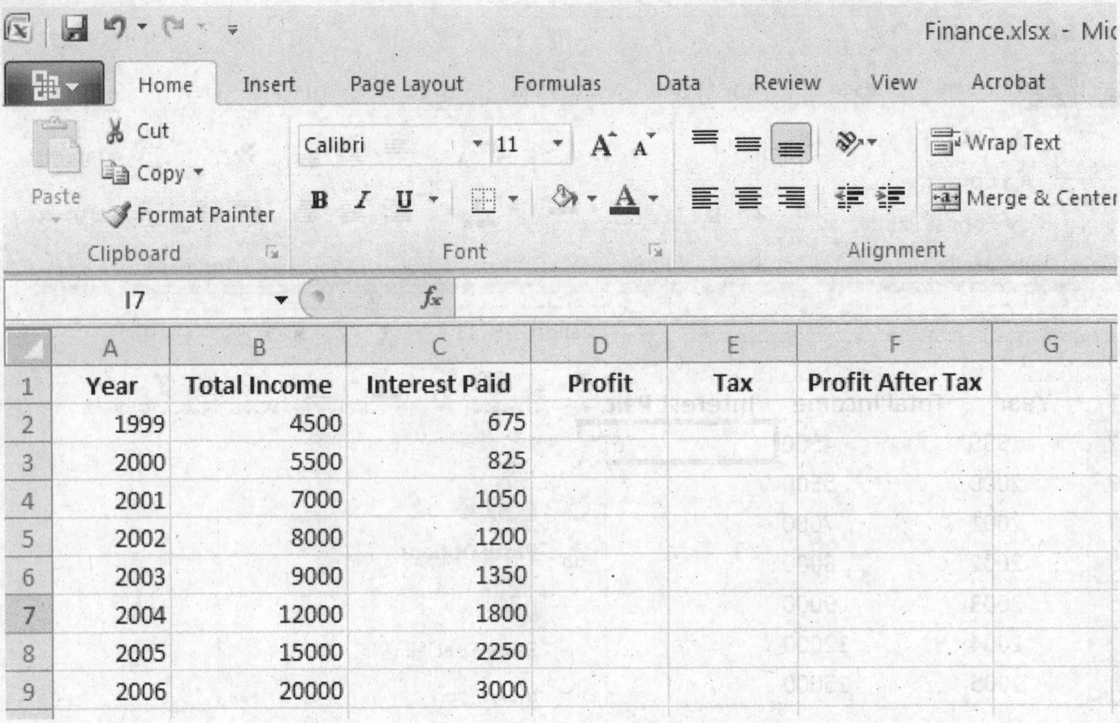

	A	B	C	D	E	F	G
1	Year	Total Income	Interest Paid	Profit	Tax	Profit After Tax	
2	1999	4500	675				
3	2000	5500	825				
4	2001	7000	1050				
5	2002	8000	1200				
6	2003	9000	1350				
7	2004	12000	1800				
8	2005	15000	2250				
9	2006	20000	3000				

copied in our formula. Is it not great? Excel has changed the cell address for you. This is called relative addressing and is a very useful feature of Excel.

10. Similar pasting in the cells from C4 to C9 can also be done.
11. Once done your worksheet should look like the one shown next.

Remember

1. You can take out the dotted lines blinking around the cell C2 by pressing the Esc key.

One look at the worksheet and you will notice that something is wrong. Some figures have no decimals and some have one. This does not look good. So what will you do? You will make them uniform. This is how:

1. Highlight all the cells from C2 to C9.
2. From the Home menu, click at General in Number panel.
3. Choose the category of Number to make all the cell data into 2 digits of numbers.
4. All your cells now have 2 places of decimals, as shown below.

Now that we have all the figures of Column **C** ready, we can proceed ahead to the next column, i.e., **D**. This column has "Profit", which is nothing but the difference of "Income" and "Interest". So let us calculate that.

Click at cell **D2** and put the formula

=SUM(B2 – C2)

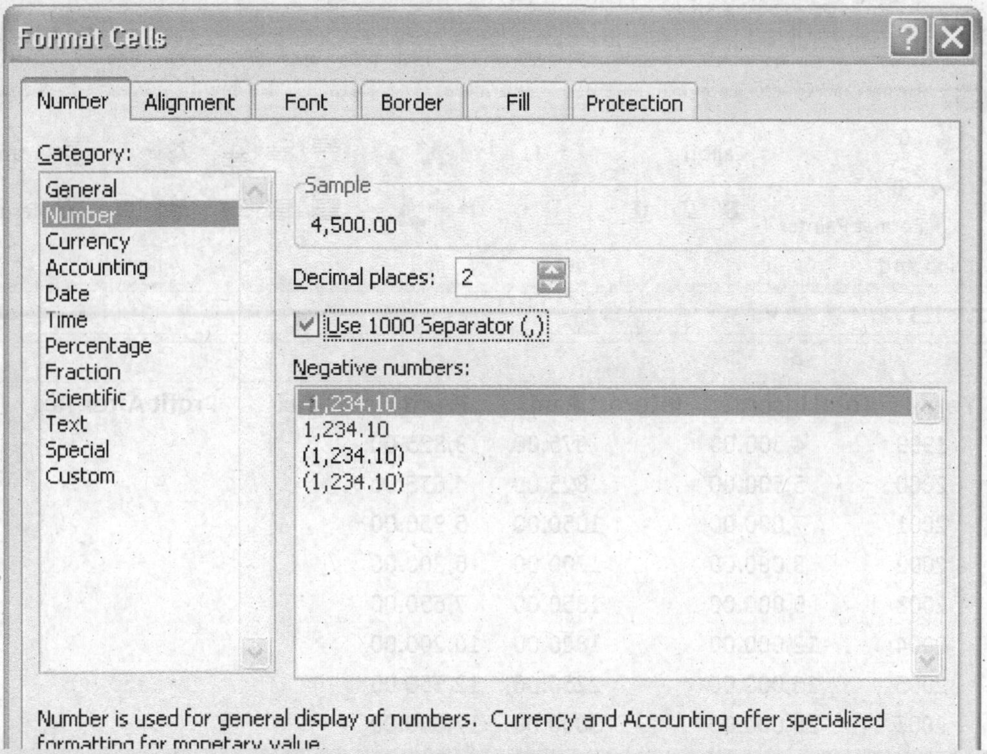

Format Cells
Number
Alignment
Font
Border
Fill
Protection
Category:
General
Number
Currency
Accounting
Date
Time
Percentage
Fraction
Scientific
Text
Special
Custom
Sample
4,500.00
Decimal places: 2
Use 1000 Separator (,)
Negative numbers:
-1,234.10
1,234.10
(1,234.10)
(1,234.10)
Number is used for general display of numbers. Currency and Accounting offer specialized

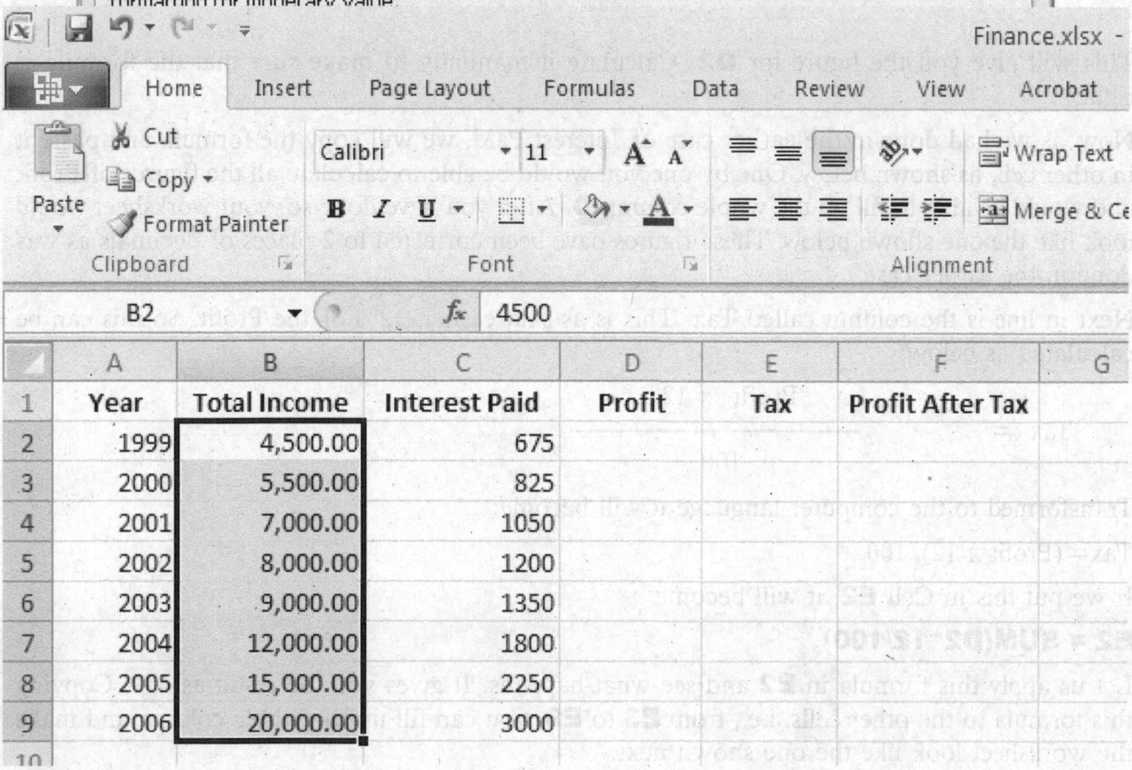

Finance.xlsx -
Home
Insert
Page Layout
Formulas
Data
Review
View
Acrobat
Cut
Copy
Paste
Format Painter
Clipboard
Calibri
11
Font
Wrap Text
Merge & Ce
Alignment
B2
4500
Year
Total Income
Interest Paid
Profit
Tax
Profit After Tax
1999 4,500.00 675
2000 5,500.00 825
2001 7,000.00 1050
2002 8,000.00 1200
2003 9,000.00 1350
2004 12,000.00 1800
2005 15,000.00 2250
2006 20,000.00 3000

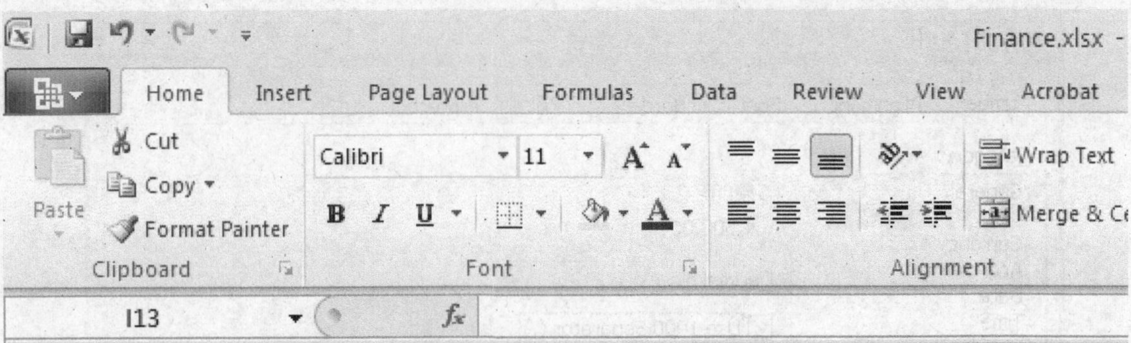

	A	B	C	D	E	F
1	Year	Total Income	Interest Paid	Profit	Tax	Profit After Tax
2	1999	4,500.00	675.00	3,825.00		
3	2000	5,500.00	825.00	4,675.00		
4	2001	7,000.00	1050.00	5,950.00		
5	2002	8,000.00	1200.00	6,800.00		
6	2003	9,000.00	1350.00	7,650.00		
7	2004	12,000.00	1800.00	10,200.00		
8	2005	15,000.00	2250.00	12,750.00		
9	2006	20,000.00	3000.00	17,000.00		

This will give you the figure for **D2**. Calculate it manually to make sure that the formula is right.

Now, as we had done in the earlier case of Interest Paid, we will copy the formula and paste it in other cell, as shown below. One by one you would be able to calculate all the figures of Profit and would be able to fill up the whole column **D**. After you have done so, your worksheet would look like the one shown below. These figures have been corrected to 2 places of decimals as was done in the earlier case.

Next in line is the column called Tax. This is as said earlier, 12% of the Profit. So this can be calculated as below:

$$\text{Tax} = \frac{\text{Profit} \times 12}{100}$$

Transformed to the computer language it will become:

Tax= (Profit x 12)/100

If we put this in Cell **E2**, it will become:

E2 = SUM(D2*12/100)

Let us apply this formula in **E2** and see what happens. It gives you the result as 459. Copying this formula to the other cells, i.e., from **E3** to **E9**, you can fill up the whole column and make the worksheet look like the one shown next.

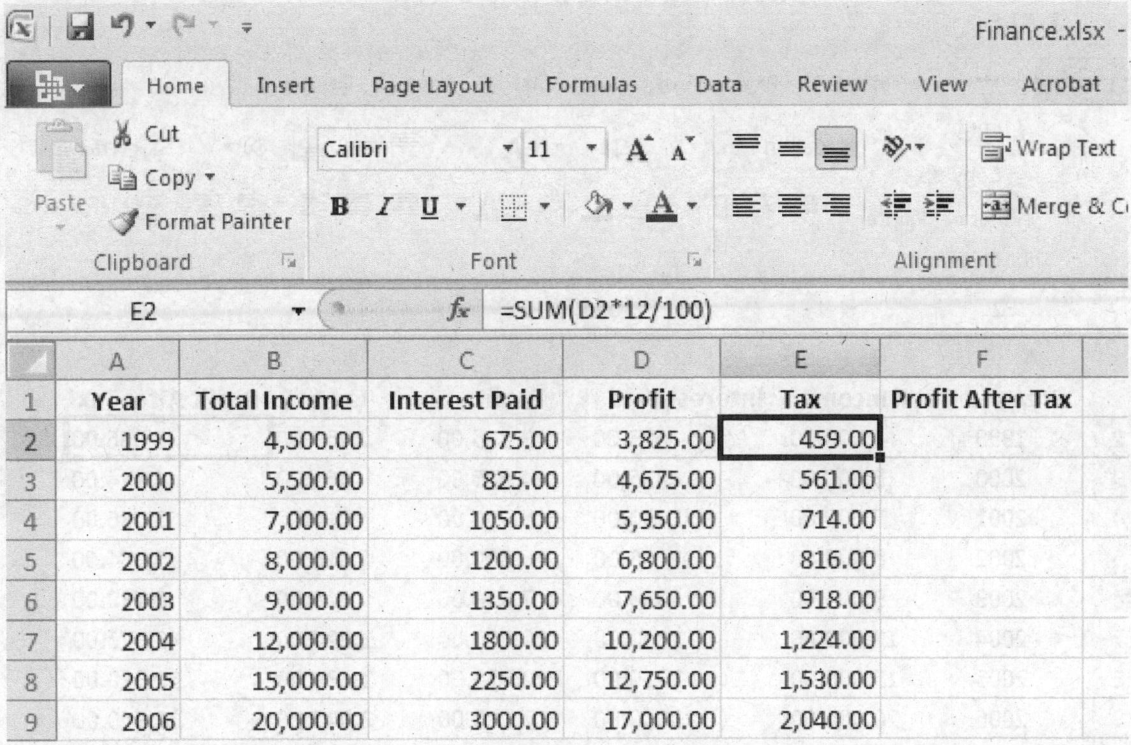

	A	B	C	D	E	F
1	Year	Total Income	Interest Paid	Profit	Tax	Profit After Tax
2	1999	4,500.00	675.00	3,825.00	459.00	
3	2000	5,500.00	825.00	4,675.00	561.00	
4	2001	7,000.00	1050.00	5,950.00	714.00	
5	2002	8,000.00	1200.00	6,800.00	816.00	
6	2003	9,000.00	1350.00	7,650.00	918.00	
7	2004	12,000.00	1800.00	10,200.00	1,224.00	
8	2005	15,000.00	2250.00	12,750.00	1,530.00	
9	2006	20,000.00	3000.00	17,000.00	2,040.00	

The last column in this case is the "Profit After Tax", which can be calculated after subtracting "Tax" from the "Profit". This calculation I am not showing here, since I assume that you should be able to do this easily. However, your resultant worksheet should look like the one shown next.

You think the worksheet is complete. No. You still have to do the column totals without which the whole worksheet looks incomplete.

For this follow the following steps.

1. Click at cell B10 to get the total of figures from B2 to B9.
2. Now click at Σ symbol in the Home menu.
3. It will search for the numeric cells above and put the formula for the same and highlight the cells it has selected.
4. It will wait for your Ok in the form of Enter to put the result.
5. Press Enter to get the total in the cell B10, as shown below.

Similarly all the other columns can be summed up showing the result as shown next.

Now you can say that your worksheet is complete. But, supposing we want to make any change. This is done deliberately to show you the main advantage of Excel software.

Supposing, we change the figure of the year 2003 from 9,000 to 9,200, which we can assume that it was wrongly given to us or was a typing mistake. It is shown next. Try changing this figure in the cell **B6** and see the resultant effect. What have you noticed? Well since all the figures

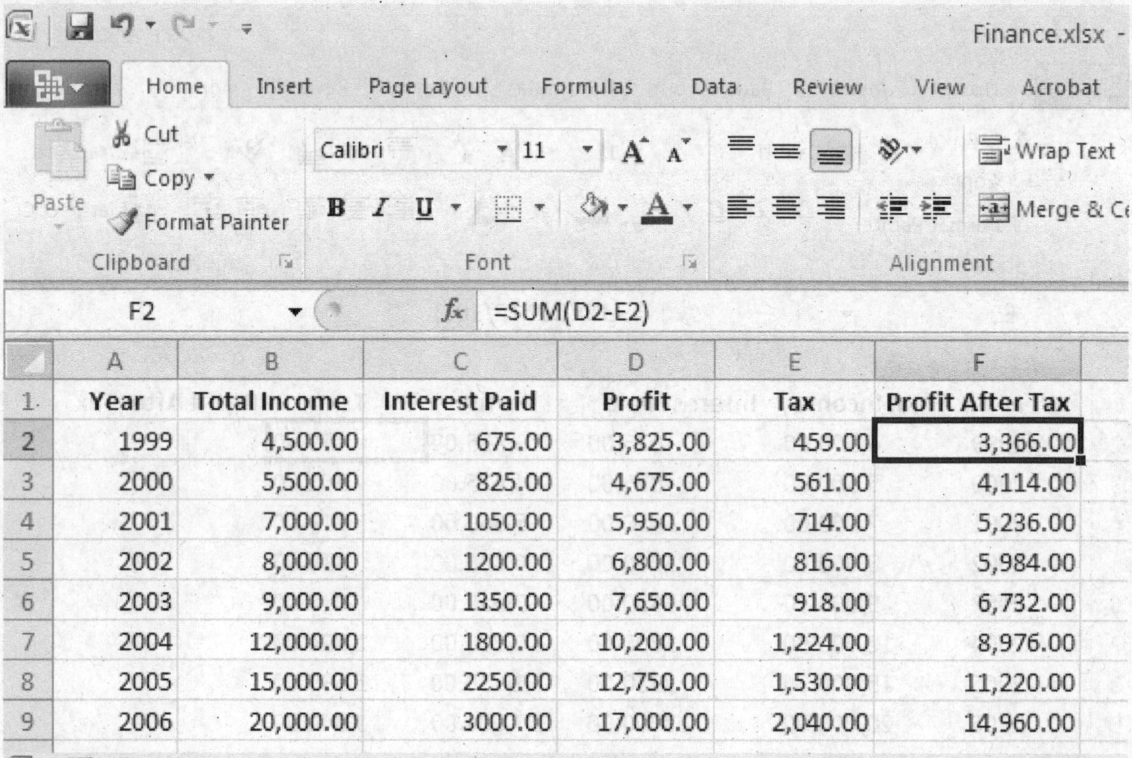

	A	B	C	D	E	F
1	Year	Total Income	Interest Paid	Profit	Tax	Profit After Tax
2	1999	4,500.00	675.00	3,825.00	459.00	3,366.00
3	2000	5,500.00	825.00	4,675.00	561.00	4,114.00
4	2001	7,000.00	1050.00	5,950.00	714.00	5,236.00
5	2002	8,000.00	1200.00	6,800.00	816.00	5,984.00
6	2003	9,000.00	1350.00	7,650.00	918.00	6,732.00
7	2004	12,000.00	1800.00	10,200.00	1,224.00	8,976.00
8	2005	15,000.00	2250.00	12,750.00	1,530.00	11,220.00
9	2006	20,000.00	3000.00	17,000.00	2,040.00	14,960.00

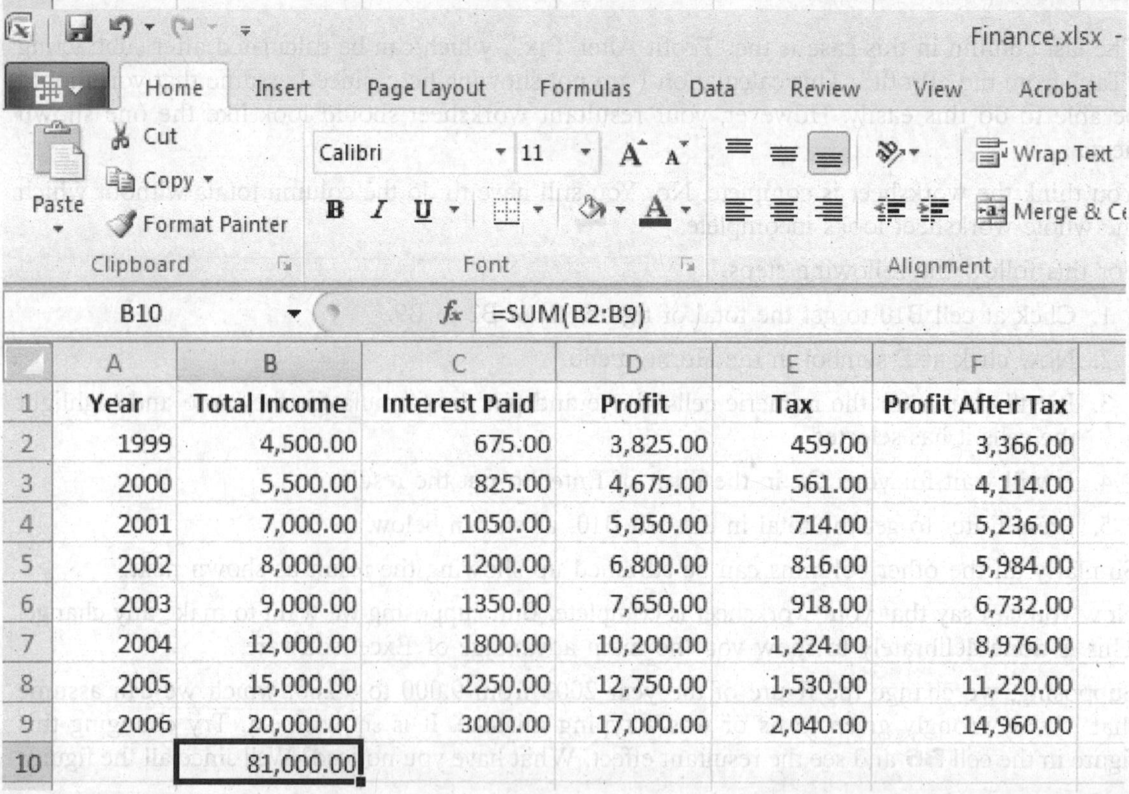

	A	B	C	D	E	F
1	Year	Total Income	Interest Paid	Profit	Tax	Profit After Tax
2	1999	4,500.00	675.00	3,825.00	459.00	3,366.00
3	2000	5,500.00	825.00	4,675.00	561.00	4,114.00
4	2001	7,000.00	1050.00	5,950.00	714.00	5,236.00
5	2002	8,000.00	1200.00	6,800.00	816.00	5,984.00
6	2003	9,000.00	1350.00	7,650.00	918.00	6,732.00
7	2004	12,000.00	1800.00	10,200.00	1,224.00	8,976.00
8	2005	15,000.00	2250.00	12,750.00	1,530.00	11,220.00
9	2006	20,000.00	3000.00	17,000.00	2,040.00	14,960.00
10		81,000.00				

are mostly inter-linked, if you change one figure all the relative figures change automatically. This is the main advantage of Excel or for that an electronic spreadsheet.

Now if you apply this to the accounting department and assume that these figures relate to actual working of the finance department. Try changing the figures of one voucher and the poor accountant would have to sit probably the whole night to recalculate all the totals in the Balance Sheet. But, now with this kind of spreadsheet, this can be done in a flash.

Coming back to our worksheet. There are 3 things more to be done. Firstly, we will decorate it using the options available in Excel 2010. After seeing a preview of our worksheet and we will print it on our printer. For decorating in Excel 2010, wc havc thc command called Conditional Formatting, which is on the Home menu. It has various options which can be used. I have gone for the one which is of color scales and have applied one of them. See the result next.

You are free to choose any one of them and decorate your worksheet as you wish. As you move your mouse over the options the resultant effect on the worksheet is also shown, which helps you in making the decisions.

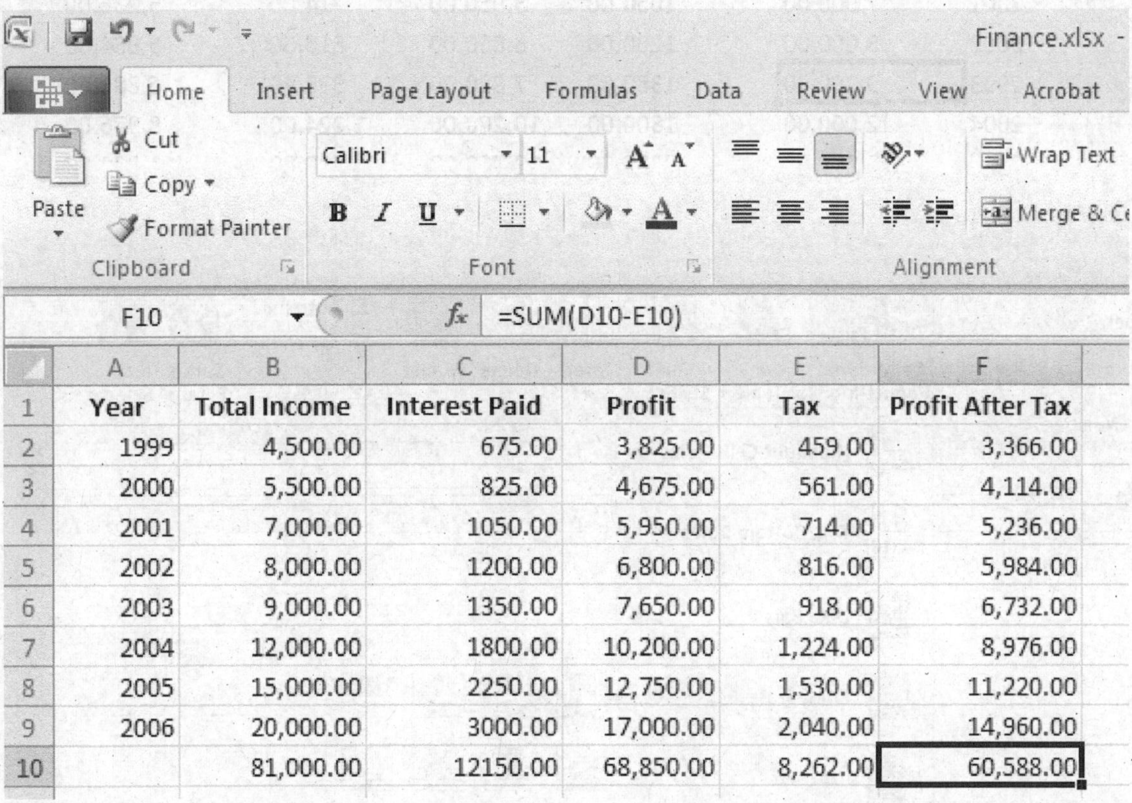

	A	B	C	D	E	F
1	Year	Total Income	Interest Paid	Profit	Tax	Profit After Tax
2	1999	4,500.00	675.00	3,825.00	459.00	3,366.00
3	2000	5,500.00	825.00	4,675.00	561.00	4,114.00
4	2001	7,000.00	1050.00	5,950.00	714.00	5,236.00
5	2002	8,000.00	1200.00	6,800.00	816.00	5,984.00
6	2003	9,000.00	1350.00	7,650.00	918.00	6,732.00
7	2004	12,000.00	1800.00	10,200.00	1,224.00	8,976.00
8	2005	15,000.00	2250.00	12,750.00	1,530.00	11,220.00
9	2006	20,000.00	3000.00	17,000.00	2,040.00	14,960.00
10		81,000.00	12150.00	68,850.00	8,262.00	60,588.00

Now that you have to print it on your printer to see the final result. But, before that we would like to see its **Preview**. This command is part of the **Print** command which is available under the **Options button**.

The preview of the worksheet is shown next.

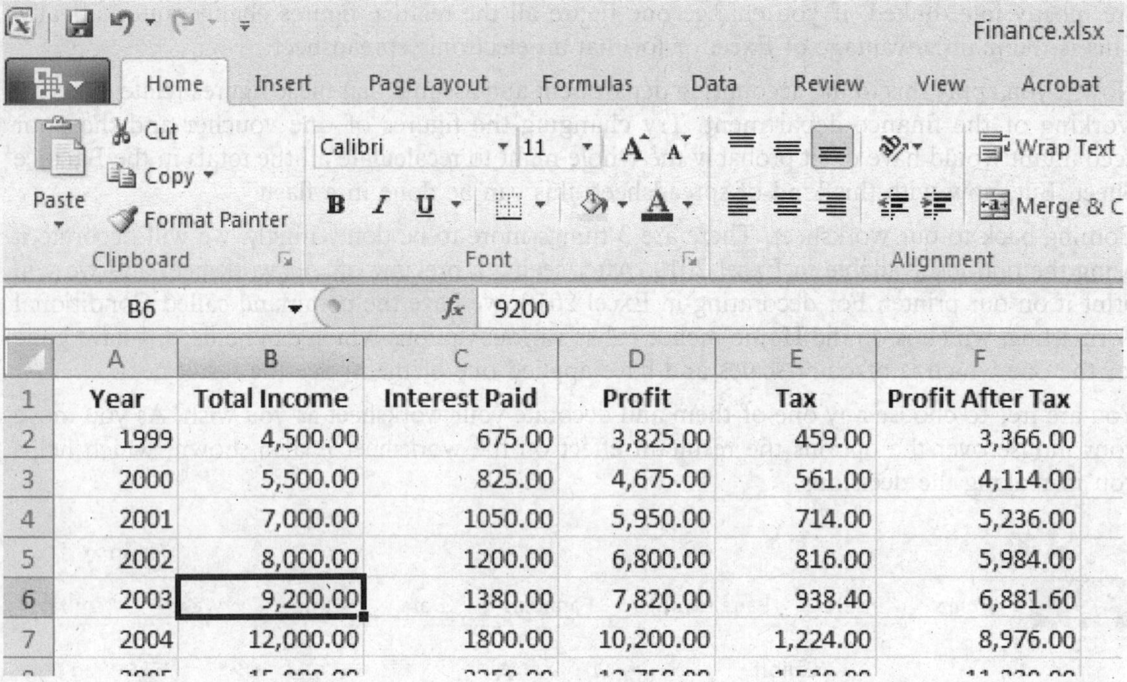
Finance.xlsx
Home
Insert
Page Layout
Formulas
Data
Review
View
Acrobat
Cut
Copy
Paste
Format Painter
Clipboard
Calibri
11
Font
Wrap Text
Merge & C
Alignment
B6
9200
Year | Total Income | Interest Paid | Profit | Tax | Profit After Tax
1999 | 4,500.00 | 675.00 | 3,825.00 | 459.00 | 3,366.00
2000 | 5,500.00 | 825.00 | 4,675.00 | 561.00 | 4,114.00
2001 | 7,000.00 | 1050.00 | 5,950.00 | 714.00 | 5,236.00
2002 | 8,000.00 | 1200.00 | 6,800.00 | 816.00 | 5,984.00
2003 | 9,200.00 | 1380.00 | 7,820.00 | 938.40 | 6,881.60
2004 | 12,000.00 | 1800.00 | 10,200.00 | 1,224.00 | 8,976.00

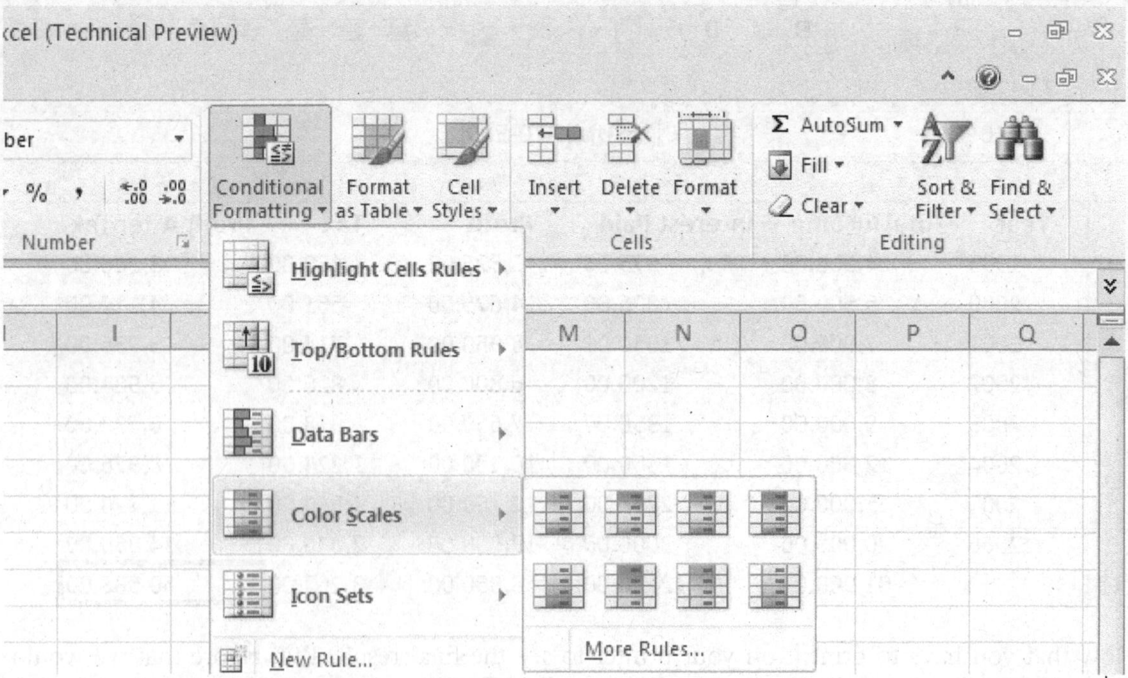
xcel (Technical Preview)
Conditional Formatting
Format as Table
Cell Styles
Insert
Delete
Format
Cells
AutoSum
Fill
Clear
Sort & Filter
Find & Select
Editing
Number
Highlight Cells Rules
Top/Bottom Rules
Data Bars
Color Scales
Icon Sets
New Rule...
More Rules...

Year	Total Income	Interest Paid	Profit	Tax	Profit After Tax
1999	4,500.00	675.00	3,825.00	459.00	3,366.00
2000	5,500.00	825.00	4,675.00	561.00	4,114.00
2001	7,000.00	1050.00	5,950.00	714.00	5,236.00
2002	8,000.00	1200.00	6,800.00	816.00	5,984.00
2003	9,200.00	1380.00	7,820.00	938.40	6,881.60
2004	12,000.00	1800.00	10,200.00	1,224.00	8,976.00
2005	15,000.00	2250.00	12,750.00	1,530.00	11,220.00
2006	20,000.00	3000.00	17,000.00	2,040.00	14,960.00
	81,200.00	12180.00	69,020.00	8,282.40	60,737.60

FORMULAS THAT MAKE DECISIONS

There will be a time when you want Excel to carry out one task under certain circumstances and another task if those circumstances don't apply. If you are familiar with any programming language, it is the case of IF, WHEN or IF, THEN. You have a similar IF function in Excel.

How the IF function works

In its simplest form, the IF function tests the value of a cell and does one thing if the test is positive (**TRUE**) and another if the test is negative (**FALSE**). It requires three arguments: the test data, the action to perform if the test is TRUE and the action to perform if the test is FALSE. You supply the arguments one after the other within the function's parentheses, separating them with commas (no spaces are to be given). The text which you want to appear as it is, i.e., TRUE or FALSE should be given under quotes, reference of cells like **C5**, etc., should be as it is.

Apply this formula in cell **B6** and see the result:

1. Select cell B6, type the following in place of formula and press Enter:

   = IF(B2=0, TRUE, FALSE)

   Excel checks whether the value in cell B2 is zero (the test), and because it isn't zero, it ignores TRUE (the action to perform if the test is TRUE) and displays FALSE (the action to perform if the test is FALSE) in cell B6.

2. Double-click cell B6, change formula to

   = IF(B2>1000, TRUE, FALSE)

   and press Enter. The entry in cell B6 instantly changes from FALSE to TRUE because the value in cell B2 is greater than one thousand; that is, the test is TRUE.

Both the options can be seen next.

Now this was very simple. Isn't it. However, you can also build tests that involve other functions. Suppose that in our Finance worksheet, we say that the Tax has to be a minimum of 1000, which means that if the Tax is less than 1000 it has to be put as 1000 and if it more that 1000, then the figure will stand as it is.

For this perform the following steps.

1. Click at any entry in E and select to insert a column from Insert Menu.
2. Use the Cut, Paste and Format buttons to restore the entries now in E2:E9 to F2:F9.
3. Click at F2 and apply the formula

   =IF(E2>1000, E2, 1000)

   This means that you are asking the system to check if it is above 1000, One of the two possibilities will arise:

TRUE This means that the figure in cell is more than 1000, then the column will be replaced by the figure in **E2**, which means that it is not changed.

FALSE This means that the figure in the cell **E2** is less than 1000, then the second condition will be met, i.e., figure in cell **F2** will be replaced with the figure of 1000.

Repeat this for all the other cells of column **F**. The easiest way out to repeat the formula in each column.

B6 | fx =IF(B2=0, TRUE, FALSE)

	A	B	C	D	E	F
1	Year	Total Income	Interest Paid	Profit	Tax	Profit After Tax
2	1999	4,500.00	675.00	3,825.00	459.00	3,366.00
3	2000	5,500.00	825.00	4,675.00	561.00	4,114.00
4	2001	7,000.00	1050.00	5,950.00	714.00	5,236.00
5	2002	8,000.00	1200.00	6,800.00	816.00	5,984.00
6	2003	FALSE	0.00	0.00	0.00	0.00

B6 | fx =IF(B2>1000, TRUE, FALSE)

	A	B	C	D	E	F
1	Year	Total Income	Interest Paid	Profit	Tax	Profit After Tax
2	1999	4,500.00	675.00	3,825.00	459.00	3,366.00
3	2000	5,500.00	825.00	4,675.00	561.00	4,114.00
4	2001	7,000.00	1050.00	5,950.00	714.00	5,236.00
5	2002	8,000.00	1200.00	6,800.00	816.00	5,984.00
6	2003	TRUE	0.15	0.85	0.10	0.75
7	2004	12,000.00	1800.00	10,200.00	1,224.00	8,976.00

Review Questions

1. Describe the working of the copying formula.
2. Describe the process of saving a worksheet.
3. How formulas can be used to take decision.
4. Describe the complete process of creating a worksheet.

5

Advanced Techniques of Microsoft Excel 2010

INTRODUCTION

So far we have used the various commands in Microsoft Excel 2010. Now, we look at the commands which are not very commonly used.

STYLES

Create a Style by Example

1. Select cell containing desired formats.
2. Click Cell Styles in the Home Panel.
3. It will show the various style sheet options available.
4. In the end there is an option of Create New Style which allows you to create one of your own.
3. Type a name for style in Style Name: The style's formats in Style includes box.

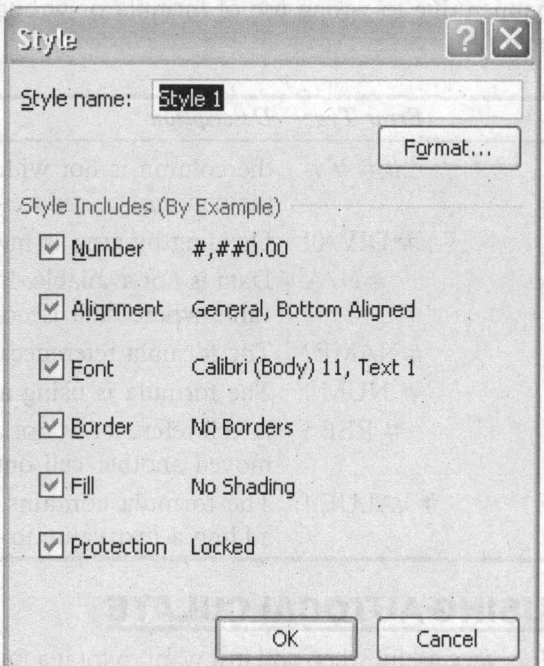

Exclude formats of selected cell from style:

1. Deselect Style Includes (by example) options: Number, Alignment, Font, Border, Fill, Protection
2. Click Ok.

FUNCTIONS IN EXCEL

They establish relationships between two or more cells. If you want to add the values in cells A3 and A4 and put the result in cell A5, move to the cell A5 and type =A3+A4 and press Enter. The result is displayed immediately in cell A5. Another way to achieve the same result is to move to cell A5 and type +, point to cell A3, type +, then point to A4, and press Enter. The easiest way to achieve this operation is to point to A5, pick up the AutoSum button Σ on the toolbar. The following symbols have their specific meaning in the formulae which are used in Excel.

Symbol	*Description*	*Symbol*	*Description*
:	Reference operator	,	Argument operator
–	Negation	%	Percentage sign
^	Exponent	*	Multiplication
/	Division	+	Addition
–	Subtraction	&	Text concatenation
>	Greater than	<	Less than
>=	Greater than or equal to	<=	Less than or equal to
<>	Not equal to		

While working with the formulae you would come across the various errors too, which could happen due to wrong use of formula or wrong typing. The following are the common type of errors.

Error Type	*Description*
# # # #	the column is not wide enough to display the number so either widen the column, or reduce the font size or change the numeric format.
# DIV/0!	Dividing by zero is invalid
# N/A	Data is not available. It happens usually when you refer to a function or value where data is not available
# NAME?	The formula references a name that is unknown to Excel
# NUM !	The formula is using an invalid number
# REF !	A cell reference is not available may be because you deleted that cell or moved another cell onto it.
# VALUE !	The formula contains an invalid operator or argument, for example, adding a text value to a numeric value

USING AUTOCALCULATE

It is very useful when you just want to total a number of columns but have the total in a particular field. The result will be displayed in Excel status bar and not in any cell. You can just view the sum. Perform the following steps to see the result.

1. Select the range whose total you want.
2. Right click at Status bar of the worksheet.
3. From the sub menu that appears, click at Sum.
4. The sum total would be displayed on the Status bar alongwith the sub menu, as shown next.

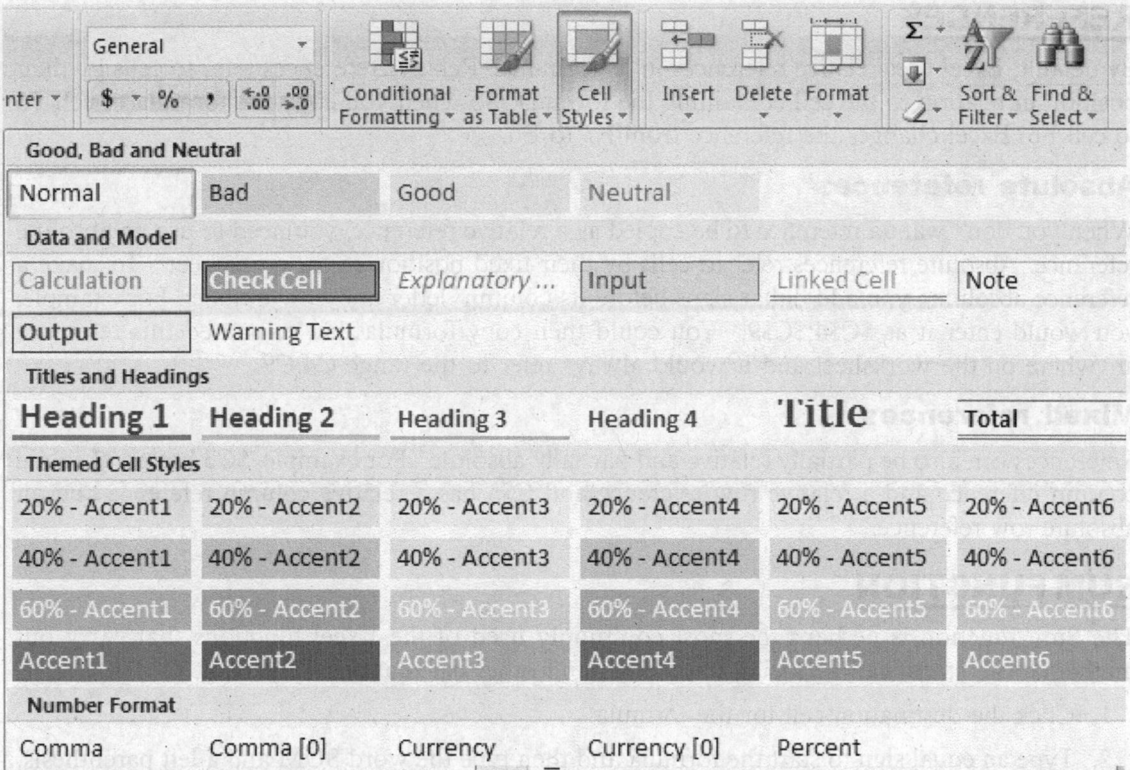
General
nter
$ % ,
Conditional Formatting
Format as Table
Cell Styles
Insert
Delete
Format
Sort & Filter
Find & Select
Good, Bad and Neutral
Normal
Bad
Good
Neutral
Data and Model
Calculation
Check Cell
Explanatory ...
Input
Linked Cell
Note
Output
Warning Text
Titles and Headings
Heading 1
Heading 2
Heading 3
Heading 4
Title
Total
Themed Cell Styles
20% - Accent1
20% - Accent2
20% - Accent3
20% - Accent4
20% - Accent5
20% - Accent6
40% - Accent1
40% - Accent2
40% - Accent3
40% - Accent4
40% - Accent5
40% - Accent6
60% - Accent1
60% - Accent2
60% - Accent3
60% - Accent4
60% - Accent5
60% - Accent6
Accent1
Accent2
Accent3
Accent4
Accent5
Accent6
Number Format
Comma
Comma [0]
Currency
Currency [0]
Percent

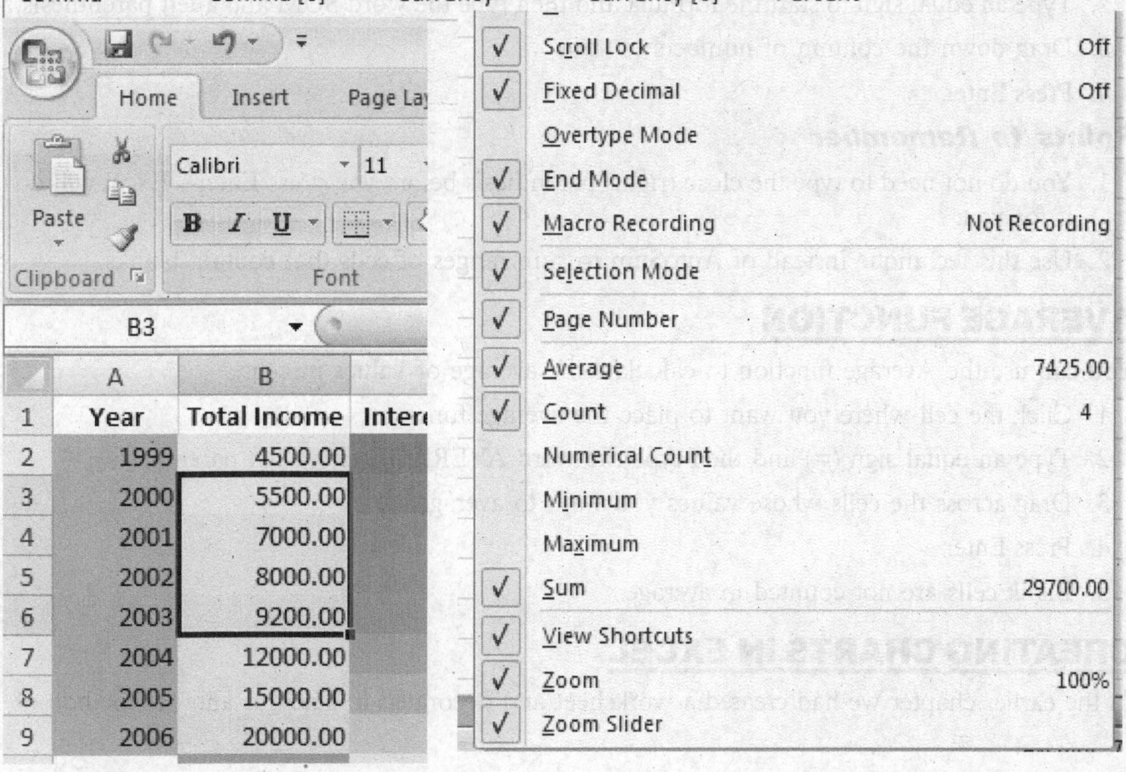
Home
Insert
Page Lay
Paste
Calibri
11
Clipboard
Font
B3
A
B
Year
Total Income
Intere
1999 4500.00
2000 5500.00
2001 7000.00
2002 8000.00
2003 9200.00
2004 12000.00
2005 15000.00
2006 20000.00
Scroll Lock Off
Fixed Decimal Off
Overtype Mode
End Mode
Macro Recording Not Recording
Selection Mode
Page Number
Average 7425.00
Count 4
Numerical Count
Minimum
Maximum
Sum 29700.00
View Shortcuts
Zoom 100%
Zoom Slider

REFERENCES

By default, Excel uses relative references in its formulae. Relative references refer to cells by their position in relation to the cell containing the formula. So when you copy the formula in cell F5 to cell F6, Excel changes the reference from E5 to E6.

Absolute references

When you don't want a reference to be copied as a relative reference, you need to use an absolute reference. Absolute references refer to cells by their fixed position in the worksheet. To make a reference absolute, you add dollar signs before its column letter and now number. For example, you would enter it as $C$4:$C$9. You could then copy formula that contained this reference anywhere on the worksheet and it would always refer to the range C4:C9.

Mixed references

References can also be partially relative and partially absolute. For example, $C3 has an absolute column reference and a relative row reference and C$3 has a relative column reference and an absolute row reference.

SUM FUNCTION

The Sum function is perhaps the most commonly used of the Excel functions that carry out mathematical, statistical, financial, date, time, and other calculations.

1. Click the destination cell for the formula.
2. Type an equal sign to start the formula and then type the word SUM and a left parenthesis.
3. Drag down the column of numbers to sum.
4. Press Enter.

Points to Remember

1. You do not need to type the close (right) parenthesis before you press Enter—Excel will do it for you.
2. Use this technique instead of AutoSum to sum ranges of cells that contain blanks.

AVERAGE FUNCTION

You can use the Average function to calculate the average of values in cells.

1. Click the cell where you want to place the average function.
2. Type an equal sign (=) and then type the word AVERAGE and a left parenthesis.
3. Drag across the cells whose values you want to average.
4. Press Enter.
5. Blank cells are not counted in average.

CREATING CHARTS IN EXCEL

In the earlier chapter we had created a worksheet and decorated it. There is another method of

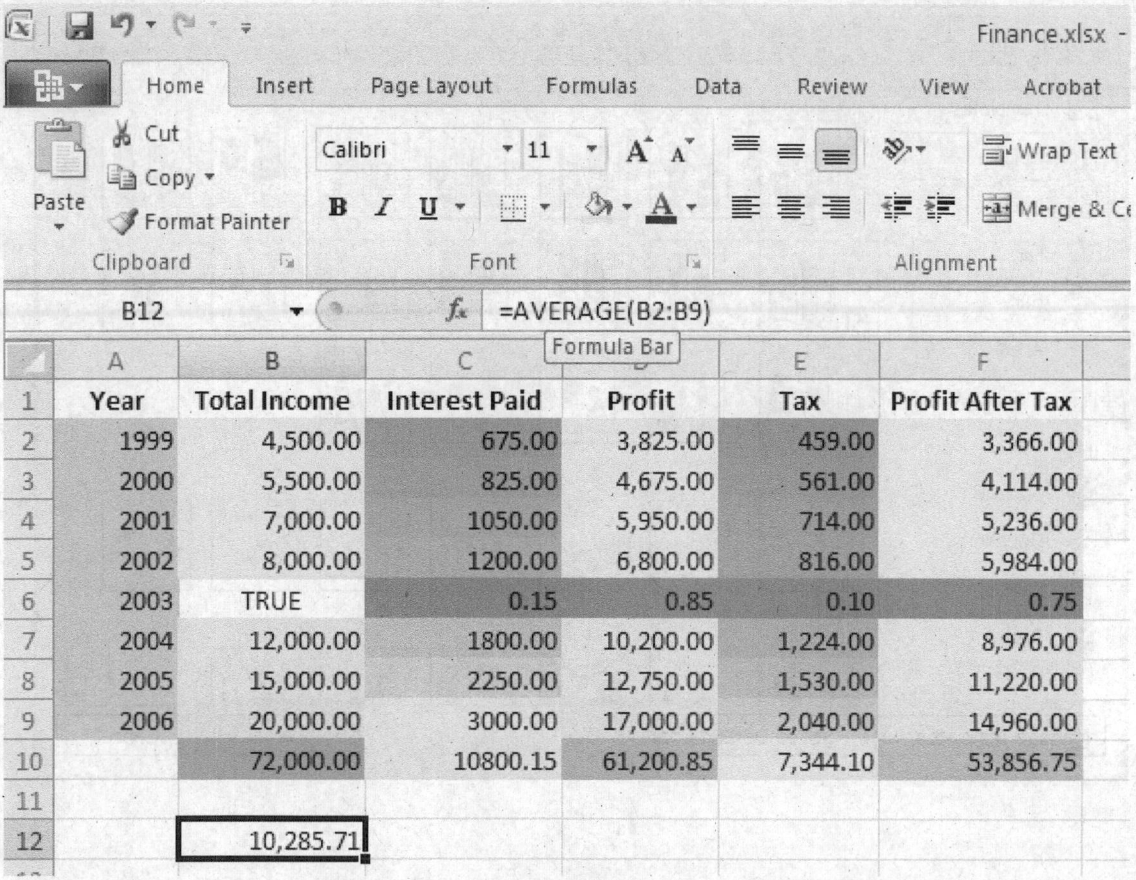

	A	B	C	D	E	F
1	Year	Total Income	Interest Paid	Profit	Tax	Profit After Tax
2	1999	4,500.00	675.00	3,825.00	459.00	3,366.00
3	2000	5,500.00	825.00	4,675.00	561.00	4,114.00
4	2001	7,000.00	1050.00	5,950.00	714.00	5,236.00
5	2002	8,000.00	1200.00	6,800.00	816.00	5,984.00
6	2003	TRUE	0.15	0.85	0.10	0.75
7	2004	12,000.00	1800.00	10,200.00	1,224.00	8,976.00
8	2005	15,000.00	2250.00	12,750.00	1,530.00	11,220.00
9	2006	20,000.00	3000.00	17,000.00	2,040.00	14,960.00
10		72,000.00	10800.15	61,200.85	7,344.10	53,856.75
11						
12		10,285.71				

presenting this worksheet and that is by converting it into graphics and specially in the form of **Charts** in Excel.

Let us use the same worksheet to make charts of the same. Different type of charts which can be created using Excel 2010 are shown here. Each one of them has various options underneath which can be chosen. For example, the 3-D column chart of the worksheet created earlier would be as shown below.

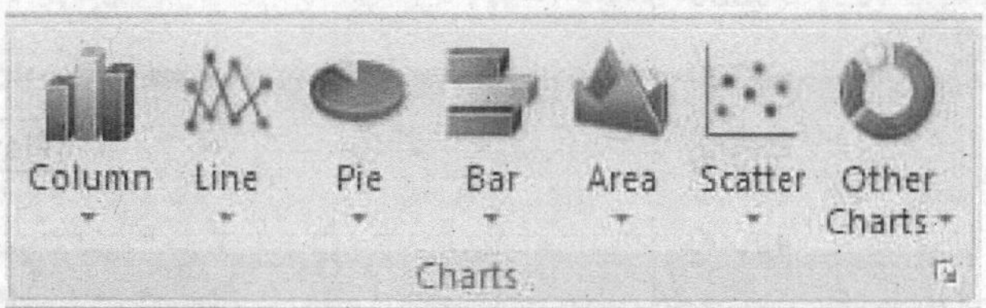

Similary you can create other type of charts. All these charts with their options can also be seen under All Chart Types under Other Charts.

AUDITING A WORKBOOK

To avoid bogus results from incorrect formulas, you can have Excel identify the cells that have supplied data for a formula. That way, you can easily see whether all the cells you wanted have been included in the calculation.

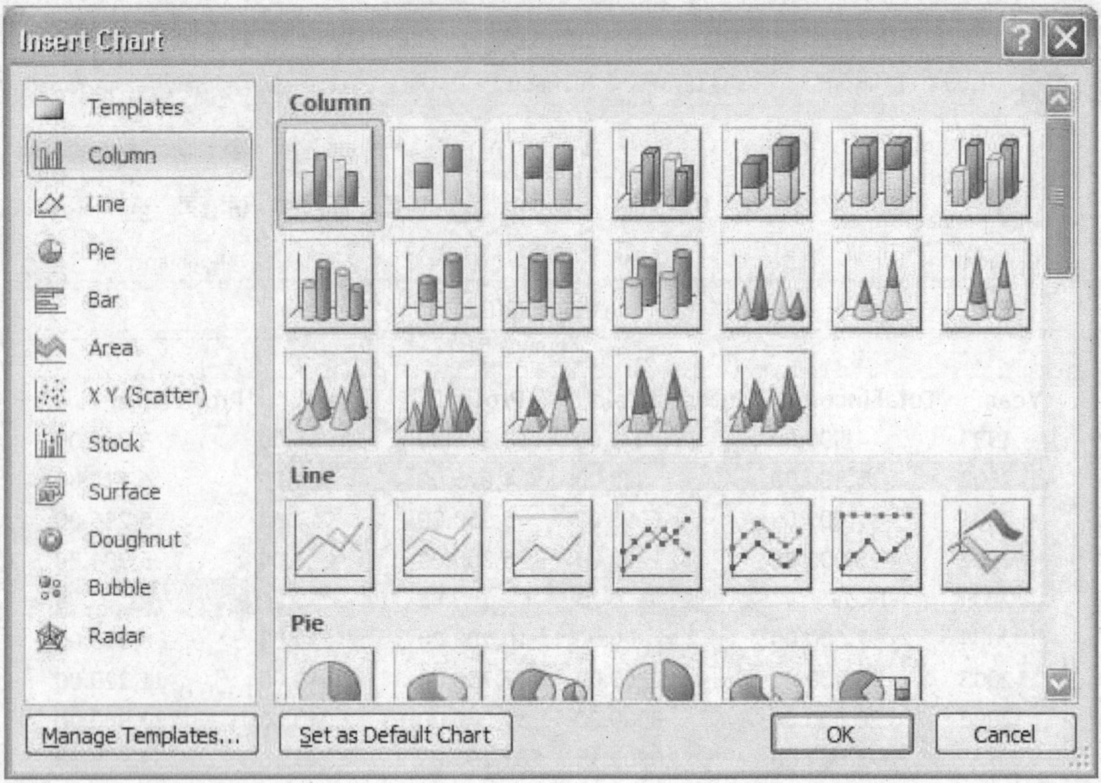
Insert Chart
Templates
Column
Line
Pie
Bar
Area
X Y (Scatter)
Stock
Surface
Doughnut
Bubble
Radar
Column
Line
Pie
Manage Templates...
Set as Default Chart
OK
Cancel

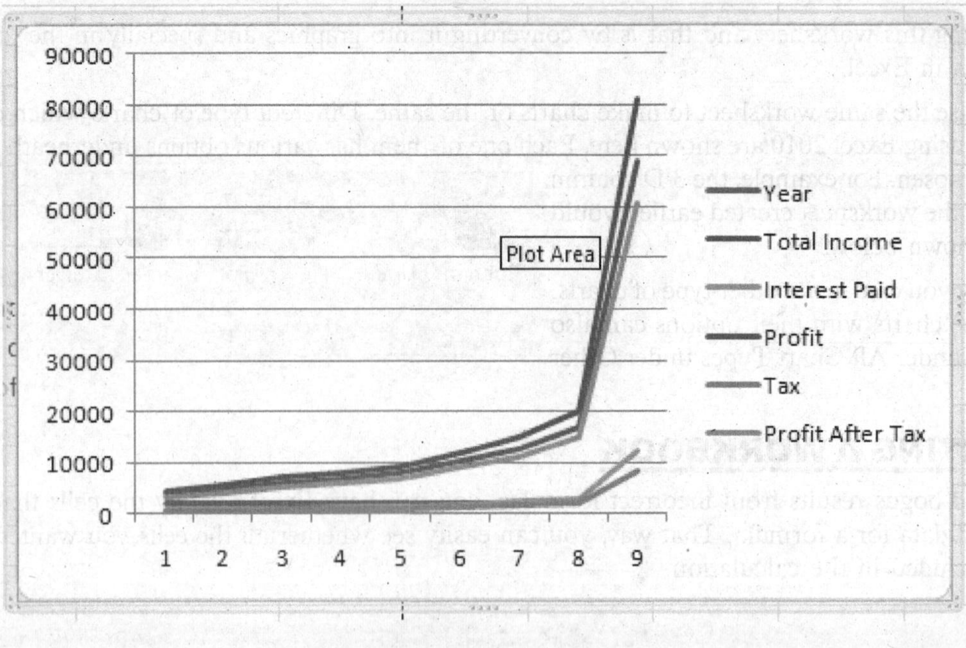
90000
80000
70000
60000
50000
40000
30000
20000
10000
0
1 2 3 4 5 6 7 8 9
Plot Area
Year
Total Income
Interest Paid
Profit
Tax
Profit After Tax

To Trace the Precedents for a Formula

1. Select the cell or cells that contain the formulas.
2. From the Formulas menu, choose Trace Precedents from Formula Auditing submenu.
3. Choose Trace Precedents again to view an additional level of precedents, if one exists.
4. This is shown below.

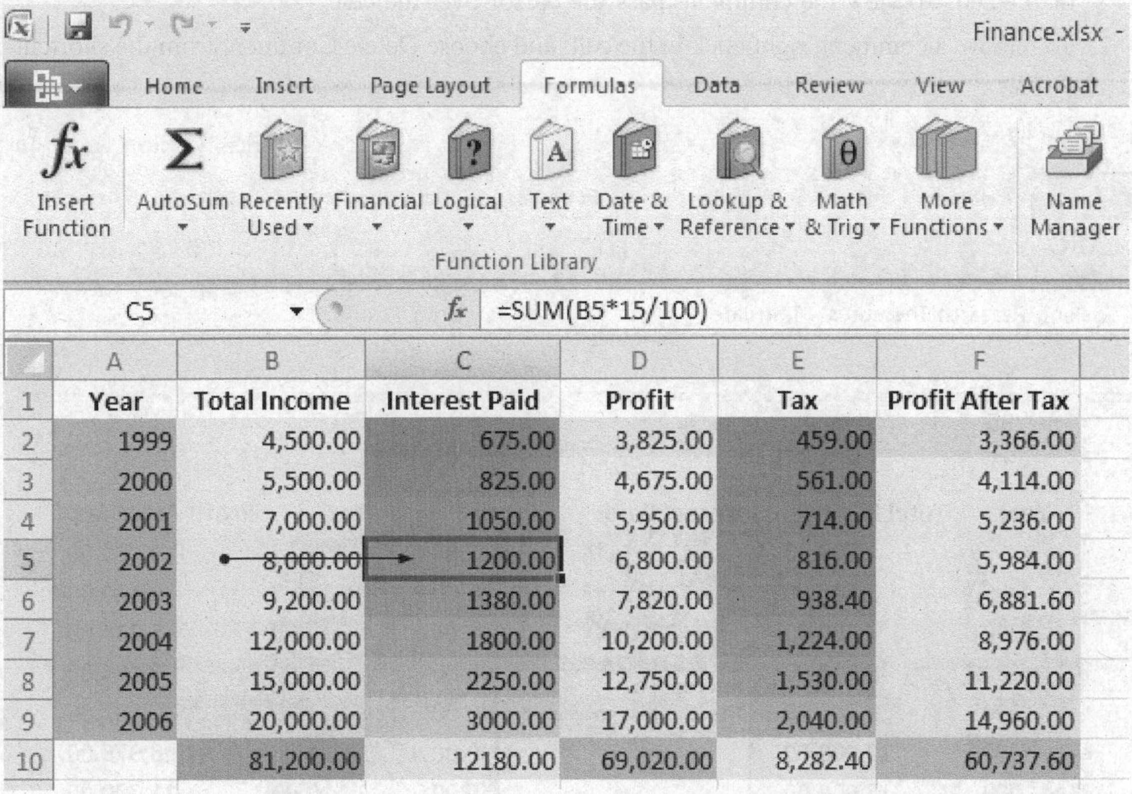

	A	B	C	D	E	F
1	Year	Total Income	Interest Paid	Profit	Tax	Profit After Tax
2	1999	4,500.00	675.00	3,825.00	459.00	3,366.00
3	2000	5,500.00	825.00	4,675.00	561.00	4,114.00
4	2001	7,000.00	1050.00	5,950.00	714.00	5,236.00
5	2002	8,000.00	1200.00	6,800.00	816.00	5,984.00
6	2003	9,200.00	1380.00	7,820.00	938.40	6,881.60
7	2004	12,000.00	1800.00	10,200.00	1,224.00	8,976.00
8	2005	15,000.00	2250.00	12,750.00	1,530.00	11,220.00
9	2006	20,000.00	3000.00	17,000.00	2,040.00	14,960.00
10		81,200.00	12180.00	69,020.00	8,282.40	60,737.60

Remember

1. To clear the arrows that have appeared to show the cells that are included in the formula, choose Remove All Arrows from the Auditing submenu menu.
2. The Auditing toolbar contains Trace Precedents and Remove All Arrows buttons. To view the Auditing toolbar, choose Show Auditing Toolbar from the Auditing submenu.

COMMENTS INSERTING

A comment is an annotation that you attach to a cell to provide information about the cell's contents. This capability enables several people to review the same worksheet and attach their comments.

To Insert a Comment

1. Select the cell to which you want to attach a comment.

2. From the Review menu, choose New Comment from Comments panel.
3. In the yellow text box that opens and displays the text for the comment.
4. Click in another cell to close the text box.

Remember

1. A comment is indicated by a comment marker (a small red triangle) at the upper right corner of the cell. To view the comment, pass the cursor over the cell.
2. To remove a comment, right-click in the cell, and choose Delete Comment from the shortcut menu.

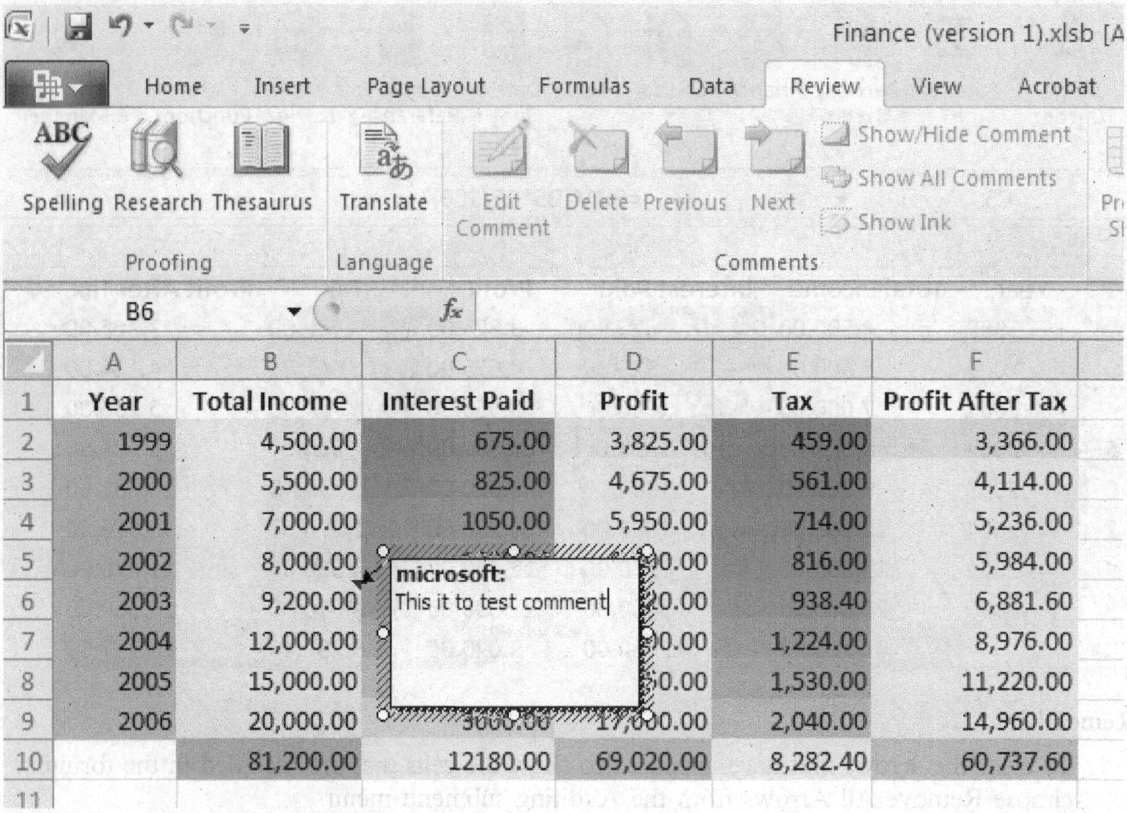

OUTLINES

Outline a Worksheet Automatically

1. Select a single cell to outline or the entire worksheet
2. Select a range of cells to outline
3. Click Data menu, Group and Outline command, and click at Group.

An outline created with outline symbols to the left of the row heading and/or above column headings.

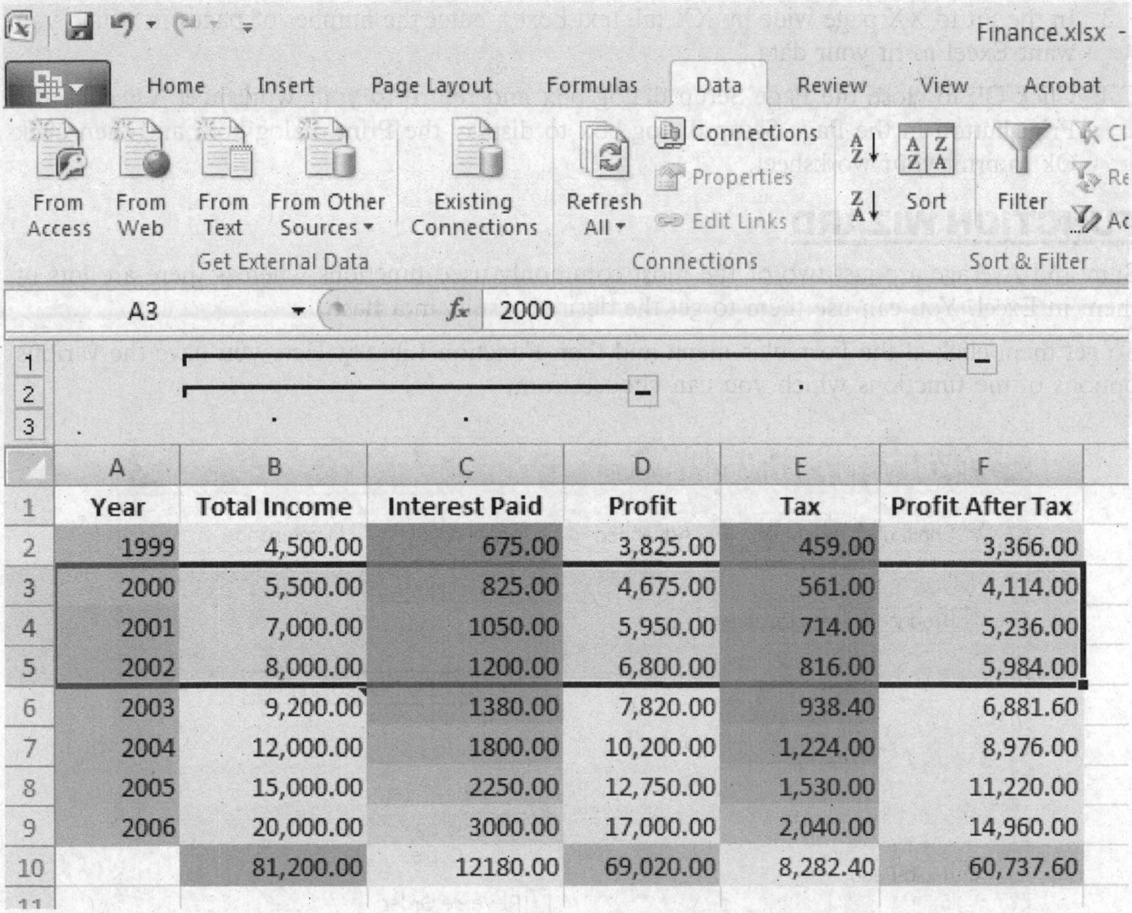

Clear Entire Outline

1. Select any cell in outline
2. Click at Data menu, Outline and Ungroup command, and Clear Outline.

WORKSHEET FITTING ON A PAGE

If your worksheet is too large to print on one page even after you change the orientation and margins, you might consider using the Fit to option.

This option shrinks the worksheet to make it fit on the specified number of pages. You can specify the document's width and height.

Follow these steps to scale a worksheet to fit on a page:

1. Open the Page Setup menu and choose Page Setup and Print Area. The Page Setup dialog box appears.
2. Click the Page tab to display the Page options.

3. In the Fit to XX page wide by XX tall text boxes, enter the number of pages in which you want Excel to fit your data.
4. Click Ok to close the Page Setup dialog box and return to your worksheet. Or click the Print button in the Page Setup dialog box to display the Print dialog box, and then click Ok to print your worksheet.

FUNCTION WIZARD

Sum and Average are just two of the most commonly used functions whereas there are lots of them in Excel. You can use them to get the desired results in a flash.

To get them click at the Formulas menu and then Function Library. Here you have the various options of the functions which you can choose from.

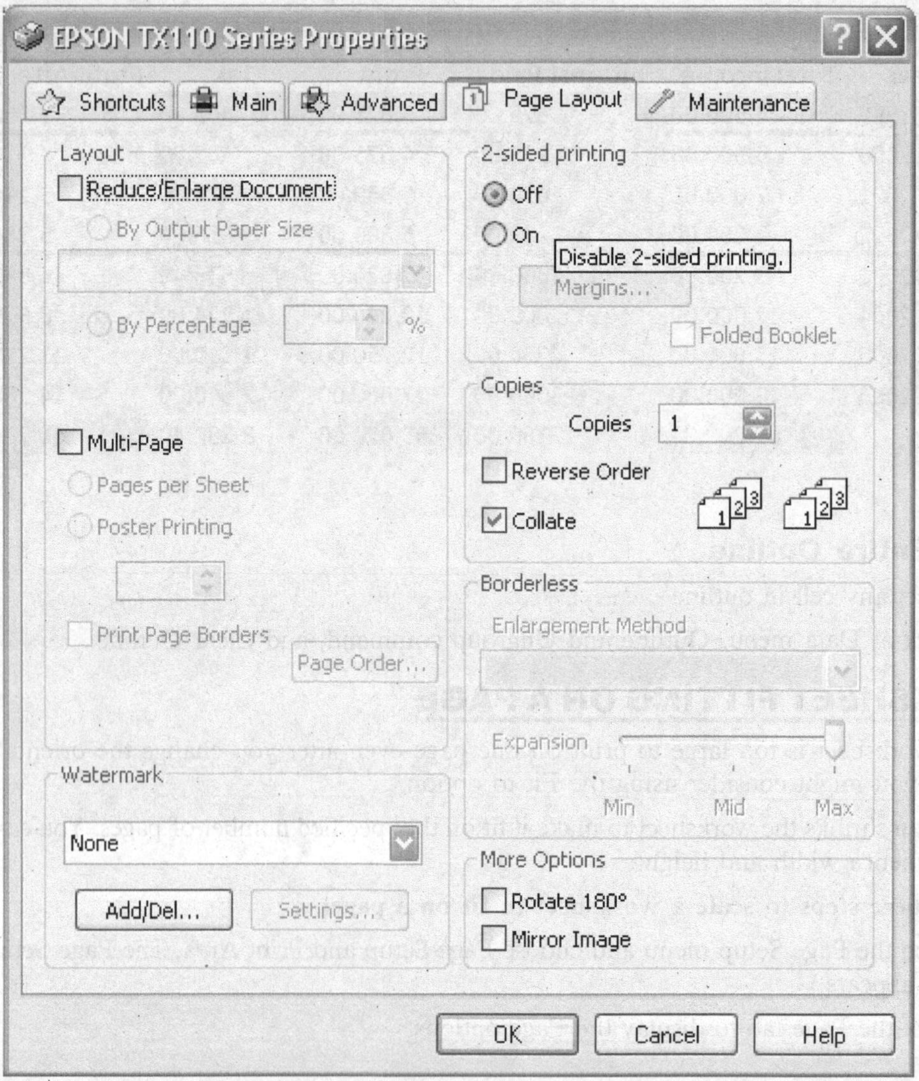

Insert Function

The Insert Function button is the option for building the formula. The Insert Function wizard takes you through the steps of building a formula.

1. Click the destination cell for the formula.
2. Click the Insert Function button.
3. In the Insert Function dialog box, select the category and then the function.
4. Click Ok.
5. Use the Insert Function Wizard to guide you in completing the formula.
6. Click Ok when you have finished.

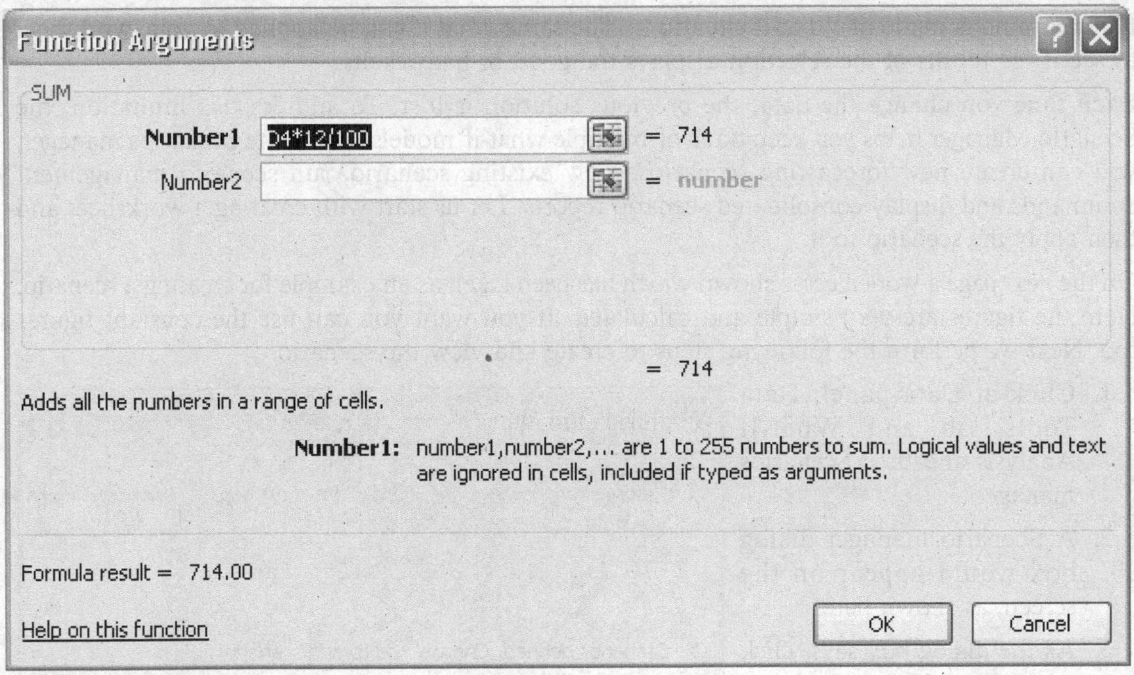

GOAL SEEKING

Usually after you create a formula, you can type in new data to see how the formula calculates the new result. However, Excel also offers a feature known as Goal Seeking. With this, you specify the value you want a formula to calculate, and then Excel changes the data in thr formula's cell references to tell you what values you need to achieve that goal.

To use Goal Seeking, follow these steps.

1. Click a the cell that contains a formula.
2. Click the Data tab.
3. Click the What-If Analysis Icon in the Data Tools group.
4. Click Goal Seek.

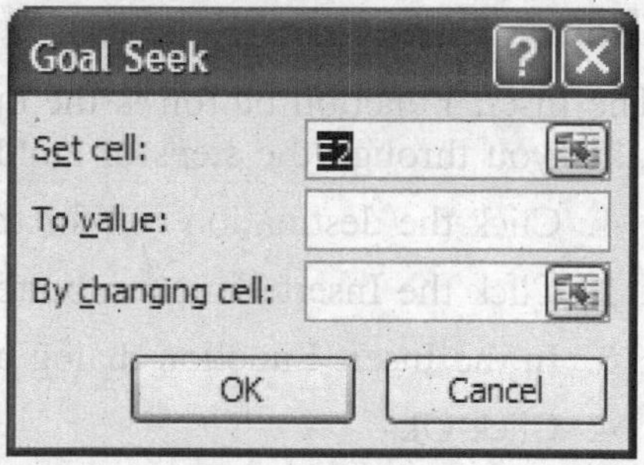

5. Click in the To Value text box and type a number that you want to appear in the formula stored in the cell that you clicked in Step 1.
6. Click in the By Changing Cell text box and click one cell that contains data used by the formula you choose in Step 1.
7. Click Ok.
8. Click Ok (to keep the changes) or click Cancel (to display the origianl vlaue your spreadsheet had before you choose the Goal Seek command)

SCENARIOS MANAGER

Human mind is made of What-if situations. The same what-if can be applied to your worksheet to see if the results of the selection displays the good or bad results.

Each time you change the data, the previous solution is lost. To address this limitation, the Scenario Manager helps you keep track of multiple what-if models. Using the Scenarios manager, you can create new forecasting scenarios, view existing scenario, run scenario management commands and display consolidated scenario reports. Let us start with creating a worksheet and then apply the scenario to it.

On the next page a worksheet is shown which has been taken as an example for creating a scenario. Here the figures are very simple and calculated. If you want you can use the constant figures too. Next we perform the following steps to create and view the scenario.

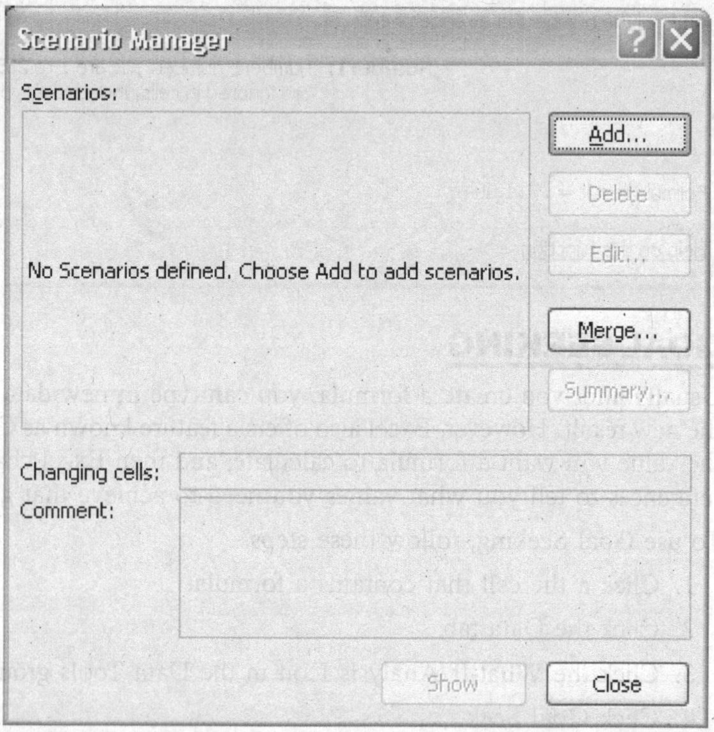

1. Click at Data panel, Data Tools tab and What-If Analysis and then Scenarios manager.
2. A Scenario manager dialog box would appear on the screen, as shown here.
3. As the dialog box says, click at Add to add a scenario.
4. This gives rise to another dialog box, which is called Add scenario.
5. In this dialog box, you have to firstly name the screnario.
6. I have named it as Good.
7. You can type the cell names or choose them by clicking at those cells. I have chosen cells from E2 to E4.

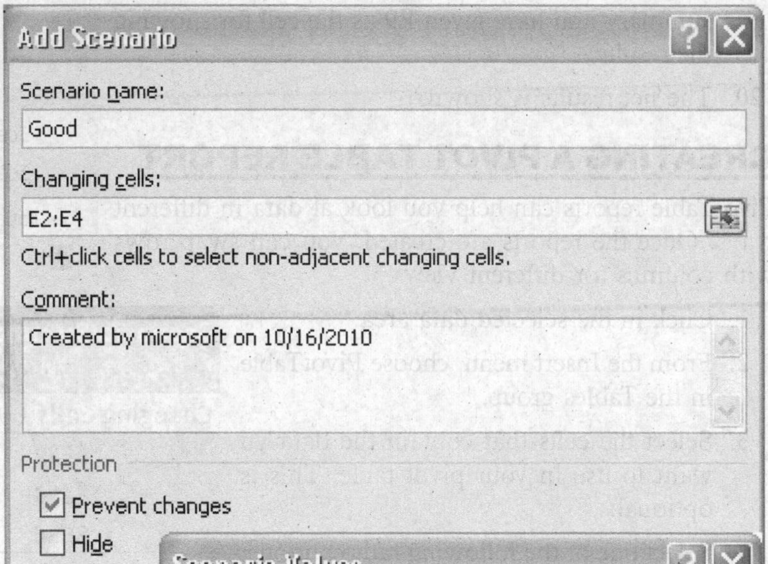

8. Click OK to add your scenario to the Scenario Manager. You'll see the Scenario Values dialog box, which asks you for your model's variables. The default values are the numbers that were already in the cells.
9. Type the various values which you want to see in the scenario.
10. Click Add to create a second scenario. If you do not want another set, just click at Ok.

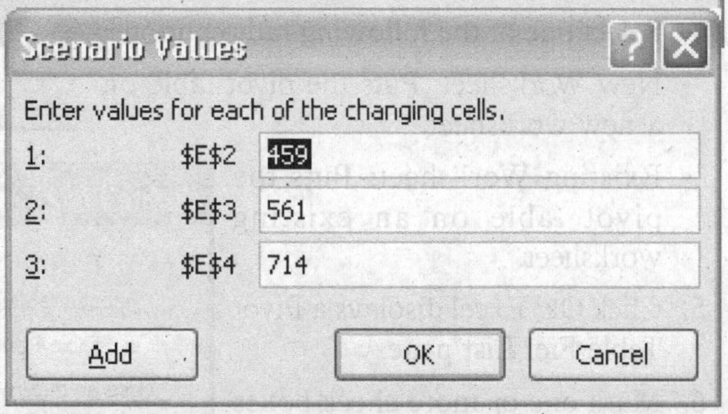

11. This will return you to the scenario manager with your scenario added to it.
12. As mentioned you can add another scenario to it.
13. Now we will see how this scenario works. For this click at Show.
14. Excel substitutes the values in the scenario for the variables in your worksheet and displays the results in your worksheet, as shown on the next page.

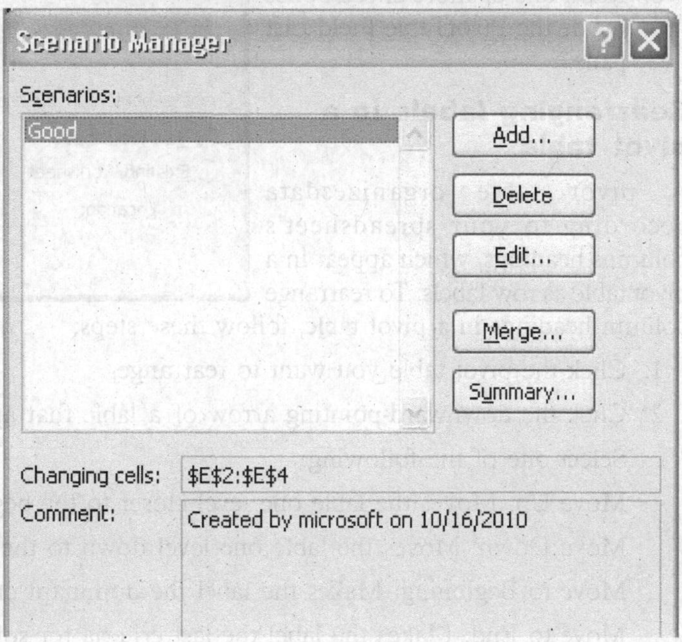

15. Next step is of having the Scenario Reports.
16. For this you choose the button called Summary from the Scenario Manager dialog box.
17. For this you will have to click at a cell where the summary would be placed.
18. You also have to define whether you want the summary or the PivtoTable report. Click any one of the two.
19. I have taken here Scenario

summary and have given E9 as the cell for showing the results.

20. The net results is shown.

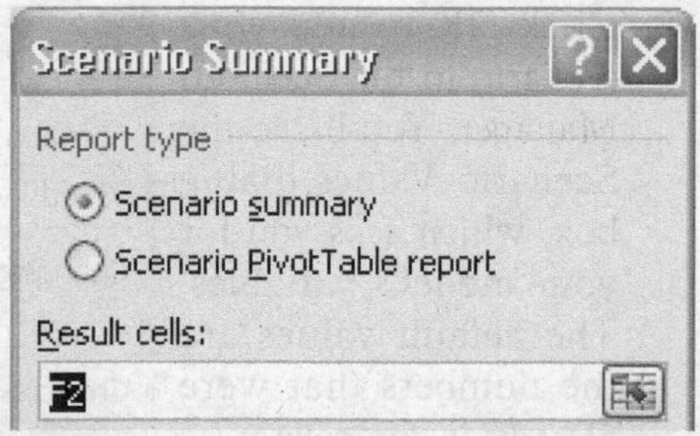

Scenario Summary		
	Current Values:	Good
Changing Cells:		
$E$2	459.00	459.00
$E$3	561.00	561.00
$E$4	714.00	714.00
Result Cells:		
$F$2	3,366.00	3,366.00

CREATING A PIVOT TABLE REPORT

PivotTable reports can help you look at data in different ways. Once the reports are created, you can swap rows with columns for different views.

1. Click in the selected data area.
2. From the Insert menu, choose PivotTable in the Tables group.
3. Select the cells that contain the data yu want to use in your pivot table. This is optional.
4. Select one of the following radio buttons:
   - New Worksheet: Puts the pivot table on a new worksheet.
   - Existing Worksheet: Puts the pivot table on an existing worksheet.
5. Click Ok, Excel displays a Pivot Table Fiel List pane.
6. Mark one or more check boxes inside the PivotTable Field List pane.

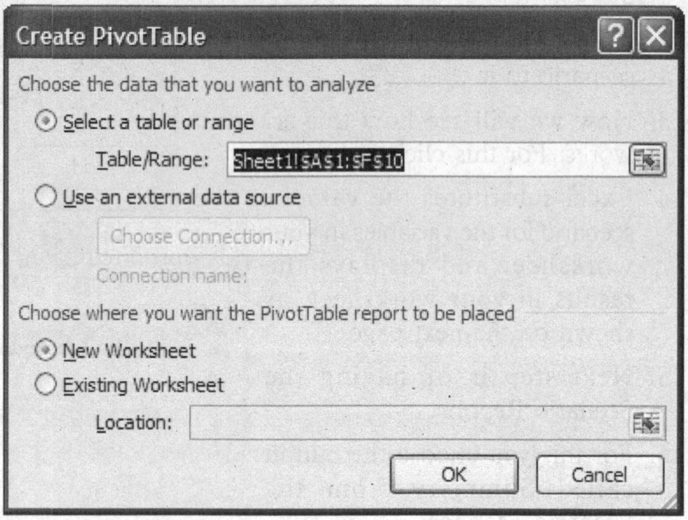

Rearranging labels in a pivot table

A pivot table organizesdata according to your spreadsheet's columns headings, which appear in a pivot table as row labels. To rearrange column headings in a pivot table, follow these steps:

1. Click the pivot table you want to rearrange.
2. Click the downward-pointing arrow of a lable that appears under the Row Labels group.

   Select one of the following:

   Move Up: Moves the lable one level closer to the beginning.

   Move Down: Moves the lable one level down to the end.

   Move to Beginning: Makes the label the dominant criteria for sorting data.

   Move to End: Makes the label the last criteria for sorting data.

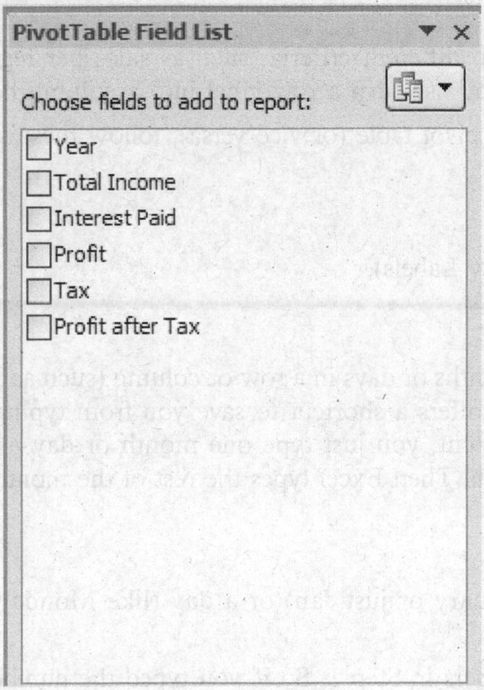

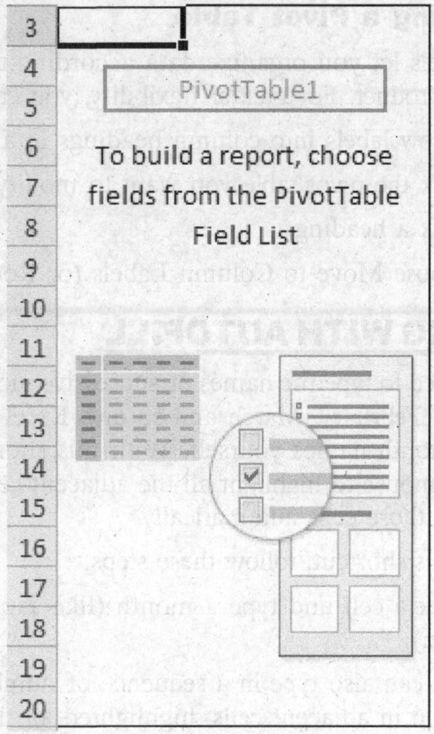

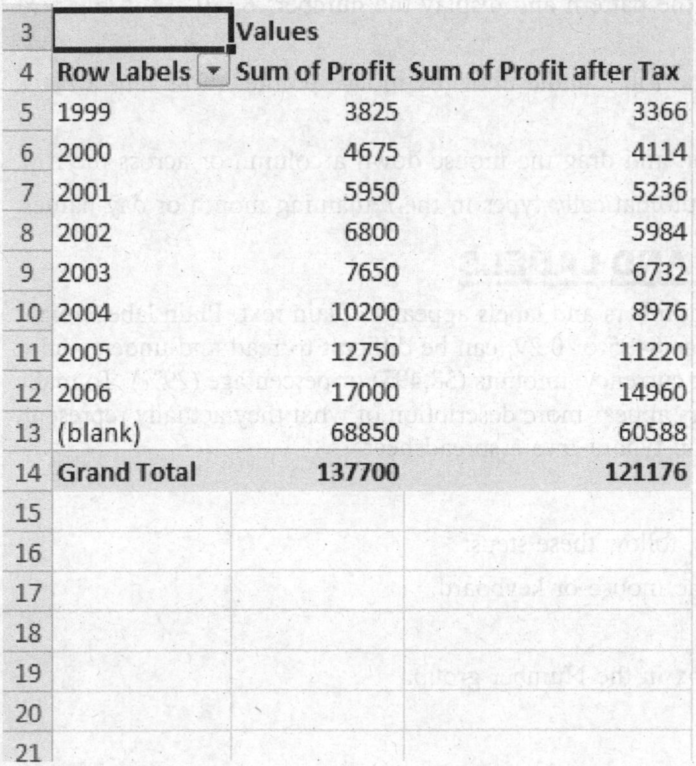

		Values	
4	Row Labels	Sum of Profit	Sum of Profit after Tax
5	1999	3825	3366
6	2000	4675	4114
7	2001	5950	5236
8	2002	6800	5984
9	2003	7650	6732
10	2004	10200	8976
11	2005	12750	11220
12	2006	17000	14960
13	(blank)	68850	60588
14	**Grand Total**	**137700**	**121176**

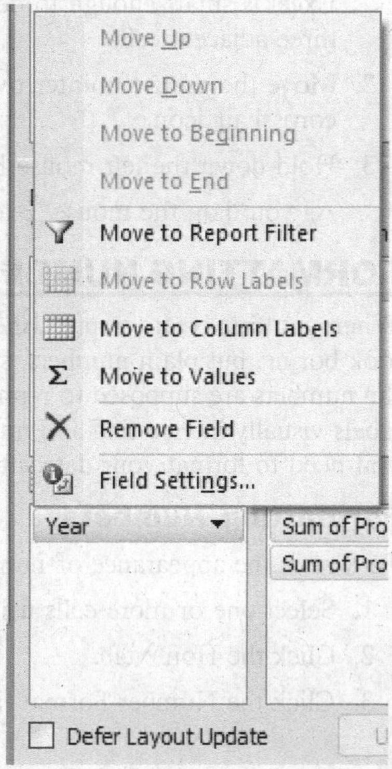

Modifying a Pivot Table

Row labels let you organize data according to different criteria, such as sales per region and then by product. For greater flexibility, you can also turn a row label into a column heading.

To turn row labels into column headings in a pivot table (or vice versa), follow these steps:

1. Click the pivot table you want to modify.
2. Click a heading.
3. Choose Move to Column Labels (or Row Labels).

TYPING WITH AUTOFILL

If you need to type the names of successive months or days in a row or column (such as January, February, February, March and so on). Excel offers a shortcut to save you from typing all the day or month names yourself. With this shortcut, you just type one month or day and them drag the mouse to highlight all the adjacent cell. Then Excel types the rest of the month or day names in those cells automatically.

To use this shortcut, follow these steps:

1. Click a cell and type a month (like January or just Jan) or a day (like Monday or just Mon).

   You can also type in a sequence of numbers in Step 1. So if you typed the numbers 2, 4, and 6 in adjacent cells, highlighted all these adjacent cells, and grabbed the Fill Handle, Excel is smart enough to detect the pattern and display the numbers 8, 10, 12 in the next three adjacent cells.
2. Move the mouse pointer over the Fill Handle until the mouse pointer turns into a black corosshair icon.
3. Hold down the left mouse button and drag the mouse down a column or across the row.

   As you drag the mouse, Excel automatically types in the remaining month or day names.

FORMATTING NUMBERS AND LABELS

When you first create a spreadsheet, numbers and labels appear as plain text. Plain labels might look boring, but plain numbers, such as 8495 or 0.29, can be difficult to read and understand it the numbers are supposed to represent currency amounts ($8,495) or percentage (29%). To make labels visually intersesting and numbers appear more description of what they actually represent, you need to format your data after you type it into a spreadsheet.

Formatting Numbers

To format the appearance of numbers, follow these steps:

1. Select one or more cells using the mouse or keyboard.
2. Click the Home tab.
3. Click the Number Format list box in the Number group.

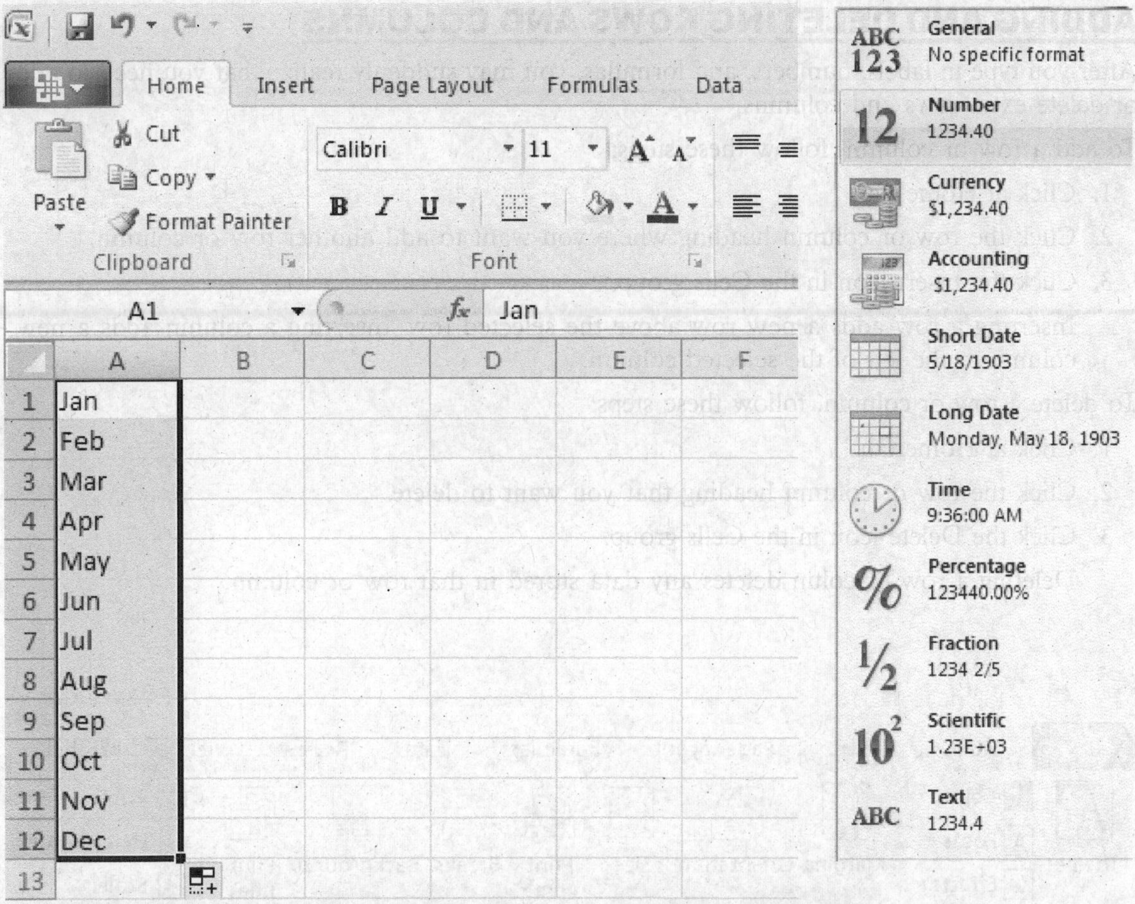

CHANGING THE SIZE OF ROWS AND COLUMNS

If you need to resize a row or columns to a precise value, it's easier to type a specific value into the Row Height or Column Width dialog box instead. To type a value into a Row Height or Column Width dialog box, follow hes steps:

1. Click the Home tab.
2. Click the row or column heading that you want to resize. Excel highlights your entire row or column.
3. Click the Format icon that appears in the Cells group. A pull-down menu appears.
4. Click Height, if you select a row, or Width, if you selected a column.
5. Type a vlaue and then click Ok.

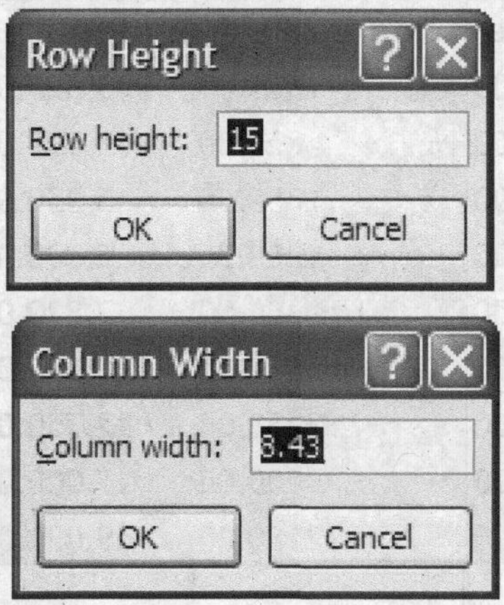

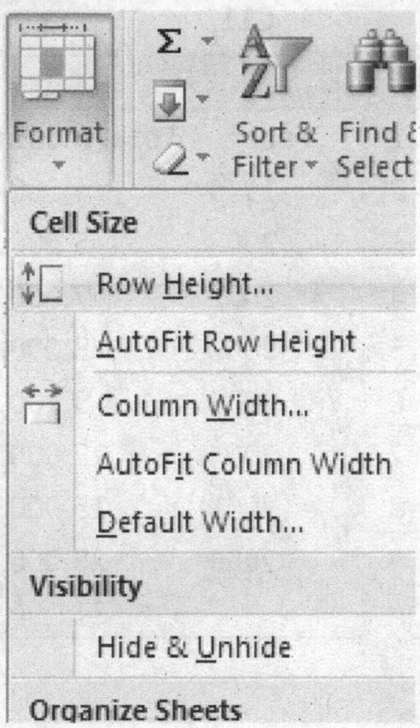

ADDING AND DELETING ROWS AND COLUMNS

After you type in labels, numbers, and formulas, you may suddenly realize that you need to add or delete extra rows and columns.

To add a row or column, follow these steps:

1. Click at Home Tab.
2. Click the row or column heading where you want to add another row or column.
3. Click the Insert icon in the Cells group.

   Inserting a row adds a new row above the selected row. Inserting a column adds a new column to the left of the selected column.

To delete a row or column, follow these steps:

1. Click at Home tab.
2. Click the row or column heading that you want to delete.
3. Click the Delete icon in the Cells group.

   Deleting a row or colun deletes any data stored in that row or column.

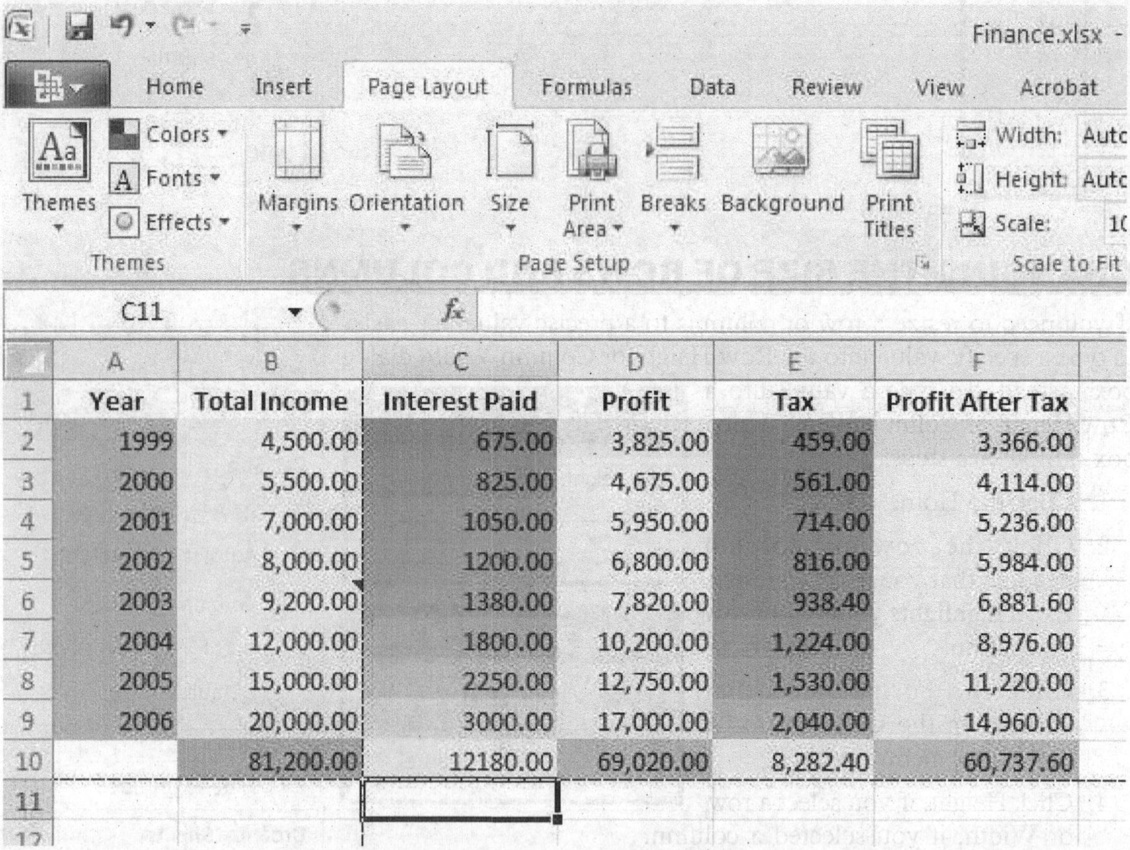

INSERTING (AND REMOVING) PAGE BREAKS

One problem with large spreadsheets is that when you print them out, parts may get cut off when printed on separate pages. To correct this problem, you can tell Excel exactly where page breaks should occur.

To insert page breaks, follow these steps:

1. Move the cursor in the cell to define where the vertical and horizontal page breaks will appear.
2. Click the Page Layout tab.
3. Click the Breaks icon in the Page Setup group.
4. Choose Insert Page Break.

   Excel inserts a horizontal page directly above the cell you selected in Step 1 and a vertical page break to the left of that cell, too.

To remove a page break, follow these steps:

1. Choose one of the following:
   - To remove a horizontal page break: Click in any cell that appears directly below that horizontal page break.
   - To remove a vertical page break: Click in any cell that appears directly to the right of the vertical page break and directly underneath the horizontal page break.
   - To remove both a vertical and horizontal page break: Click in the cell that appears to the right of the vertical page break and directly underneath the horizontal page break.
2. Click the Page Layout tab.
3. Click the Breaks icon in the Page Setup group.
4. Choose Remove Page Break. Excel removes your chosen page break.

APPLYING THEMES

You can quickly and easily format an entire document to give it a professional and modern look by applying a document theme. A document theme is a set of formatting choices that include a set of theme colors, a set of theme fonts (including heading and body text fonts), and a set of theme effects (including lines and fill effects).

Apply a Document Theme

You can change the document theme that is applied by default in Office programs, such as Word, Excel, and PowerPoint, by selecting another predefined document theme or a custom document theme. Document themes that you apply immediately affect the styles that you can use in your document.

Do one of the following:

- On the Page Layout tab, in the Themes group, click Themes.
- To apply a predefined document theme, click the document theme that you want to use under Built-In.

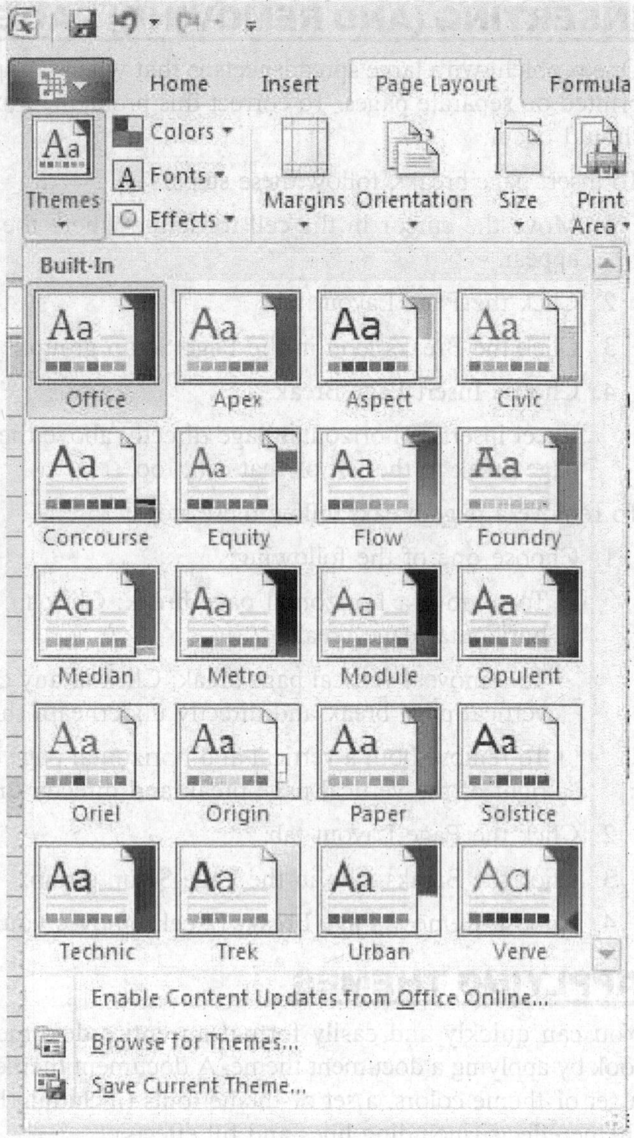

- To apply a custom document theme, click the document theme that you want to use under Custom.
- Custom is available only if you created one or more custom document themes.
- If a document theme that you want to use is not listed, click Browse for Themes to find it on your computer or a network location.

Customize a Document Theme

To customize a document theme, you start by changing the colors, the fonts, or the line and fill effects that are used. Changes that you make to one or more of these theme components immediately affect the styles that you have applied in the active document. If you want to apply these changes to new documents, you can save them as a custom document theme.

Customize the Theme Colors

Theme colors contain four text and background colors, six accent colors, and two hyperlink colors. The colors in the Theme Colors button represent the current text and background colors. The set of colors that you see next to the Theme Colors name after you click the Theme Colors button represent the accent and hyperlink colors for that theme. When you change any of these colors to create your own set of theme colors, the colors that are shown in the Theme Colors button and next to the Theme Colors name will change accordingly.

Customize the Theme Fonts

Theme fonts contain a heading font and a body text font. When you click the Theme Fonts button, you can see the name of the heading font and body text font that is used for each theme font below the Theme Fonts name. You can change both of these fonts to create your own set of theme fonts.

Select a Set of Theme Effects

Theme effects are sets of lines and fill effects. When you click the Theme Effects button, you can see the lines and fill effects that are used for each set of theme effects in the graphic that is displayed with the Theme Effects name. Although you cannot create your own set of theme effects, you can choose the one that you want to use in your own document theme.

Save a Document Theme

Any changes that you make to the colors, the fonts, or the line and fill effects of a document theme can be saved as a custom document theme that you can apply to other documents.

ADD OR REMOVE A SHEET BACKGROUND

In Microsoft Office Excel, you can use a picture as a sheet background for display purposes only. A sheet background is not printed, and it is not retained in an individual worksheet or in an item that you save as a Web page. Because a sheet background is not printed, it cannot be used as a watermark. You can, however, mimic a watermark by inserting a graphic in a header or footer.

Add a Sheet Background

1. Click the worksheet that you want to display with a sheet background. Make sure that only one worksheet is selected.
2. On the Page Layout tab, in the Page Setup group, click Background.
3. Select the picture that you want to use for the sheet background, and then click Insert.
4. The selected picture is repeated to fill the sheet.

Remove a Sheet Background

1. Click the worksheet that is displayed with a sheet background. Make sure that only one worksheet is selected.
2. On the Page Layout tab, in the Page Setup group, click Background.

CONVERT TEXT TO COLUMNS

You can convert text to columns in Excel by using the Wizard called Convet Text to Columns. For this select the text which you want to convert and select the wizard from Data menu and Text to Columns from Data Tools tab. Rest is easy. Just follow the three steps shown on next pages.

PROTECT WORKSHEET OR WORKBOOK ELEMENTS

To prevent a user from accidentally or deliberately changing, moving, or deleting important data, you can protect certain worksheet (worksheet: The primary document that you use in Excel to store and work with data. Also called a spreadsheet. A worksheet consists of cells that are organized into columns and rows; a worksheet is always stored in a workbook.) or workbook elements, with or without a password.

Workbook and worksheet element protection should not be confused with workbook-level password security. Element protection cannot protect a workbook from users who have malicious intent.

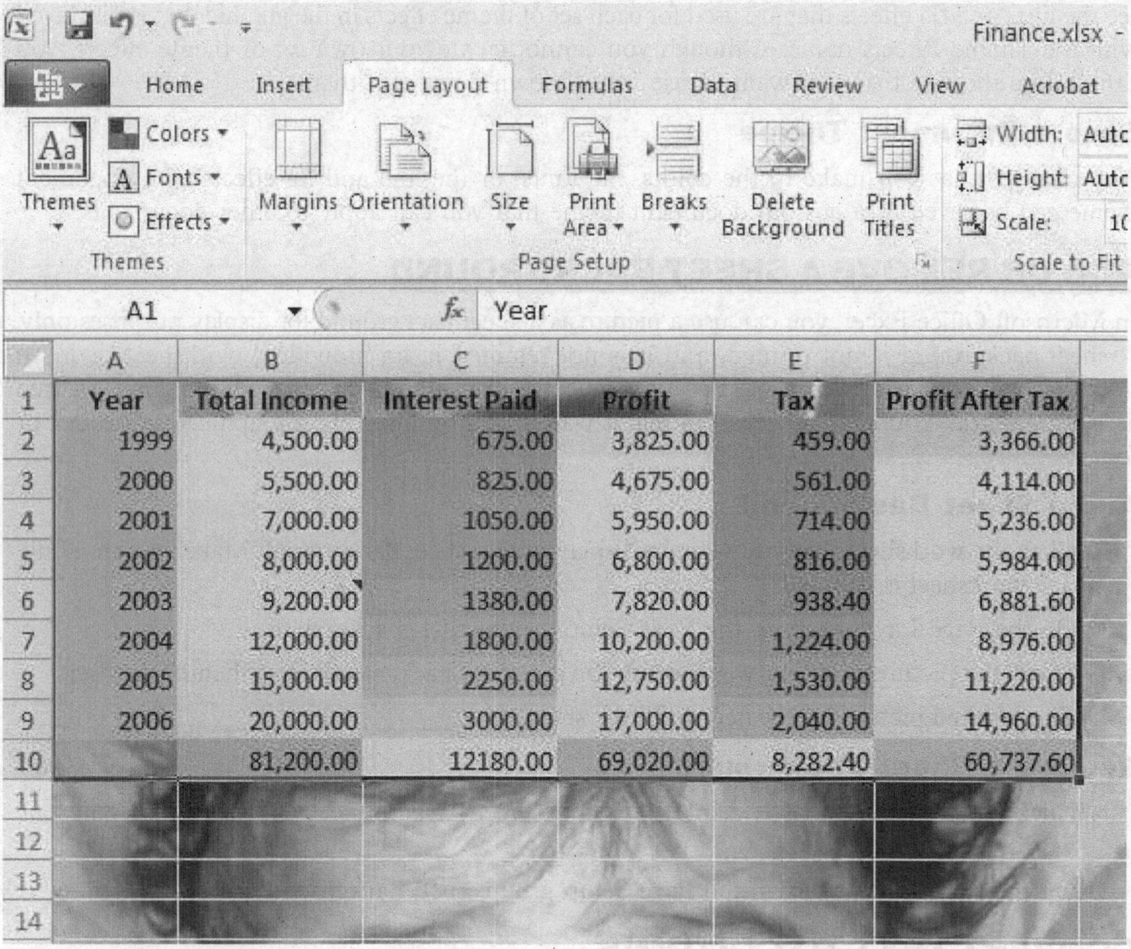

	A	B	C	D	E	F
1	Year	Total Income	Interest Paid	Profit	Tax	Profit After Tax
2	1999	4,500.00	675.00	3,825.00	459.00	3,366.00
3	2000	5,500.00	825.00	4,675.00	561.00	4,114.00
4	2001	7,000.00	1050.00	5,950.00	714.00	5,236.00
5	2002	8,000.00	1200.00	6,800.00	816.00	5,984.00
6	2003	9,200.00	1380.00	7,820.00	938.40	6,881.60
7	2004	12,000.00	1800.00	10,200.00	1,224.00	8,976.00
8	2005	15,000.00	2250.00	12,750.00	1,530.00	11,220.00
9	2006	20,000.00	3000.00	17,000.00	2,040.00	14,960.00
10		81,200.00	12180.00	69,020.00	8,282.40	60,737.60

Protect Worksheet Elements

1. Select the worksheet that you want to protect.
2. To unlock any cells or ranges that you want other users to be able to change, do the following:
    1. Select each cell or range that you want to unlock.
    2. On the Home tab, in the Cells group, click Format, and then click Format Cells.
    3. On the Protection tab, clear the Locked check box, and then click OK.
3. To hide any formulas that you don't want to be visible, do the following:
    1. In the worksheet, select the cells that contain the formulas that you want to hide.
    2. On the Home tab, in the Cells group, click Format, and then click Format Cells.
    3. On the Protection tab, select the Hidden check box, and then click OK.
4. To unlock any graphic objects (such as pictures, clip art, shapes, or Smart Art graphics) that you want users to be able to change, do the following:

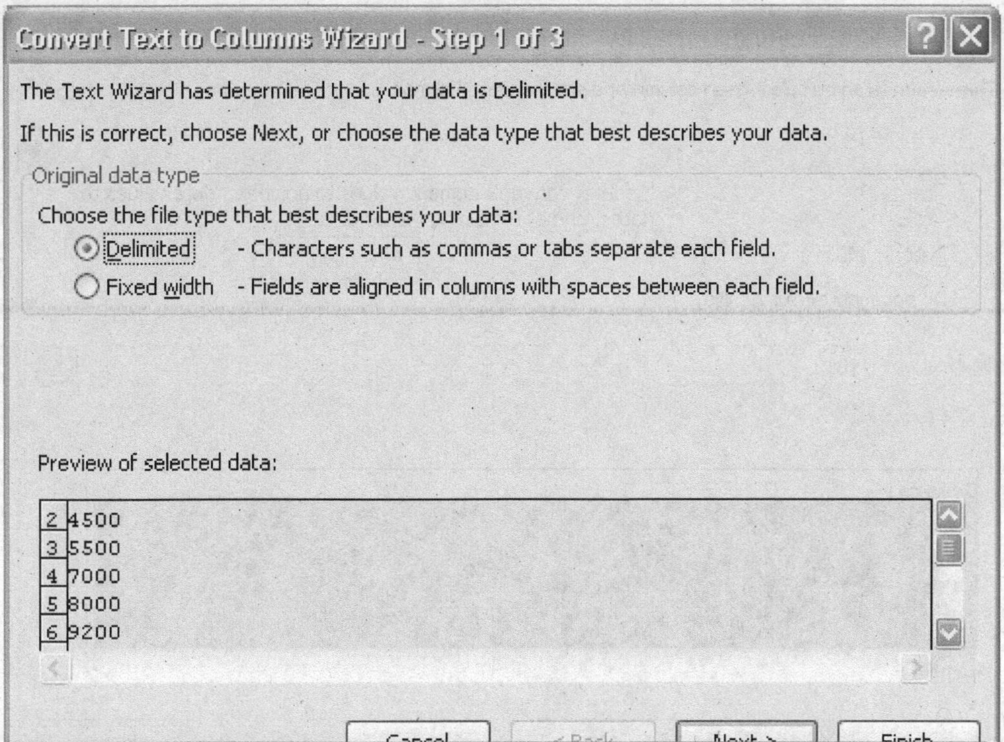
Convert Text to Columns Wizard - Step 1 of 3
The Text Wizard has determined that your data is Delimited.
If this is correct, choose Next, or choose the data type that best describes your data.
Original data type
Choose the file type that best describes your data:
Delimited - Characters such as commas or tabs separate each field.
Fixed width - Fields are aligned in columns with spaces between each field.
Preview of selected data:
2 4500
3 5500
4 7000
5 8000
6 9200

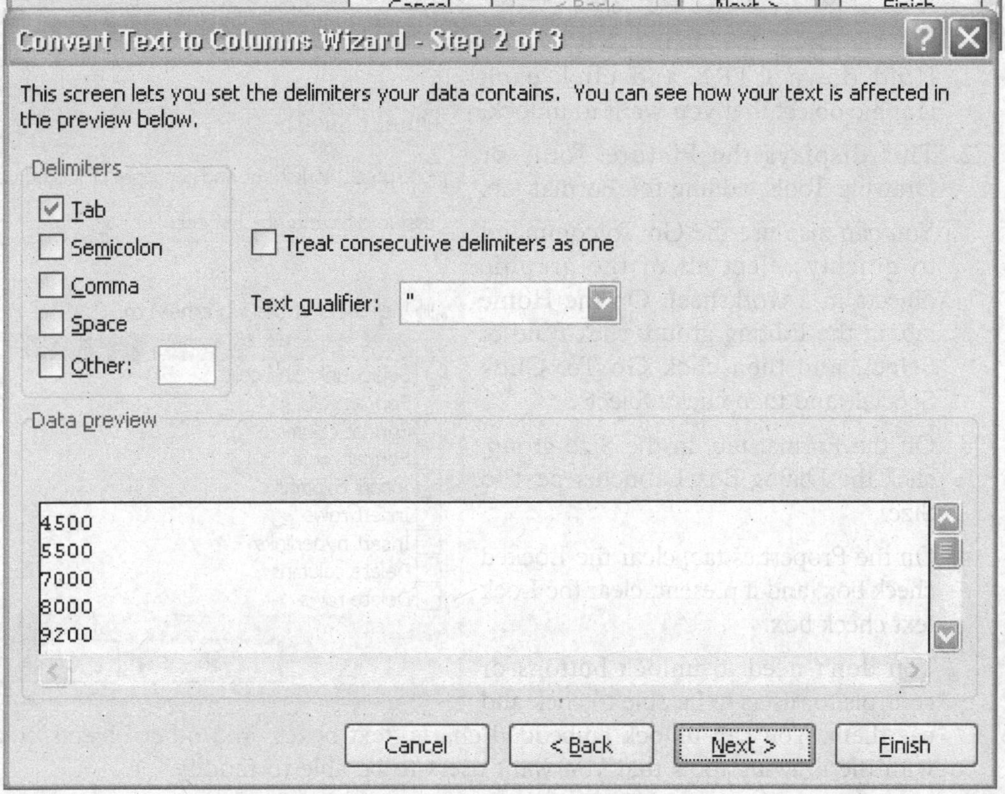
Convert Text to Columns Wizard - Step 2 of 3
This screen lets you set the delimiters your data contains. You can see how your text is affected in the preview below.
Delimiters
Tab
Semicolon
Comma
Space
Other:
Treat consecutive delimiters as one
Text qualifier: "
Data preview
4500
5500
7000
8000
9200
Cancel
< Back
Next >
Finish

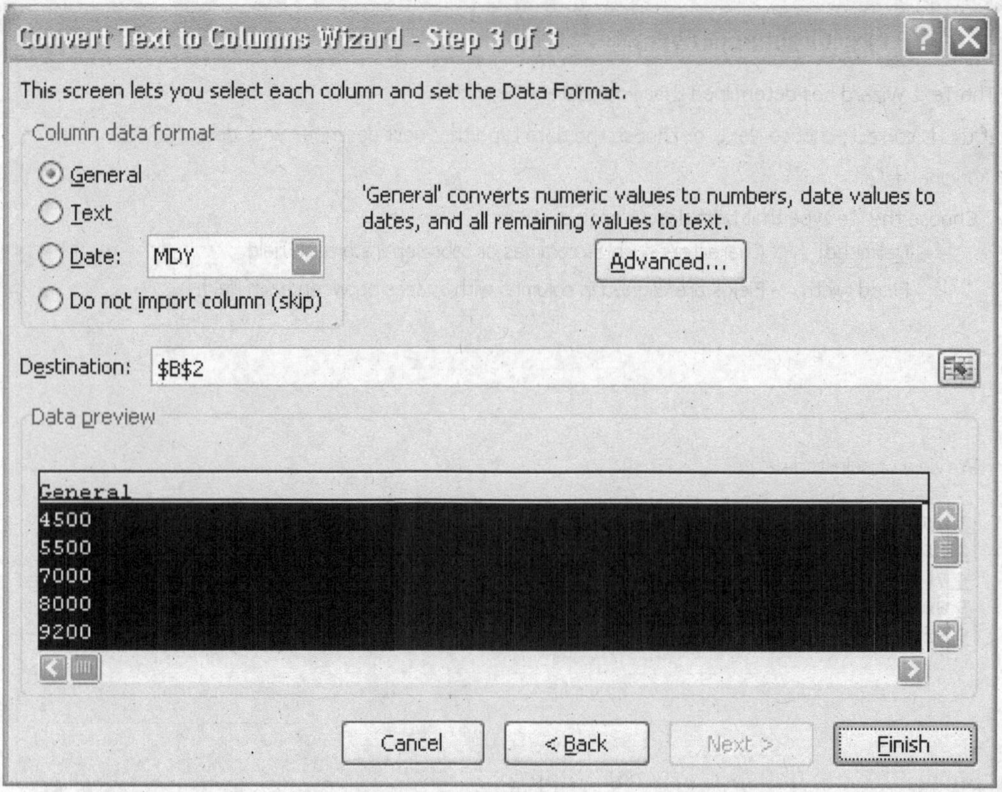

1. Hold down CTRL and click each graphic object that you want to unlock.
2. This displays the Picture Tools or Drawing Tools, adding the Format tab.

   You can also use the Go To command to quickly select all of the graphic objects in a worksheet. On the Home tab, in the Editing group, click Find & Select, and then click Go To. Click Special, and then click Objects.
3. On the Format tab, in the Size group, click the Dialog Box Launcher next to Size.
4. On the Properties tab, clear the Locked check box, and if present, clear the Lock text check box.

   You don't need to unlock buttons or controls for users to be able to click and use them. You can unlock embedded charts, text boxes, and other objects created with the drawing tools that you want users to be able to modify.

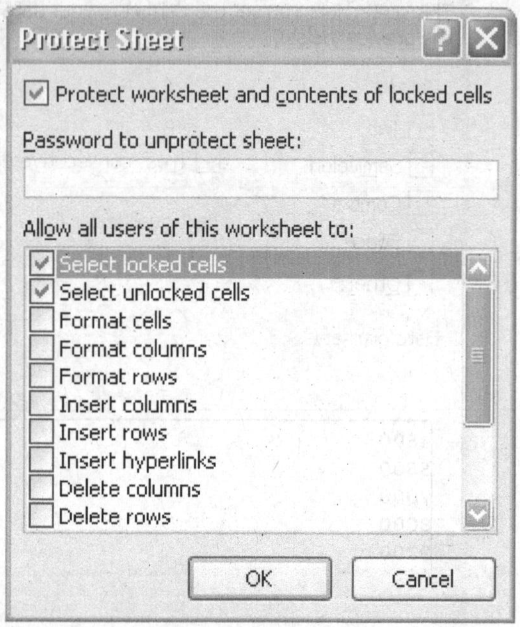

5. On the Review tab, in the Changes group, click Protect Sheet.
6. In the Allow all users of this worksheet to list, select the elements that you want users to be able to change.

Worksheet elements

Clear this check box	To prevent users from
Select locked cells	Moving the pointer to cells for which the Locked check box is selected on the Protection tab of the Format Cells dialog box. By default, users are allowed to select locked cells.
Select unlocked cells	Moving the pointer to cells for which the Locked check box is cleared on the Protection tab of the Format Cells dialog box. By default, users are allowed to select unlocked cells, and they can press the TAB key to move between the unlocked cells on a protected worksheet.
Format cells	Changing any of the options in the Format Cells or Conditional Formatting dialog boxes. If you applied conditional formats before you protected the worksheet, the formatting continues to change when a user enters a value that satisfies a different condition.
Format columns	Using any of the column formatting commands, including changing column width or hiding columns (Home tab, Cells group, Format button).
Format rows	Using any of the row formatting commands, including changing row height or hiding rows (Home tab, Cells group, Format button).
Insert columns	Inserting columns.
Insert rows	Inserting rows.
Insert hyperlinks	Inserting new hyperlinks (hyperlink: Colored and underlined text or a graphic that you click to go to a file, a location in a file, a Web page on the World Wide Web, or a Web page on an intranet. Hyperlinks can also go to newsgroups and to Gopher, Telnet, and FTP sites.), even in unlocked cells.
Delete columns	Deleting columns. Note If Delete columns is protected and Insert columns is not also protected, a user can insert columns that he or she cannot delete.
Delete rows	Deleting rows. Note If Delete rows is protected and Insert rows is not also protected, a user can insert rows that he or she cannot delete.
Sort	Using any commands to sort data (Data tab, Sort & Filter group). Note Users can't sort ranges that contain locked cells on a protected worksheet, regardless of this setting.
Use AutoFilter	Using the drop-down arrows to change the filter on ranges when AutoFilters are applied. Note Users cannot apply or remove AutoFilters on a protected worksheet, regardless of this setting.

Use PivotTable reports	Formatting, changing the layout, refreshing, or otherwise modifying PivotTable reports or creating new reports. Edit objects Doing the any of the following: • Making changes to graphic objects—including maps, embedded charts, shapes, text boxes, and controls—that you did not unlock before you protected the worksheet. For example, if a worksheet has a button that runs a macro, you can click the button to run the macro, but you cannot delete the button. • Making any changes, such as formatting, to an embedded chart. The chart continues to be updated when you change its source data. • Adding or editing comments.
Edit scenarios	Viewing scenarios that you have hidden, making changes to scenarios that you have prevented changes to, and deleting these scenarios. Users can change the values in the changing cells, if the cells are not protected, and add new scenarios.

Review Questions

1. How would you audit a worksheet? Explain.
2. Describe the process of inserting a comment in the worksheet.
3. Describe how the logical functions work in worksheet?
4. Describe how would you put Headers and Footers in a worksheet?
5. How would you merge two worksheets?
6. Describe the method of putting Outlines to worksheet.
7. How would you put labels on your rows and columns of the worksheet?
8. How would you protect your worksheet?
9. How would you name a range of cells?
10. Describe the various type of references.
11. Describe the command Goal Seek.
12. Describe the process of naming sheets.
13. How would you create a style?
14. How would you copy entries between workbooks?

6

Charts in Microsoft Excel 2010

INTRODUCTION

Various type of charts are used in Microsoft Excel 2010. In this chapter about them in details.

AVAILABLE CHART TYPES

Microsoft Office Excel 2010 supports numerous types of charts to help you display data in ways that are meaningful to your audience. When you want to create a chart or change an existing chart, you can choose from a wide range of chart subtypes available for each of the following chart types.

COLUMN CHARTS

Data that is arranged in columns or rows on a worksheet can be plotted in a column chart. Column charts are useful for showing data changes over a period of time or for illustrating comparisons among items.

In column charts, categories are typically organized along the horizontal axis and values along the vertical axis.

Column charts have the following chart subtypes:

- Clustered column and clustered column in 3-D: Clustered column charts compare values across categories. A clustered column chart displays values in 2-D vertical rectangles. A clustered column in 3-D chart displays only the vertical rectangles in 3-D format; it does not display the data in 3-D format.

  To present data in a 3-D format that uses three axes (horizontal, vertical, and depth axes) that you can modify, you should use the 3-D column chart subtype.

  You can use a clustered column chart type when you have categories that represent:

- Ranges of values (for example, item counts in a histogram).
- Specific scale arrangements (for example, a Likert scale with entries, such as strongly agree, agree, neutral, disagree, strongly disagree).

- Names that are not in any specific order (for example, item names, geographic names, or the names of people).

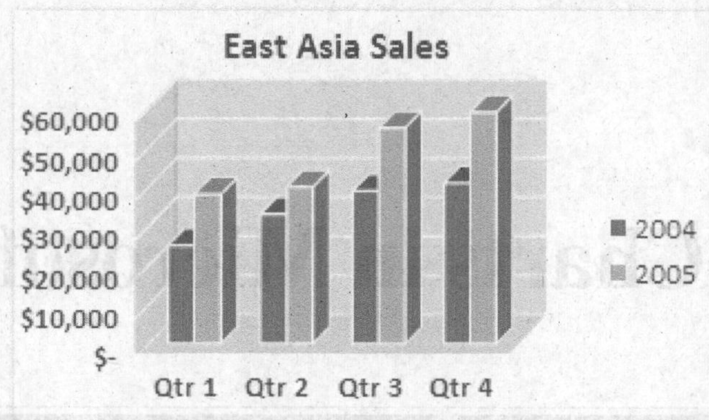

- Stacked column and stacked column in 3-D: Stacked column charts show the relationship of individual items to the whole, comparing the contribution of each value to a total across categories. A stacked column chart displays values in 2-D vertical stacked rectangles. A 3-D stacked column chart displays the vertical stacked rectangles in 3-D format; it does not display the data in 3-D format.

  You can use a stacked column chart when you have multiple data series and when you want to emphasize the total.

- 100% stacked column and 100% stacked column in 3-D: These types of column charts compare the percentage each value contributes to a total across categories. A 100% stacked column chart displays values in 2-D vertical 100% stacked rectangles. A 3-D 100% stacked column chart displays the vertical 100% stacked rectangles in 3-D format; it does not display the data in 3-D format. You can use a 100% stacked column chart when you have three or more data series and you want to emphasize the contributions to the whole, especially if the total is the same for each category.

- 3-D column. 3-D column charts use three axes that you can modify (a horizontal axis, a vertical axis, and a depth axis) and they compare data points (data points: Individual values plotted in a chart and represented by bars, columns, lines, pie or doughnut slices, dots, and various other shapes called data markers. Data markers of the same color constitute a data series.) along the horizontal and the depth axes.

  You can use a 3-D column chart when you want to compare data across the categories and across the series equally.

- Cylinder, cone, and pyramid: Cylinder, cone, and pyramid charts are available in the same clustered, stacked, 100% stacked, and 3-D chart types that are provided for rectangular column charts, and they show and compare data exactly the same way. The only difference is that these chart types display cylinder, cone, and pyramid shapes instead of rectangles.

LINE CHARTS

Data that is arranged in columns or rows on a worksheet can be plotted in a line chart. Line charts can display continuous data over time, set against a common scale, and are therefore ideal for showing trends in data at equal intervals. In a line chart, category data is distributed evenly along the horizontal axis, and all value data is distributed evenly along the vertical axis.

You should use a line chart if your category labels are text, and are representing evenly spaced values such as months, quarters, or fiscal years. This is especially true if there are multiple series—

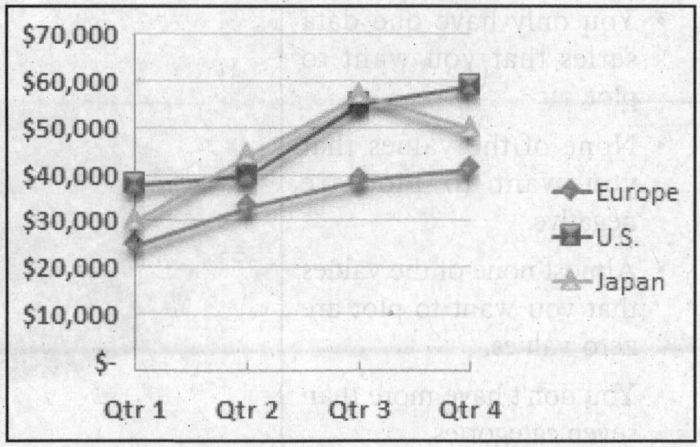

for one series, you should consider using a category chart. You should also use a line chart if you have a few evenly spaced numerical labels, especially years. If you have more than ten numerical labels, use a scatter chart instead.

Line charts have the following chart subtypes:

- Line and line with markers: Displayed with or without markers to indicate individual data values, line charts are useful to show trends over time or ordered categories, especially when there are many data points and the order in which they are presented is important. If there are many categories or the values are approximate, you should use a line chart without markers.
- Stacked line and stacked line with markers: Displayed with or without markers to indicate individual data values, stacked line charts are useful to show the trend of the contribution of each value over time or ordered categories. If there are many categories or the values are approximate, you should use a stacked line chart without markers.

  For a better presentation of this type of data, you may want to consider using a stacked area chart instead.
- 100% stacked line and 100% stacked line with markers: Displayed with or without markers to indicate individual data values, 100% stacked line charts are useful to show the trend of the percentage each value contributes over time or ordered categories. If there are many categories or the values are approximate, you should use a 100% stacked line chart without markers.

  For a better presentation of this type of data, you may want to consider using a 100% stacked area chart instead.
- 3-D line: 3-D line charts show each row or column of data as a 3-D ribbon. A 3-D line chart has horizontal, vertical, and depth axes that you can modify.

PIE CHARTS

Data that is arranged in one column or row only on a worksheet can be plotted in a pie chart. Pie charts show the size of items in one data series (data series: Related data points that are plotted in a chart. Each data series in a chart has a unique color or pattern and is represented in the chart legend. You can plot one or more data series in a chart. Pie charts have only one data series.), proportional to the sum of the items. The data points (data points: Individual values plotted in a chart and represented by bars, columns, lines, pie or doughnut slices, dots, and various other shapes called data markers. Data markers of the same color constitute a data series.) in a pie chart are displayed as a percentage of the whole pie.

Consider using a pie chart when:

- You only have one data series that you want to plot.
- None of the values that you want to plot are negative.
- Almost none of the values that you want to plot are zero values.
- You don't have more than seven categories.
- The categories represent parts of the whole pie.

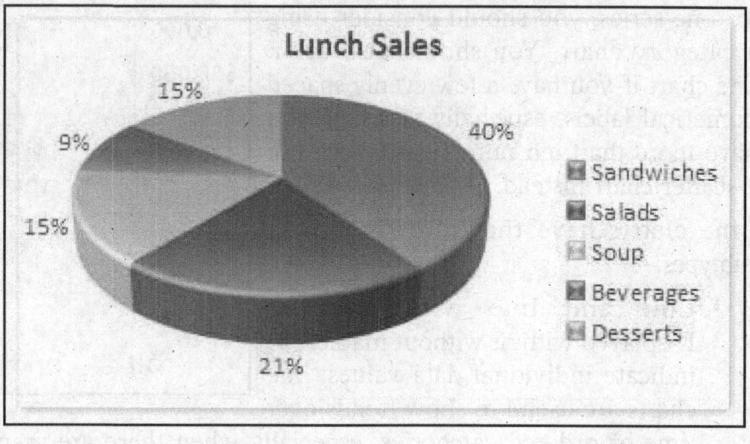

Pie charts have the following chart subtypes:

- Pie and pie in 3-D: Pie charts display the contribution of each value to a total in a 2-D or 3-D format. You can manually pull out the slices of a pie chart to emphasize them.
- Pie of pie and bar of pie: Pie of pie or bar of pie charts display pie charts with user-defined values extracted from the main pie chart and combined into a second pie or into a stacked bar. These chart types are useful when you want to make small slices in the main pie easier to see.
- Exploded pie and exploded pie in 3-D: Exploded pie charts display the contribution of each value to a total while emphasizing individual values. Exploded pie charts can be displayed in 3-D format. Because you cannot move the slices of an exploded pie individually, you may want to consider using a pie or pie in 3-D chart instead. You can then pull out the slices manually.

BAR CHARTS

Data that is arranged in columns or rows on a worksheet can be plotted in a bar chart. Bar charts illustrate comparisons among individual items.

Consider using a bar chart when:

- The axis labels are long.
- The values that are shown are durations.

Bar charts have the following chart subtypes:

- Clustered bar and clustered bar in 3-D: Clustered bar charts compare values across categories. In a clustered bar chart, the categories are typically organized along the vertical axis, and the values along the horizontal axis. A clustered bar in 3-D chart displays the horizontal rectangles in 3-D format; it does not display the data in 3-D format.
- Stacked bar and stacked bar in 3-D: Stacked bar charts show the relationship of individual items to the whole. A stacked bar in 3-D chart displays the horizontal rectangles in 3-D format; it does not display the data in 3-D format.

- 100% stacked bar and 100% stacked bar in 3-D: This type of chart compares the percentage each value contributes to a total across categories. A 100% stacked bar in 3-D chart displays the horizontal rectangles in 3-D format; it does not display the data in 3-D format.

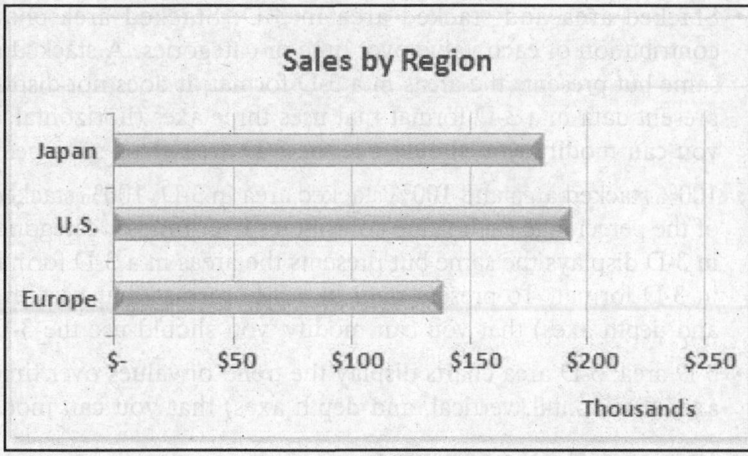

- Horizontal cylinder, cone, and pyramid: Horizontal cylinder, cone, and pyramid charts are available in the same clustered, stacked, and 100% stacked chart types that are provided for rectangular bar charts, and they show and compare data exactly the same way. The only difference is that these chart types display cylinder, cone, and pyramid shapes instead of horizontal rectangles.

AREA CHARTS

Data that is arranged in columns or rows on a worksheet can be plotted in an area chart. Area charts emphasize the magnitude of change over time, and can be used to draw attention to the total value across a trend. For example, data that represents profit over time can be plotted in an area chart to emphasize the total profit.

By displaying the sum of the plotted values, an area chart also shows the relationship of parts to a whole.

Area charts have the following chart subtypes:

- Area and area in 3-D: Area charts display the trend of values over time or categories. An area chart in 3-D displays the same but presents the areas in a 3-D format; it does not display the data in 3-D format. To present data in a 3-D format that uses three axes (horizontal, vertical, and depth axes) that you can modify, you should use the 3-D area chart subtype. As a general rule, you should consider using a line chart instead of a non-stacked area chart.

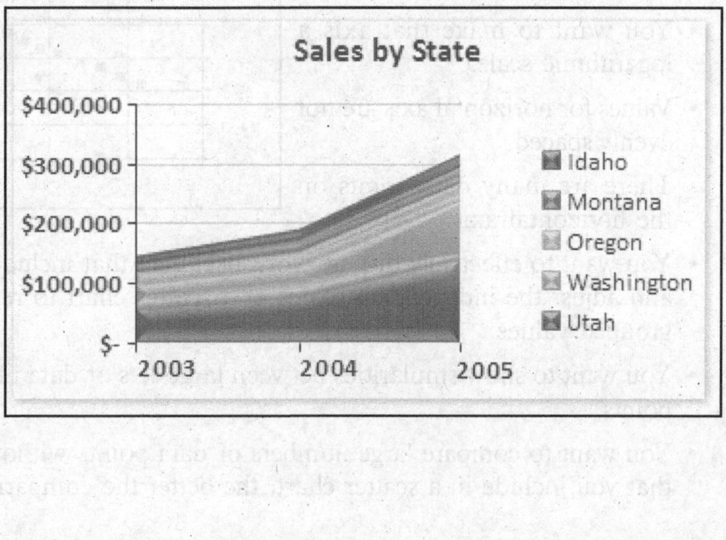

- Stacked area and stacked area in 3-D: Stacked area charts display the trend of the contribution of each value over time or categories. A stacked area chart in 3-D displays the same but presents the areas in a 3-D format; it does not display the data in 3-D format. To present data in a 3-D format that uses three axes (horizontal, vertical, and depth axes) that you can modify, you should use the 3-D area chart subtype.
- 100% stacked area and 100% stacked area in 3-D: 100% stacked area charts display the trend of the percentage each value contributes over time or categories. A 100% stacked area chart in 3-D displays the same but presents the areas in a 3-D format; it does not display the data in 3-D format. To present data in a 3-D format that uses three axes (horizontal, vertical, and depth axes) that you can modify, you should use the 3-D area chart subtype.
- 3-D area: 3-D area charts display the trend of values over time or categories by using three axes (horizontal, vertical, and depth axes) that you can modify.

XY (SCATTER) CHARTS

Data that is arranged in columns and rows on a worksheet can be plotted in an xy (scatter) chart. Scatter charts show the relationships among the numeric values in several data series, or plots two groups of numbers as one series of xy coordinates.

A scatter chart has two value axes, showing one set of numerical data along the horizontal axis (x-axis) and another along the vertical axis (y-axis). It combines these values into single data points and displays them in uneven intervals, or clusters. Scatter charts are commonly used for displaying and comparing numeric values, such as scientific, statistical, and engineering data.

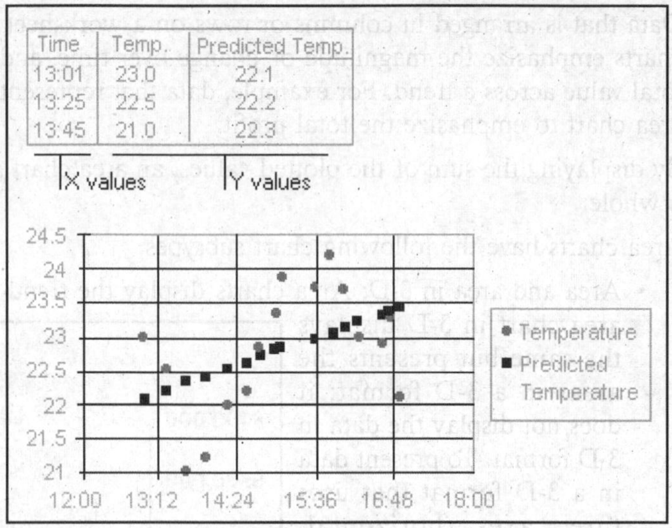

Consider using a scatter chart when:

- You want to change the scale of the horizontal axis.
- You want to make that axis a logarithmic scale.
- Values for horizontal axis are not evenly spaced.
- There are many data points on the horizontal axis.
- You want to effectively display worksheet data that includes pairs or grouped sets of values and adjust the independent scales of a scatter chart to reveal more information about the grouped values.
- You want to show similarities between large sets of data instead of differences between data points.
- You want to compare large numbers of data points without regard to time—the more data that you include in a scatter chart, the better the comparisons that you can make.

To arrange data on a worksheet for a scatter chart, you should place the x values in one row or column, and then enter the corresponding y values in the adjacent rows or columns.

Scatter charts have the following chart subtypes:

- Scatter with only markers: This type of chart compares pairs of values. Use a scatter chart without lines when you have data in a specific order.
- Scatter with smooth lines and scatter with smooth lines and markers: This type of chart can be displayed with or without a smooth curve connecting the data points. These lines can be displayed with or without markers. Use the scatter chart without markers if there are many data points.
- Scatter with straight lines and scatter with straight lines and markers: This type of chart can be displayed with or without straight connecting lines between data points. These lines can be displayed with or without markers.

STOCK CHARTS

Data that is arranged in columns or rows in a specific order on a worksheet can be plotted in a stock chart. As its name implies, a stock chart is most often used to illustrate the fluctuation of stock prices. However, this chart may also be used for scientific data. For example, you could use a stock chart to indicate the fluctuation of daily or annual temperatures. You must organize your data in the correct order to create stock charts. The way stock chart data is organized in your worksheet is very important. For example, to create a simple high-low-close stock chart, you should arrange your data with High, Low, and Close entered as column headings, in that order.

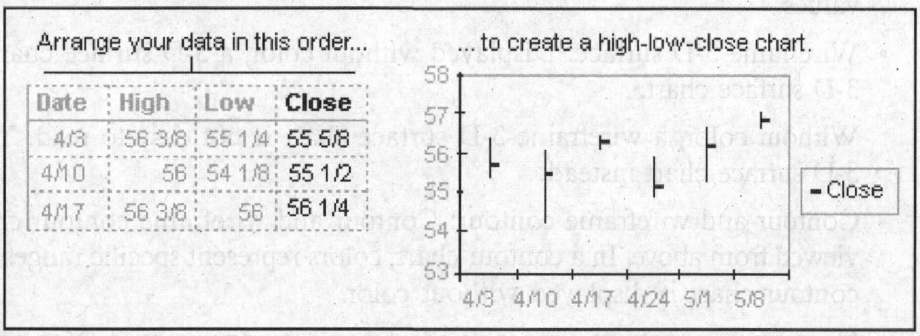

Stock charts have the following chart sub-types:

- High-low-close: The high-low-close chart is often used to illustrate stock prices. It requires three series of values in the following order: high, low, and then close.
- Open-high-low-close: This type of chart requires four series of values in the correct order (open, high, low, and then close).
- Volume-high-low-close: This type of chart requires four series of values in the correct order (volume, high, low, and then close). It measures volume by using two value axes: one for the columns that measure volume, and the other for the stock prices.
- Volume-open-high-low-close: This type of chart requires five series of values in the correct order (volume, open, high, low, and then close).

SURFACE CHARTS

Data that is arranged in columns or rows on a worksheet can be plotted in a surface chart. A surface chart is useful when you want to find optimum combinations between two sets of data. As in a topographic map, colors and patterns indicate areas that are in the same range of values.

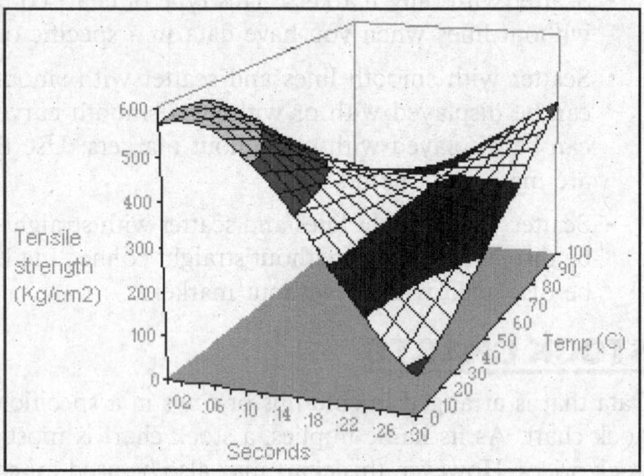

You can use a surface chart when both categories and data series are numeric values.

Surface charts have the following chart subtypes:

- 3-D surface: 3-D surface charts show trends in values across two dimensions in a continuous curve. Colors in a surface chart do not represent the data series; they represent the distinction between the values.
- Wireframe 3-D surface: Displayed without color, a 3-D surface chart is called a wireframe 3-D surface chart.

  Without color, a wireframe 3-D surface chart is not easy to read. You may want to use a 3-D surface chart instead.
- Contour and wireframe contour: Contour and wireframe contour charts are surface charts viewed from above. In a contour chart, colors represent specific ranges of values. A wireframe contour chart is displayed without color.

  Contour or wireframe contour chart are not easy to read. You may want to use a 3-D surface chart instead.

DOUGHNUT CHARTS

Data that is arranged in columns or rows only on a worksheet can be plotted in a doughnut chart. Like a pie chart, a doughnut chart shows the relationship of parts to a whole, but it can contain more than one data series (data series: Related data points that are plotted in a chart. Each data series in a chart has a unique color or pattern and is represented in the chart legend. You can plot one or more data series in a chart. Pie charts have only one data series.).

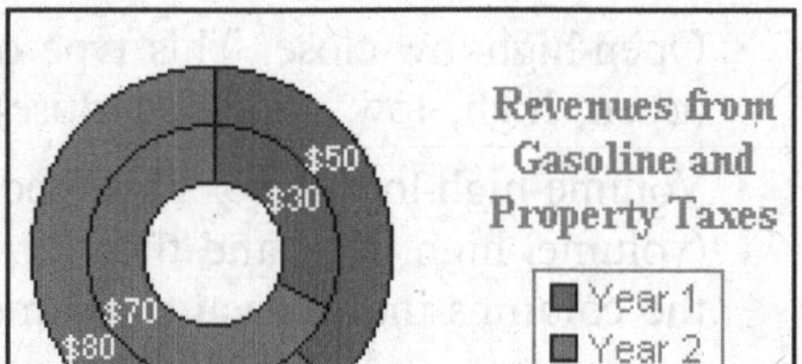

Doughnut charts are not easy to read. You may want to use a stacked column or stacked bar chart instead.

Doughnut charts have the following chart subtypes:

- Doughnut: Doughnut charts display data in rings, where each ring represents a data series.

For example, in the previous chart, the inner ring represents gas tax revenues, and the outer ring represents property tax revenues.

- Exploded Doughnut: Much like exploded pie charts, exploded doughnut charts display the contribution of each value to a total while emphasizing individual values, but they can contain more than one data series.

BUBBLE CHARTS

Data that is arranged in columns on a worksheet so that x values are listed in the first column and corresponding y values and bubble size values are listed in adjacent columns, can be plotted in a bubble chart.

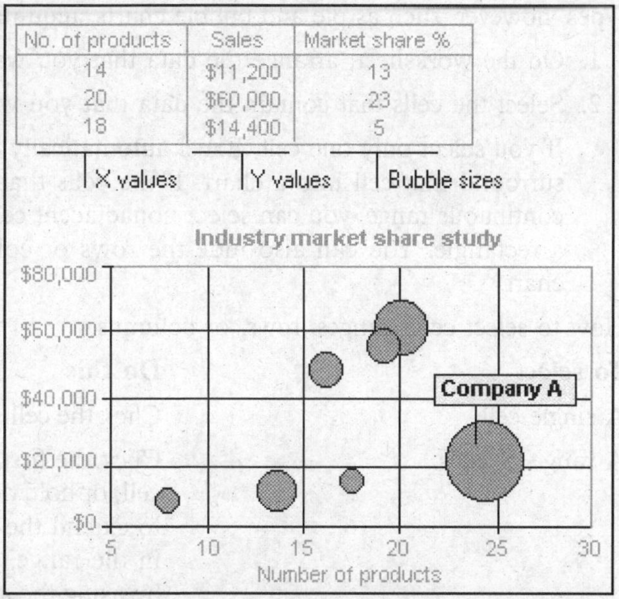

For example, you would organize your data as shown in the following example.

Bubble charts have the following chart subtypes:

- Bubble and bubble with 3-D effect: Bubble charts are similar to xy (scatter) chart, but they compare sets of three values instead of two. The third value determines the size of the bubble marker. You can choose a bubble or a bubble with a 3-D effect chart subtype.

RADAR CHARTS

Data that is arranged in columns or rows on a worksheet can be plotted in a radar chart. Radar charts compare the aggregate values of a number of data series (data series: Related data points that are plotted in a chart. Each data series in a chart has a unique color or pattern and is represented in the chart legend. You can plot one or more data series in a chart. Pie charts have only one data series.).

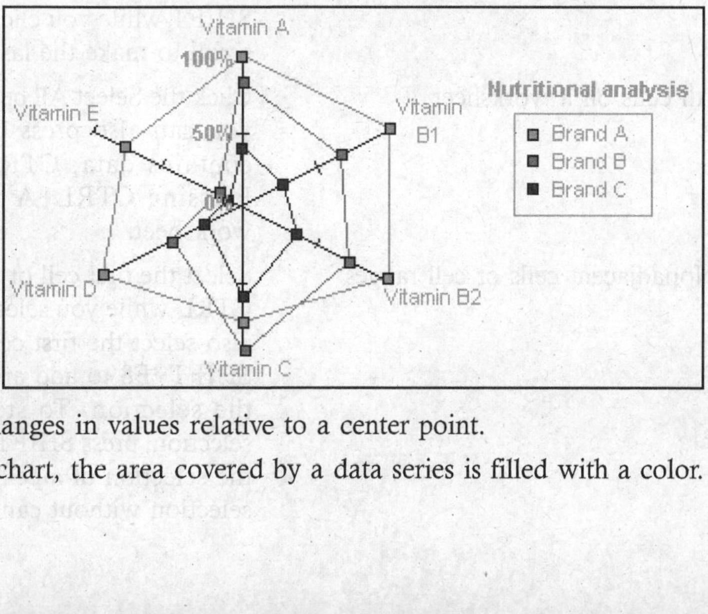

Radar charts have the following chart subtypes:

- Radar and radar with markers: With or without markers for individual data points, radar charts display changes in values relative to a center point.
- Filled radar: In a filled radar chart, the area covered by a data series is filled with a color.

CREATE A CHART

Creating a chart in Microsoft Office Excel is quick and easy. Excel provides a variety of chart types that you can choose from when you create a chart. For more information about the chart types that you can use, see Available chart types.

For most charts, such as column and bar charts, you can plot the data that you arrange in rows or columns on a worksheet (worksheet: The primary document that you use in Excel to store and work with data. Also called a spreadsheet. A worksheet consists of cells that are organized into columns and rows; a worksheet is always stored in a workbook.) in a chart. Some chart types, however, such as pie and bubble charts, require a specific data arrangement.

1. On the worksheet, arrange the data that you want to plot in a chart.
2. Select the cells that contain the data that you want to use for the chart.

   If you select only one cell, Excel automatically plots all cells containing data that directly surround that cell into a chart. If the cells that you want to plot in a chart are not in a continuous range, you can select nonadjacent cells or ranges as long as the selection forms a rectangle. You can also hide the rows or columns that you don't want to plot in the chart.

How to select cells, ranges, rows, or columns

To select	Do this
A single cell	Click the cell, or press the arrow keys to move to the cell.
A range of cells	Click the first cell in the range, and then drag to the last cell, or hold down SHIFT while you press the arrow keys to extend the selection. You can also select the first cell in the range, and then press F8 to extend the selection by using the arrow keys. To stop extending the selection, press F8 again.
A large range of cells	Click the first cell in the range, and then hold down SHIFT while you click the last cell in the range. You can scroll to make the last cell visible.
All cells on a worksheet	Click the Select All button. To select the entire worksheet, you can also press CTRL+A. Note If the worksheet contains data, CTRL+A selects the current region. Pressing CTRL+A a second time selects the entire worksheet.
Nonadjacent cells or cell ranges	Select the first cell or range of cells, and then hold down CTRL while you select the other cells or ranges. You can also select the first cell or range of cells, and then press SHIFT+F8 to add another nonadjacent cell or range to the selection. To stop adding cells or ranges to the selection, press SHIFT+F8 again.Note You cannot cancel the selection of a cell or range of cells in a nonadjacent selection without canceling the entire selection.

An entire row or column	Click the row or column heading. Row headingColumn headingYou can also select cells in a row or column by selecting the first cell and then pressing CTRL+SHIFT+ARROW key (RIGHT ARROW or LEFT ARROW for rows, UP ARROW or DOWN ARROW for columns).Note If the row or column contains data, CTRL+SHIFT+ARROW key selects the row or column to the last used cell. Pressing CTRL+SHIFT+ARROW key a second time selects the entire row or column.
Adjacent rows or columns	Drag across the row or column headings. Or select the first row or column; then hold down SHIFT while you select the last row or column.
Nonadjacent rows or columns	Click the column or row heading of the first row or column in your selection; then hold down CTRL while you click the column or row headings of other rows or columns that you want to add to the selection.
The first or last cell in a row or column	Select a cell in the row or column, and then press CTRL+ARROW key (RIGHT ARROW or LEFT ARROW for rows, UP ARROW or DOWN ARROW for columns).
The first or last cell on a worksheet or in a Microsoft Office Excel table	Press CTRL+HOME to select the first cell on the worksheet or in an Excel list. Press CTRL+END to select the last cell on the worksheet or in an Excel list that contains data or formatting.
Cells to the last used cell on the worksheet (lower-right corner)	Select the first cell, and then press CTRL+SHIFT+END to extend the selection of cells to the last used cell on the worksheet (lower-right corner).
Cells to the beginning of the worksheet	Select the first cell, and then press CTRL + SHIFT + HOME to extend the selection of cells to the beginning of the worksheet.
More or fewer cells than the active selection	Hold down SHIFT while you click the last cell that you want to include in the new selection. The rectangular range between the active cell (active cell: The selected cell in which data is entered when you begin typing. Only one cell is active at a time. The active cell is bounded by a heavy border.) and the cell that you click becomes the new selection.
	To cancel a selection of cells, click any cell on the worksheet.

On the Insert tab, in the Charts group, do one of the following:

- Click the chart type, and then click a chart subtype that you want to use.
- To see all available chart types, click a chart type, and then click All Chart Types to display the Insert Chart dialog box, click the arrows to scroll through all available chart types and chart subtypes, and then click the the ones that you want to use.

  A ScreenTip displays the chart type name when you rest the mouse pointer over any chart type or chart subtype.

- The chart is placed on the worksheet as an embedded chart (embedded chart: A chart that is placed on a worksheet rather than on a separate chart sheet. Embedded charts are beneficial when you want to view or print a chart or a PivotChart report with its source data or other information in a worksheet.). If you want to place the chart in a separate chart sheet (chart sheet: A sheet in a workbook that contains only a chart. A chart sheet is beneficial when you want to view a chart or a PivotChart report separately from worksheet data or a PivotTable report.), you can change its location.

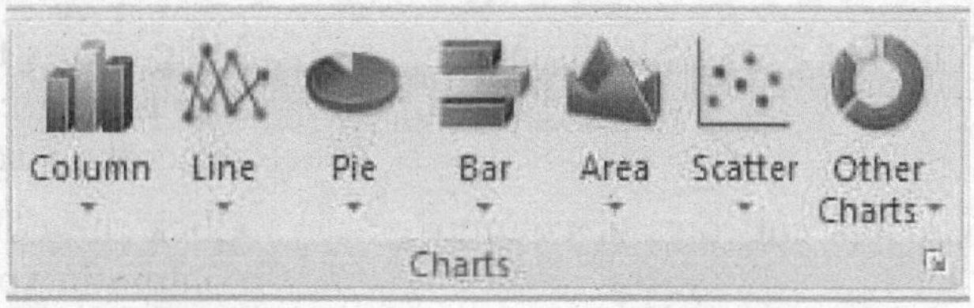

How to Change the Location of a Chart?

Click the embedded chart or the chart sheet to select it and to display the chart tools.

- On the Design tab, in the Location group, click Move Chart.
- Under Choose where you want the chart to be placed, do one of the following:
  - To display the chart in a chart sheet, click New sheet.

    If you want to replace the suggested name for the chart, you can type a new name in the New sheet box.

  - To display the chart as an embedded chart in a worksheet, click Object in, and then click a worksheet in the Object in box.
  - To quickly create a chart that is based on the default chart type, select the data that you want to use for the chart, and then press ALT+F1 or F11. When you press ALT+F1, the chart is displayed as an embedded chart; when you press F11, the chart is displayed on a separate chart sheet.
  - If you use a specific chart type frequently when you create a chart, you may want to set that chart type as the default chart type. After you select the chart type and chart subtype in the Insert Chart dialog box, click Set as Default Chart.
  - When you create a chart, the chart tools become available and the Design, Layout, and Format tabs are displayed. You can use the commands on these tabs to modify the chart so that it presents the data the way that you want. For example, use the Design tab to display the data series by row or by column, make changes to the source data of the chart, change the location of the chart, change the chart type, save a chart as a template, or select predefined layout and formatting options. Use the Layout tab to change the

display of chart elements such as chart titles and data labels, use drawing tools, or add text boxes and pictures to the chart. Use the Format tab to add fill colors, change line styles, or apply special effects.

CHANGE THE CHART TYPE OF AN EXISTING CHART

For most 2-D charts, you can change the chart type of the entire chart to give the chart a completely different look, or you can select a different chart type for any single data series (data series: Related data points that are plotted in a chart. Each data series in a chart has a unique color or pattern and is represented in the chart legend. You can plot one or more data series in a chart. Pie charts have only one data series.), which turns the chart into a combination chart. For bubble charts and most 3-D charts, you can only change the chart type of the entire chart.

Do one of the following:

- To change the chart type of the entire chart, click the chart area (chart area: The entire chart and all its elements.) or plot area (plot area: In a 2-D chart, the area bounded by the axes, including all data series. In a 3-D chart, the area bounded by the axes, including the data series, category names, tick-mark labels, and axis titles.) of the chart to display the chart tools.
- To change the chart type of a single data series, click that data series.

  This displays the chart tools, adding the Design, Layout, and Format tabs.

On the Design tab, in the Type group, click Change Chart Type.

In the Change Chart Type dialog box, do one of the following:

- Click a chart type in the first box, and then click the chart subtype that you want to use in the second box.
- If you saved a chart type as a template, click Templates, and then click the chart template that you want to use in the second box.

  You can only change the chart type of one data series at a time. To change the chart type of more than one data series in the chart, you must repeat all of the steps in this procedure for each data series.

  If you use a specific chart type frequently when you create a chart, you may want to set that chart type as the default chart type. After you select the chart type and the chart subtype in the Change Chart Type dialog box, click Set as Default Chart.

CREATE, APPLY, OR REMOVE A CHART TEMPLATE

To reuse a favorite chart type that you customized to meet your needs, you can save that chart as a chart template (*.crtx) in the charts template folder.

Instead of re-creating the chart, you can simply apply the chart template. You can also apply other types of chart templates, such as templates, that are provided by your corporation or templates that you download from Office Online.

If you no longer need a specific chart template, you can remove it from the charts template folder or you can delete it from your computer.

Save a Chart as a Chart Template

1. Click the chart that you want to save as a template.

   This displays the Chart Tools, adding the Design, Layout, and Format tabs.

2. On the Design tab, in the Type group, click Save Template.
3. In the Save in box, make sure that the Charts folder is selected.
4. In the File name box, type an appropriate name for the chart template.

Apply a Chart Template

Do one of the following:

- To create a new chart based on the template, on the Insert tab, in the Charts group, click any chart type, and then click All Chart Types.

  You can also click the Dialog Box Launcher next to Charts in the Charts group on the Insert tab.

- To make a selected chart match a template, on the Design tab, in the Type group, click Change Chart Type.

Click Templates in the first box, and then click the template that you want to use in the second box under My Templates.

If a chart template is located in a folder other than the Charts folder, click Manage Templates, locate the chart template, and then copy or move it to the Charts folder under Templates.

Remove or Delete a Chart Template

1. On the Insert tab, in the Charts group, click any chart type, and then click All Chart Types.
2. You can also click the Dialog Box Launcher next to Charts in the Charts group on the Insert tab.
3. Click Manage Templates.
4. Do one of the following:
   - To remove the chart template from the Charts folder, drag it to the folder where you want to store it.
   - To delete the chart template from your computer, right-click it, and then click Delete.

Display Hidden Data and Empty Cells in a Chart

By default, data that is hidden in rows and columns in the worksheet is not displayed in a chart, and empty cells are displayed as gaps. You can, however, display the hidden data and change the way that the empty cells are displayed. Rather then displaying gaps, you can display empty cells as zero values, or you can span the gaps with a line.

1. Click a chart in which you want to display hidden data and empty cells.

   This displays the Chart Tools, adding the Design, Layout, and Format tabs.

2. On the Design tab, in the Data group, click Select Data.

Plot Data Series from Worksheet Rows or Columns

After you create a chart, you can easily change the way that worksheet rows and columns are plotted in the chart.

1. Click the chart that contains the data that you want to plot differently.

   This displays the chart tools, adding the Design, Layout, and Format tabs.

2. On the Design tab, in the Data group.

Change the Layout or Style of a Chart

After you create a chart, you can instantly change its look. Instead of manually adding or changing chart elements or formatting the chart, you can quickly apply a predefined layout and style to your chart. Microsoft Office Excel provides a variety of useful predefined layouts and styles (or quick layouts and quick styles) that you can choose from, but you can customize a layout or style further if needed by manually changing the layout and style of individual chart elements. You cannot save a custom layout or format, but if you want to use the same layout or format again, you can save the chart as a chart template.

Select a Predefined Chart Layout

1. Click the chart that you want to format.

   This displays the Chart Tools, adding the Design, Layout, and Format tabs.

2. On the Design tab, in the Chart Layouts group, click the chart layout that you want to use.

   When the Excel window is reduced in size, chart layouts will be available in the Quick Layout gallery in the Chart Layouts group.

   To see all available layouts, click More.

Select a Predefined Chart Style

1. Click the chart that you want to format.

   This displays the Chart Tools, adding the Design, Layout, and Format tabs.

2. On the Design tab, in the Chart Styles group, click the chart style that you want to use.

   When the Excel window is reduced in size, chart styles will be available in the Chart Quick Styles gallery in the Chart Styles group.

   To see all predefined chart styles, click More.

Change the Layout of Chart Elements Manually

1. Click the chart, or select the chart element for which you want to change the layout.
2. How to select a chart element from a list of chart elements.
3. Click a chart to display the Chart Tools.
4. On the Format tab, in the Current Selection group, click the arrow next to the Chart Elements box, and then click the chart element that you want.

   This displays the Chart Tools, adding the Design, Layout, and Format tabs.

   On the Layout tab, do the one or more of the following:

- In the Labels group, click the label layout option that you want.
- In the Axes group, click the axis or gridline option that you want.
- In the Background group, click the layout option that you want.

The layout options that you select are applied to the element that you have selected. For example, if you have the entire chart selected, data labels will be applied to all data series. If you have a single data point selected, data labels will only be applied to the selected data series or data point.

Change the Style of Chart Elements Manually

1. Click the chart.

   This displays the Chart Tools, adding the Design, Layout, and Format tabs.
2. On the Format tab, in the Current Selection group, click the arrow in the Chart Elements box, and then select the chart element that you want to format.
3. In the Current Selection group, click Format Selection, and then select the formatting options that you want.

   You can also apply a quick style to individual elements, or click Shape Fill, Shape Outline, and Shape Effects in the Shape Quick Styles group on the Format tab, and then select the formatting options that you want.

Save a Chart as a Chart Template

1. Click the chart that you want to save as a template.

   This displays the Chart Tools, adding the Design, Layout, and Format tabs.
2. On the Design tab, in the Type group, click Save As Template.
3. In the Save in box, make sure that the Charts folder is selected.
4. In the File name box, type an appropriate name for the chart template.

   When you create a new chart or want to change the chart type of an existing chart, you can apply the new chart template.

How to Apply a Chart Template

Do one of the following:

- To create a new chart based on the template, on the Insert tab, in the Charts group, click any chart type, and then click All Chart Types.

  You can also click the Dialog Box Launcher next to Charts in the Charts group on the Insert tab.
- To base the chart type of a selected chart on the template, on the Design tab, in the Type group, click Change Chart Type.

  Click Templates in the first box, and then click the template that you want to use in the second box.

  If you saved a chart template in a folder other than the Charts folder, click Manage Templates, locate the chart template, and then copy or move it to the Charts folder under Templates.

Format Chart Elements

You can format individual chart elements, such as the chart area (chart area: The entire chart and all its elements.), plot area (plot area: In a 2-D chart, the area bounded by the axes, including all data series. In a 3-D chart, the area bounded by the axes, including the data series, category names, tick-mark labels, and axis titles.), data series (data series: Related data points that are plotted in a chart. Each data series in a chart has a unique color or pattern and is represented in the chart legend. You can plot one or more data series in a chart.

Pie charts have only one data series.), axes (axis: A line bordering the chart plot area used as a frame of reference for measurement. The y axis is usually the vertical axis and contains data. The x-axis is usually the horizontal axis and contains categories.), titles (titles in charts: Descriptive text that is automatically aligned to an axis or centered at the top of a chart.), data labels (data label: A label that provides additional information about a data marker, which represents a single data point or value that originates from a worksheet cell.), or legend (legend: A box that identifies the patterns or colors that are assigned to the data series or categories in a chart.).

In a chart, click the chart element that you want to format, or do the following to select the chart element from a list of chart elements:

1. Click the chart.
2. This displays the Chart Tools, adding the Design, Layout, and Format tabs.
3. On the Format tab, in the Current Selection group, click the arrow next to the Chart Elements box, and then select the chart element that you want to format.
4. On the Format tab, do any of the following:
   - To format any selected chart element, in the Current

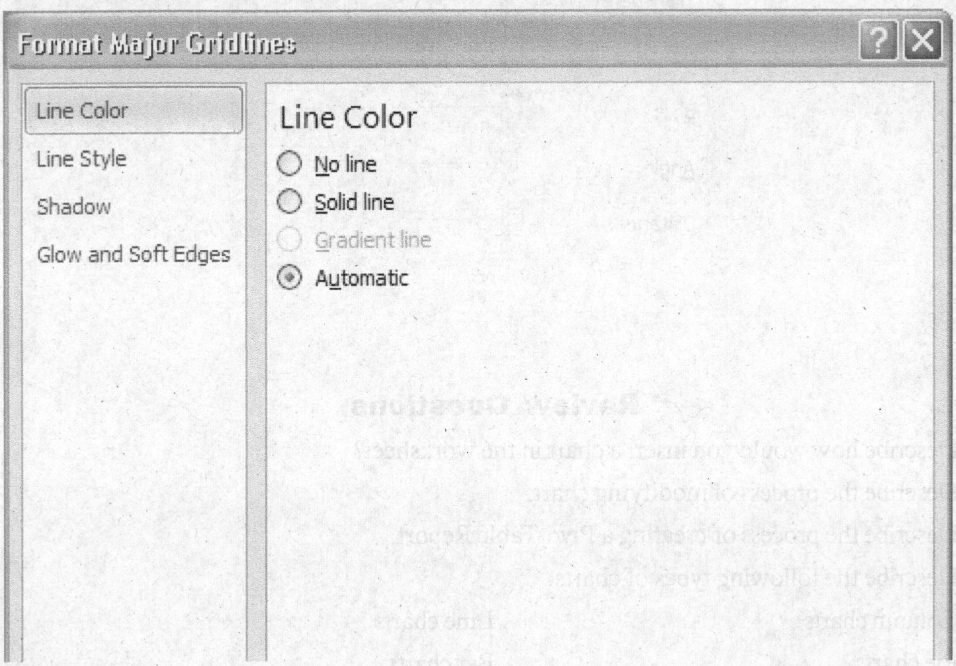

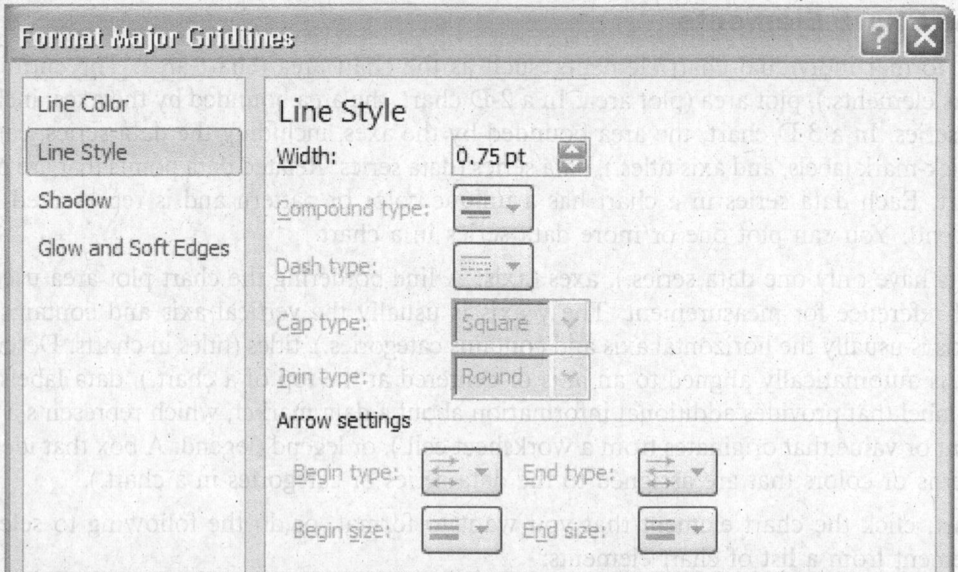

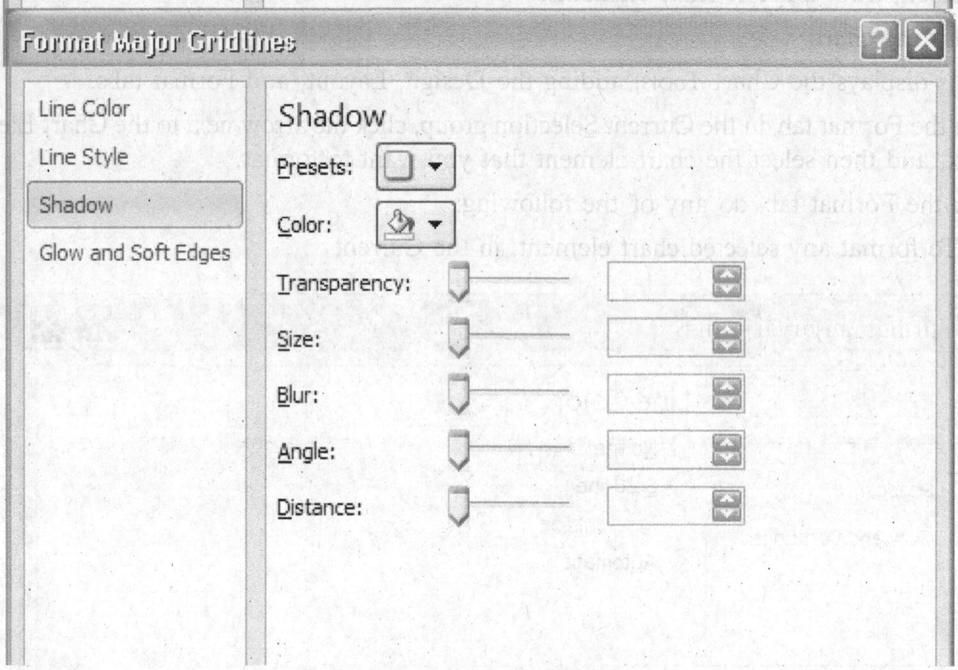

Review Questions

1. Describe how would you insert a chart in the worksheet?
2. Describe the process of modifying chart.
3. Describe the process of creating a PivotTable Report.
4. Describe the following types of charts:

   Column charts
   Line charts
   Pie charts
   Bar charts
   Area charts
   Stock charts
   Surface charts
   Doughnut charts

7

Web Based Commands of Microsoft Excel 2010

INTRODUCTION

Microsoft Excel 2010 supports the web based information. In this chapter, you would read about the various commands which can be used.

CREATE OR REMOVE A HYPERLINK

For quick access to related information in another file or on a Web page, you can insert a hyperlink (hyperlink: Colored and underlined text or a graphic that you click to go to a file, a location in a file, a Web page on the World Wide Web, or a Web page on an intranet. Hyperlinks can also go to newsgroups and to Gopher, Telnet, and FTP sites.) in a worksheet cell. You can also insert hyperlinks in specific chart elements.

CREATE A HYPERLINK TO A NEW FILE

1. On a worksheet, click the cell where you want to create a hyperlink.

   You can also select an object, such as a picture or an element in a chart that you want to use to represent the hyperlink.

2. On the Insert tab, in the Links group, click Hyperlink.

   You can also right-click the cell or graphic and then click Hyperlink on the shortcut menu, or you can press CTRL+K.

3. Under Link to, click Create New Document.

4. In the Name of new document box, type a name for the new file.

   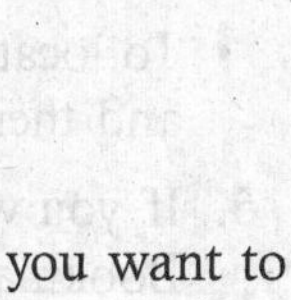

   To specify a location other than the one shown under Full path, you can type the new location before the name in the Name of new document box, or you can click Change to select the location that you want and then click OK.

5. Under When to edit, click Edit the new document later or Edit the new document now to specify when you want to open the new file for editing.

6. In the Text to display box, type the text that you that you want to use to represent the hyperlink.
7. To display helpful information when you rest the pointer on the hyperlink, click ScreenTip, type the text that you want in the ScreenTip text box, and then click OK.

CREATE A HYPERLINK TO AN EXISTING FILE OR WEB PAGE

1. On a worksheet, click the cell where you want to create a hyperlink.

   You can also select an object, such as a picture or an element in a chart that you want to use to represent the hyperlink.
2. On the Insert tab, in the Links group, click Hyperlink.

   You can also right-click the cell or object and then click Hyperlink on the shortcut menu, or you can press CTRL+K.
3. Under Link to, click Existing File or Web Page.
4. Do one of the following:
   - To select a file, click Current Folder, and then click the file that you want to link to.

     You can change the current folder by selecting a different folder in the Look in list.
   - To select a Web page, click Browsed Pages and then click the Web page that you want to link to.
   - To select a file that you recently used, click Recent Files and then click the file that you want to link to.
   - To enter the name and location of a known file or Web page that you want to link to, type that information in the Address box.
   - To locate a Web page, click Browse the Web , open the Web page that you want to link to, and then switch back to Microsoft Office Excel without closing your browser.
5. If you want to create a hyperlink to a specific location in the file or on the Web page, click Bookmark, and then double-click the bookmark (bookmark: A location or selection of text in a file that you name for reference purposes. Bookmarks identify a location within your file that you can later refer or link to.) that you want.

   The file or Web page that you are linking to must have a bookmark.
6. In the Text to display box, type the text that you want to use to represent the hyperlink.
7. To display helpful information when you rest the pointer on the hyperlink, click ScreenTip, type the text that you want in the ScreenTip text box, and then click OK.

CREATE A HYPERLINK TO A SPECIFIC LOCATION IN A WORKBOOK

To link to a location in the current workbook or another workbook, you can either define a name (name: A word or string of characters that represents a cell, range of cells, formula, or constant value. Use easy-to-understand names, such as Products, to refer to hard to understand ranges, such as Sales!C20:C30.) for the destination (destination: General term for the name of the element you go to from a hyperlink.) cells or use a cell reference.

1. To use a name, you must name the destination cells in the destination workbook.

   How to name a cell or a range of cells

   - Select the cell, range of cells, or nonadjacent selections (nonadjacent selection: A selection of two or more cells or ranges that don't touch each other. When plotting nonadjacent selections in a chart, make sure that the combined selections form a rectangular shape.) that you want to name.
   - Click the Name box at the left end of the formula bar (formula bar: A bar at the top of the Excel window that you use to enter or edit values or formulas in cells or charts. Displays the constant value or formula stored in the active cell.).
   - In the Name box, type the name for the cells, and then press ENTER.

     Names cannot contain spaces and must begin with a letter.

2. On a worksheet of the source (source file: The file that contains information that was used to create a linked or embedded object. When you update the information in the source file, you can also update the linked object in the destination file.) workbook, click the cell where you want to create a hyperlink.

   You can also select an object, such as a picture or an element in a chart that you want to use to represent the hyperlink.

3. On the Insert tab, in the Links group, click Hyperlink.

   You can also right-click the cell or object and then click Hyperlink on the shortcut menu, or you can press CTRL+K.

4. Under Link to, do one of the following:

   - To link to a location in your current workbook, click Place in This Document.
   - To link to a location in another workbook, click Existing File or Web Page, locate and select the workbook that you want to link to, and then click Bookmark.

5. Do one of the following:

   - In the Or select a place in this document box, under Cell Reference, click the sheet that you want to link to, type the cell reference in the Type in the cell reference box, and then click OK.
   - In the list under Defined Names, click the name that represents the cells that you want to link to, and then click OK.

6. In the Text to display box, type the text that you want to use to represent the hyperlink.
7. To display helpful information when you rest the pointer on the hyperlink, click ScreenTip, type the text that you want in the ScreenTip text box, and then click OK.

CREATE A CUSTOM HYPERLINK BY USING THE HYPERLINK FUNCTION

You can use the HYPERLINK function to create a hyperlink that opens a document that is stored on a network server, an intranet (intranet: A network within an organization that uses Internet technologies (such as the HTTP or FTP protocol). By using hyperlinks, you can explore objects, documents, pages, and other destinations on the intranet.), or the Internet. When you click the cell that contains the HYPERLINK function, Excel opens the file that is stored at the location of the link.

CREATE A HYPERLINK TO AN E-MAIL ADDRESS

When you click a hyperlink to an e-mail address, your e-mail program automatically starts and creates an e-mail message with the correct address in the To box, provided that you have an e-mail program installed.

1. On a worksheet, click the cell where you want to create a hyperlink.

   You can also select an object, such as a picture or an element in a chart that you want to use to represent the hyperlink.
2. On the Insert tab, in the Links group, click Hyperlink.

   You can also right-click the cell or object and then click Hyperlink on the shortcut menu, or you can press CTRL+K.
3. Under Link to, click E-mail address.
4. In the E-mail address box, type the e-mail address that you want.
5. In the Subject box, type the subject of the e-mail message.

   Some Web browsers (Web browser: Software that interprets HTML files, formats them into Web pages, and displays them. A Web browser, such as Windows Internet Explorer, can follow hyperlinks, transfer files, and play sound or video files that are embedded in Web pages.) and e-mail programs may not recognize the subject line.
6. In the Text to display box, type the text that you want to use to represent the hyperlink.
7. To display helpful information when you rest the pointer on the hyperlink, click ScreenTip, type the text that you want in the ScreenTip text box, and then click OK.

   You can also create a hyperlink to an e-mail address in a cell by typing the address directly in the cell. For example, a hyperlink is created automatically when you type an e-mail address such as someone@example.com.

DELETE A HYPERLINK

To delete a hyperlink, do one of the following:

- To delete a hyperlink and the text that represents it, right-click the cell that contains the hyperlink, and then click Clear Contents on the shortcut menu.
- To delete a hyperlink and the graphic that represents it, hold down CTRL and click the graphic, and then press DELETE.

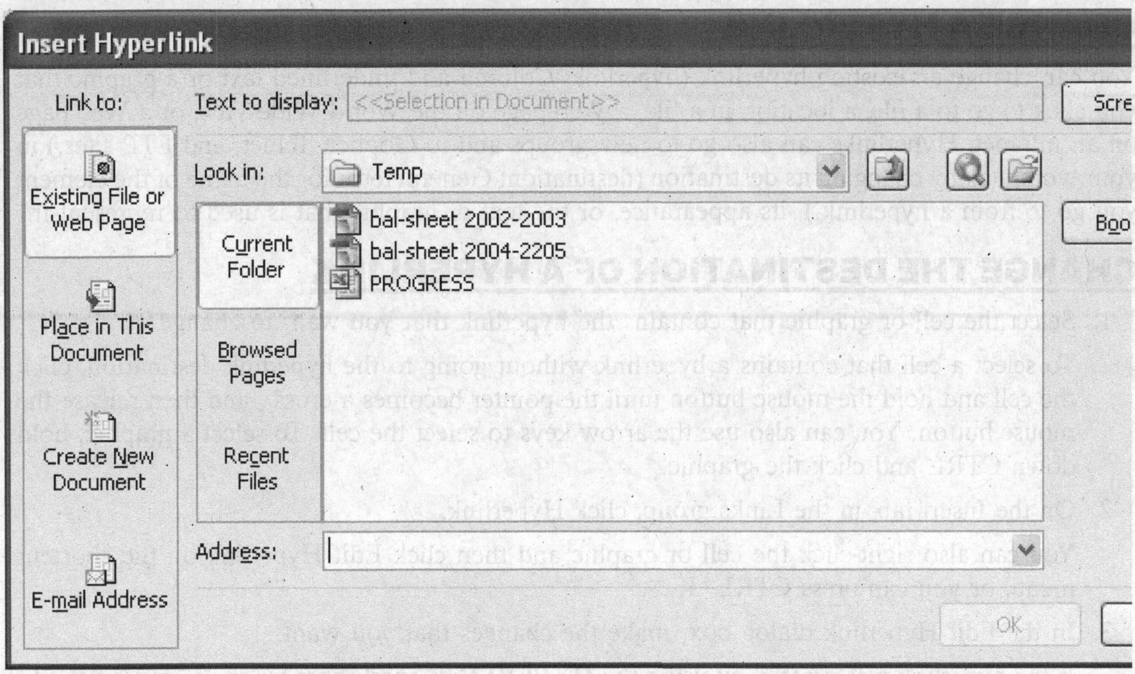

- To turn off a single hyperlink, right-click the hyperlink, and then click Remove Hyperlink on the shortcut menu.
- To turn off several hyperlinks at once, do the following:

1. In a blank cell, type the number 1.
2. Right-click the cell, and then click Copy on the shortcut menu.
3. Hold down CTRL and select each hyperlink that you want to turn off.

   To select a cell that has a hyperlink in it without going to the hyperlink destination, click the cell and hold the mouse button until the pointer becomes a cross , and then release the mouse button.
4. On the Home tab, in the Clipboard group, click the arrow below Paste, and then click Paste Special.
5. Under Operation, click Multiply, and then click OK.

COPY OR MOVE A HYPERLINK

Right-click the hyperlink (hyperlink: Colored and underlined text or a graphic that you click to go to a file, a location in a file, a Web page on the World Wide Web, or a Web page on an intranet. Hyperlinks can also go to newsgroups and to Gopher, Telnet, and FTP sites.) that you want to copy or move, and then click Copy or Cut on the shortcut menu.

Right-click the cell that you want to copy or move the hyperlink to, and then click Paste on the shortcut menu.

CHANGE A HYPERLINK

You can change an existing hyperlink (hyperlink: Colored and underlined text or a graphic that you click to go to a file, a location in a file, a Web page on the World Wide Web, or a Web page on an intranet. Hyperlinks can also go to newsgroups and to Gopher, Telnet, and FTP sites.) in your workbook by changing its destination (destination: General term for the name of the element you go to from a hyperlink.), its appearance, or the text or graphic that is used to represent it.

CHANGE THE DESTINATION OF A HYPERLINK

1. Select the cell or graphic that contains the hyperlink that you want to change.

   To select a cell that contains a hyperlink without going to the hyperlink destination, click the cell and hold the mouse button until the pointer becomes a cross , and then release the mouse button. You can also use the arrow keys to select the cell. To select a graphic, hold down CTRL and click the graphic.

2. On the Insert tab, in the Links group, click Hyperlink.

   You can also right-click the cell or graphic and then click Edit Hyperlink on the shortcut menu, or you can press CTRL+K.

3. In the Edit Hyperlink dialog box, make the changes that you want.

   If the hyperlink was created by using the HYPERLINK worksheet function, you must edit the formula to change the destination. Select the cell that contains the hyperlink, and then click the formula bar (formula bar: A bar at the top of the Excel window that you use to enter or edit values or formulas in cells or charts. Displays the constant value or formula stored in the active cell.) to edit the formula.

CHANGE THE APPEARANCE OF HYPERLINK TEXT

You can change the appearance of all hyperlink text in the current workbook by changing the cell style for hyperlinks.

1. On the Home tab, in the Styles group, click Cell Styles.
2. Under Data and Model, do the following:
   - To change the appearance of hyperlinks that have not been clicked to go to their destinations, right-click Hyperlink, and then click Modify.
   - To change the appearance of hyperlinks that have been clicked to go to their destinations, right-click Followed Hyperlink, and then click Modify.

     The Hyperlink cell style is available only when the workbook contains a hyperlink. The Followed Hyperlink cell style is available only when the workbook contains a hyperlink that has been clicked.
3. In the Style dialog box, click Format.
4. On the Font tab and Fill tab, select the formatting options that you want, and then click OK.

Notes

- The options that you select in the Format Cells dialog box appear as selected under Style

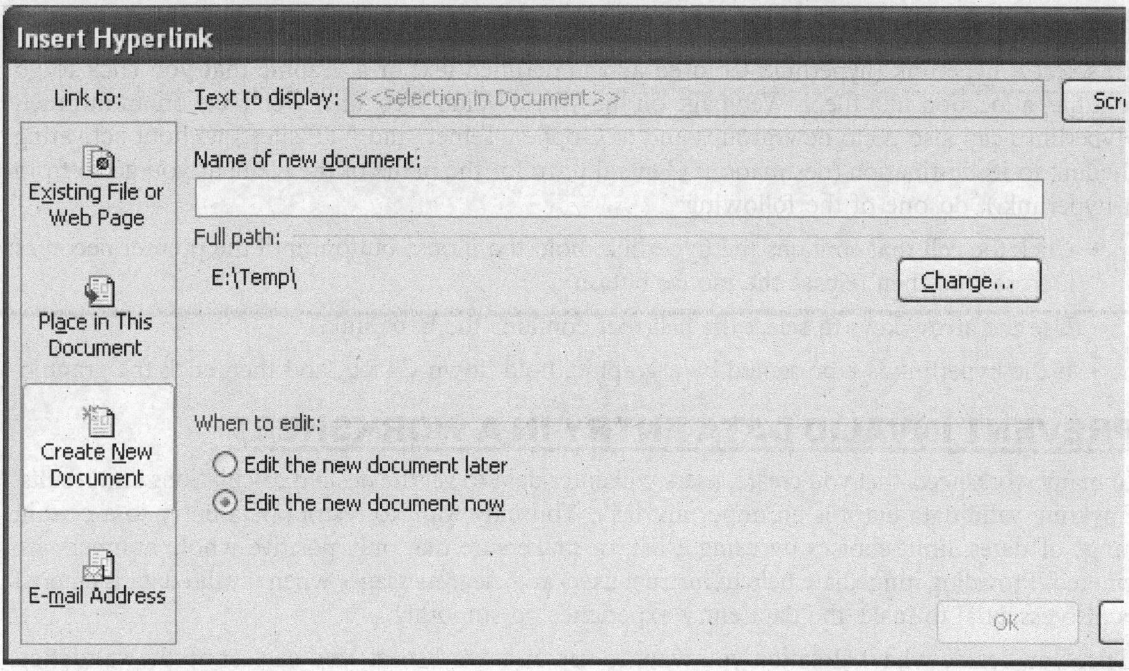

includes in the Style dialog box. You can clear the check boxes for any options that you don't want to apply.

- Changes that you make to the Hyperlink and Followed Hyperlink cell styles apply to all hyperlinks in the current workbook. You cannot change the appearance of individual hyperlinks.

CHANGE THE TEXT OR GRAPHIC FOR A HYPERLINK

Select the cell or graphic that contains the hyperlink that you want to change.

Tip To select a cell that contains a hyperlink without going to the hyperlink destination, click the cell and hold the mouse button until the pointer becomes a cross , and then release the mouse button. You can also use the arrow keys to select the cell. To select a graphic, hold down CTRL and click the graphic.

Do one or more of the following:

- To change the hyperlink text, click in the formula bar (formula bar: A bar at the top of the Excel window that you use to enter or edit values or formulas in cells or charts. Displays the constant value or formula stored in the active cell.), and then edit the text.
- To change the format of a graphic, right-click it, and then click the option that you need to change its format.
- To change text in a graphic, double-click the selected graphic, and then make the changes that you want.
- To change the graphic that represents the hyperlink, insert a new graphic, make it a hyperlink with the same destination, and then delete the old graphic and hyperlink.

SELECT A HYPERLINK WITHOUT ACTIVATING THE LINK

To select a hyperlink (hyperlink: Colored and underlined text or a graphic that you click to go to a file, a location in a file, a Web page on the World Wide Web, or a Web page on an intranet. Hyperlinks can also go to newsgroups and to Gopher, Telnet, and FTP sites.) without activating the link to its destination (destination: General term for the name of the element you go to from a hyperlink.), do one of the following:

- Click the cell that contains the hyperlink, hold the mouse button until the pointer becomes a cross, and then release the mouse button.
- Use the arrow keys to select the cell that contains the hyperlink.
- If the hyperlink is represented by a graphic, hold down CTRL, and then click the graphic.

PREVENT INVALID DATA ENTRY IN A WORKSHEET

In many worksheets that you create, users will enter data to get the desired calculations and results. Ensuring valid data entry is an important task. You may want to restrict data entry to a certain range of dates, limit choices by using a list, or make sure that only positive whole numbers are entered. Providing immediate help to instruct users and clear messages when invalid data is entered is also essential to make the data entry experience go smoothly.

Once you decide what validation you want to use on a worksheet, you can set up the validation by doing the following:

1. Select one or more cells to validate.
2. On the Data tab, in the Data Tools group, click Data Validation.

   The Data Validation dialog box is displayed.

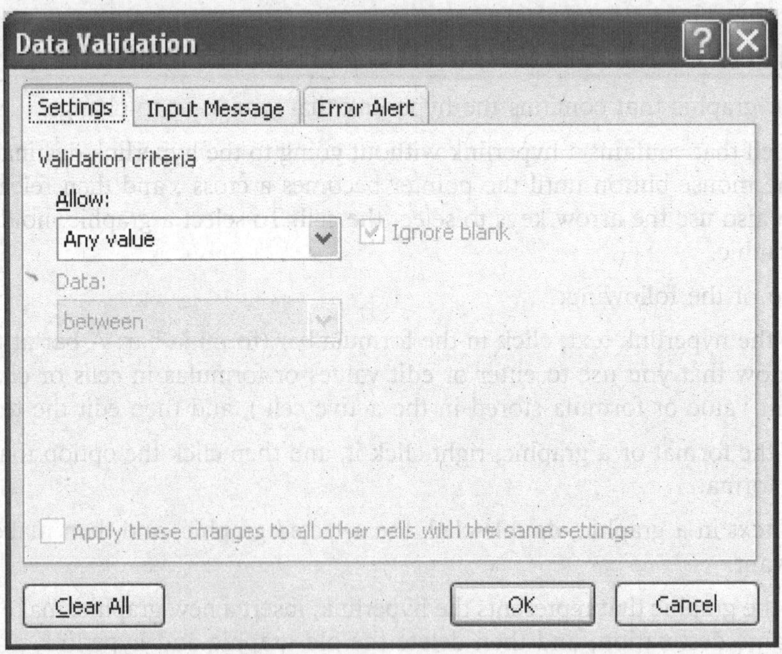

3. Click the Settings tab.
4. To specify the type of validation that you want, do one of the following:

Allow values from a list

1. In the Allow box, select List.
2. Click the Source box and then type the list values separated by the Microsoft Windows list separator character (commas by default).

   For example:

   - To limit entry to a question, such as "Do you have children?", to two choices, type Yes, No.
   - To limit a vendor's quality reputation to three ratings, type Low, Average, High.

3. You can also create a list of values from a range of cells. For more information, see Create a drop-down list from a range of cells.

   The width of the drop-down list is determined by the width of the cell that has the data validation. You may need to adjust the width of that cell to prevent truncating the width of valid entries that are wider than the width of the drop-down list.

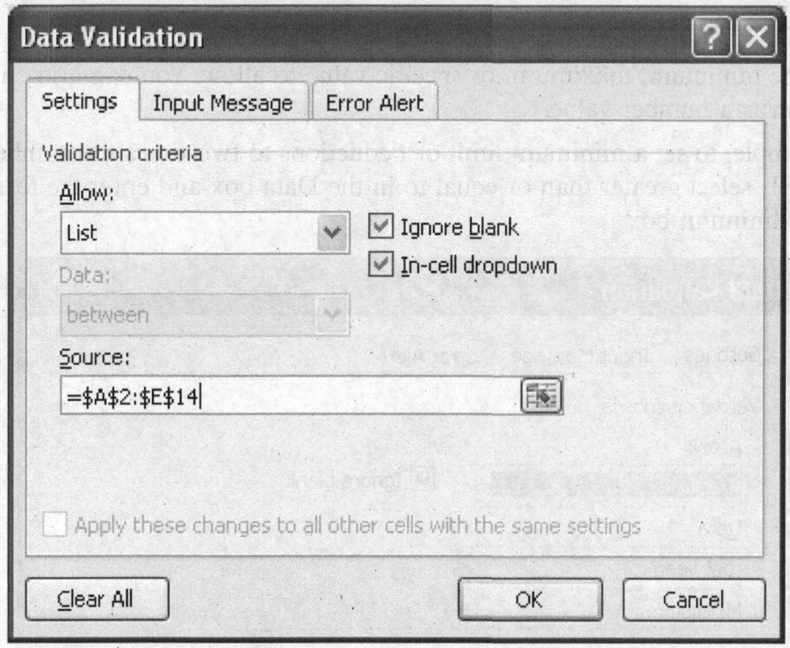

Make sure that the In-cell dropdown check box is selected.

Allow a whole number within limits

1. In the Allow box, select Whole Number.
2. In the Data box, select the type of restriction that you want. For example, to set upper and lower limits, select between.

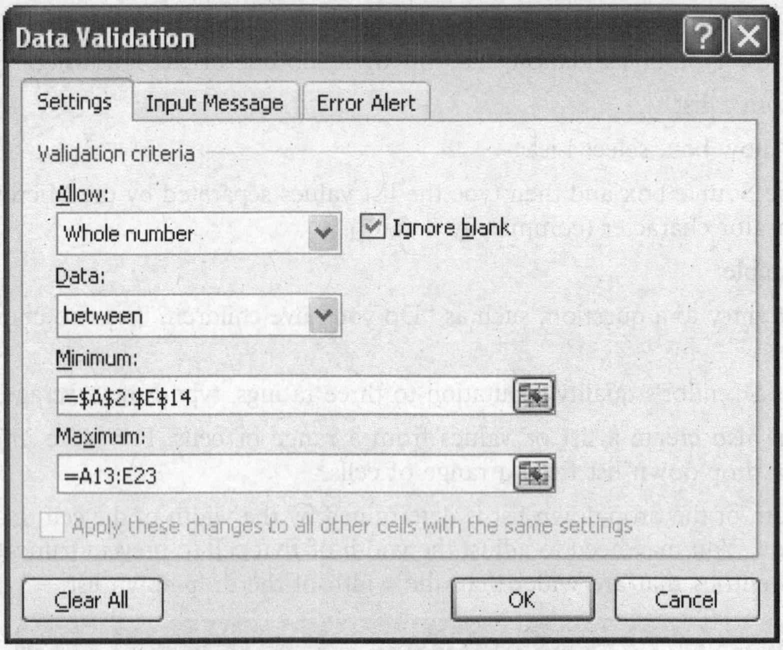

3. Enter the minimum, maximum, or specific value to allow. You can also enter a formula that returns a number value.

   For example, to set a minimum limit of deductions to two times the number of children in cell F1, select greater than or equal to in the Data box and enter the formula, =2*F1, in the Minimum box.

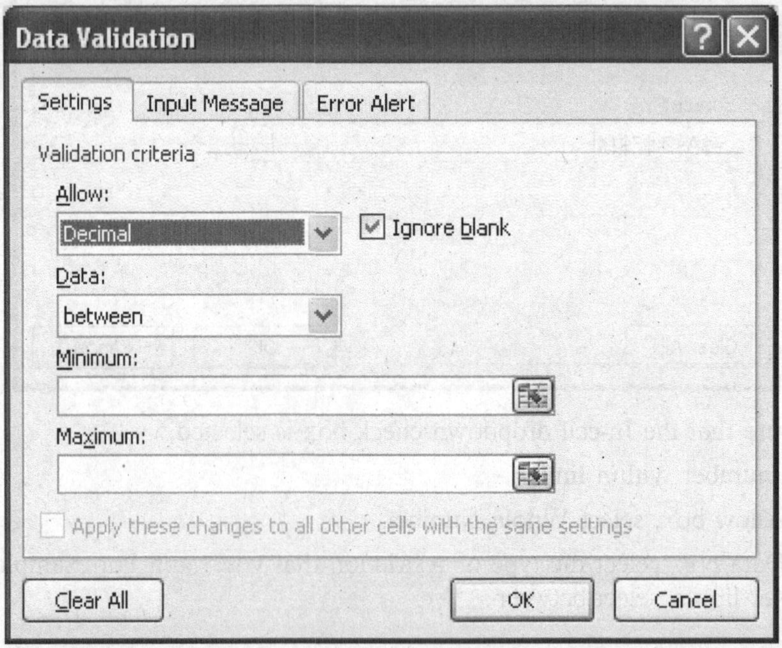

Allow a decimal number within limits

1. In the Allow box, select Decimal.
2. In the Data box, select the type of restriction that you want. For example, to set upper and lower limits, select between.
3. Enter the minimum, maximum, or specific value to allow. You can also enter a formula that returns a number value.

   For example, to set a maximum limit for commissions and bonuses of 6% of a salesperson's salary in cell E1, select less than or equal to in the Data box and enter the formula, =E1*6%, in the Maximum box.

   To allow a user to enter percentages, for example 20%, select Decimal in the Allow box, select the type of restriction that you want in the Data box, enter the minimum, maximum, or specific value as a decimal, for example .2, and then display the data validation cell as a percentage by selecting the cell and clicking Percent Style in the Number group on the Sheet tab.

Allow a date within a timeframe

1. In the Allow box, select Date.
2. In the Data box, select the type of restriction that you want. For example, to allow dates after a certain day, select greater than.
3. Enter the start, end, or specific date to allow. You can also enter a formula that returns a date.

   For example, to set a time frame between today's date and 3 days from today's date, select between in the Data box, enter =TODAY() in the Minimum box, and enter =TODAY()+3 in the Maximum box.

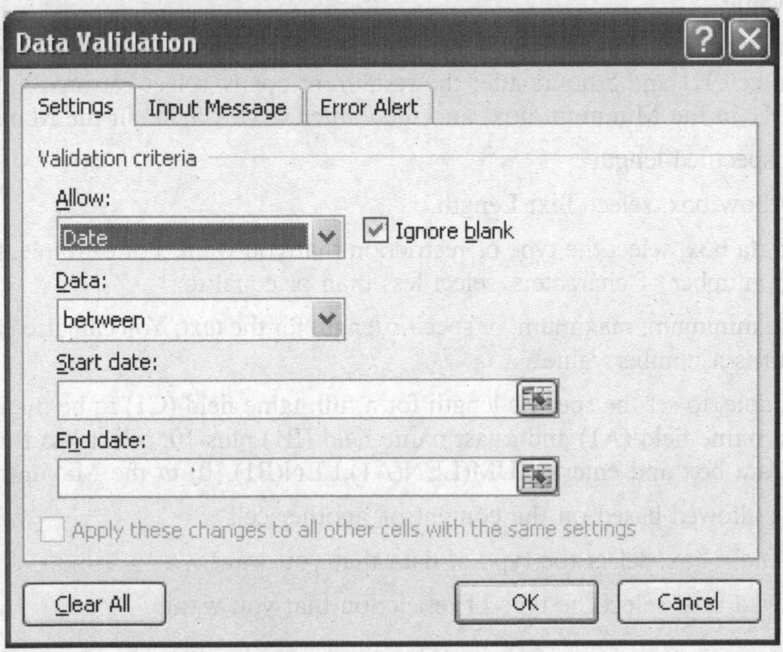

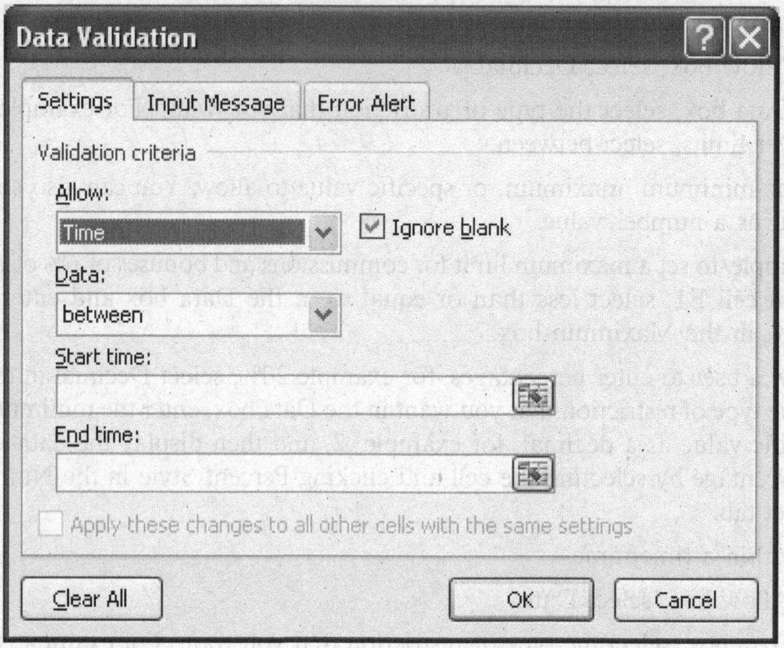

Allow a time within a timeframe

1. In the Allow box, select Time.
2. In the Data box, select the type of restriction that you want. For example, to allow times before a certain time of day, select less than.
3. Enter the start, end, or specific time to allow. You can also enter a formula that returns a time value.

   For example, to set a time frame for serving breakfast between the time when the restaurant opens in cell H1 and 5 hours after the restaurant opens, select between in the Data box, enter =H1 in the Minimum box, and then enter =H1+"5:00" in the Maximum box.

Allow text of a specified length

1. In the Allow box, select Text Length.
2. In the Data box, select the type of restriction that you want. For example, to allow up to a certain number of characters, select less than or equal to.
3. Enter the minimum, maximum, or specific length for the text. You can also enter a formula that returns a number value.

   For example, to set the specific length for a full name field (C1) to be the current length of a first name field (A1) and a last name field (B1) plus 10, select less than or equal to in the Data box and enter =SUM(LEN(A1),LEN(B1),10) in the Maximum box.

Calculate what's allowed based on the content of another cell

1. In the Allow box, select the type of data that you want.
2. In the Data box, select the type of restriction that you want.

3. In the box or boxes below the Data box, click the cell that you want to use to specify what's allowed.

   For example, to allow entries for an account only if the result won't go over the budget in cell E4, select Decimal for Allow, select less than or equal to for Data, and in the Maximum box, enter =E4.

Use a formula to calculate what's allowed

1. In the Allow box, select Custom.
2. In the Formula box, enter a formula that calculates a logical value (TRUE for valid or FALSE for invalid entries). For example:

To make sure that	**Enter this formula**
The cell for the picnic account (B1) can only be updated if nothing is budgeted for the discretionary account (D1) and the total budget (D2) is less than the $40,000 allocated.	=AND(D1=0,D2<40000)
The cell containing a product description (B2) only contains text.	=ISTEXT(B2)
For the cell containing a projected advertising budget (B3), the subtotal for subcontractors and services (E1) must be less than or equal to $800, and the total budget amount (E2) must also be less than or equal to $97,000.	=AND(E1<=800,E2<=97000)
The cell containing an employee age (B4) is always greater than the number of full years of employment (F1) plus 18 (the minimum age of employment).	=IF(B4>F1+18,TRUE,FALSE)

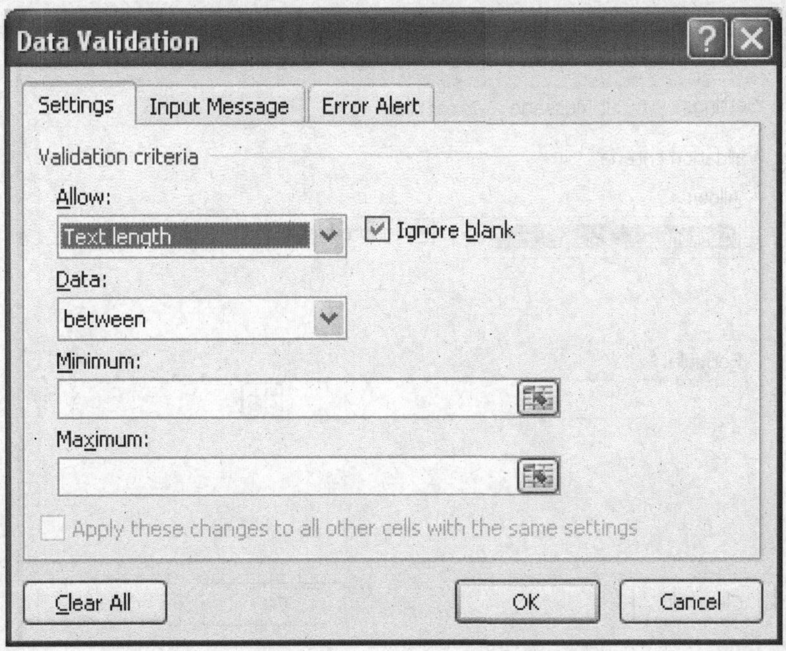

All the data in the cell range A1:A20 contains unique values.

=COUNTIF($A$1:$A$20,A1)=1

You must enter the formula in the data validation for cell A1, and then fill the cells A2 though A20 so that the data validation for each cell in the range has a similar formula, but the second argument to the COUNTIF function will match the current cell.

The cell containing a product code name (B5) always begins with the standard prefix of ID- and is at least 10 characters in length.

=AND(LEFT(B5, 3) ="ID-",LEN(B5) > 9)

3. To specify how you want to handle blank (null) values, select or clear the Ignore blank check box.

   If your allowed values are based on a cell range with a defined name, and there is a blank cell anywhere in the range, setting the Ignore blank check box allows any values to be entered in the validated cell. This is also true for any cells referenced by validation formulas: if any referenced cell is blank, setting the Ignore blank check box allows any values to be entered in the validated cell.

4. Optionally, display an input message when the cell is clicked.

   How?

   1. Click the Input Message tab.
   2. Make sure the Show input message when cell is selected check box is selected.
   3. Fill in the title and text for the message.

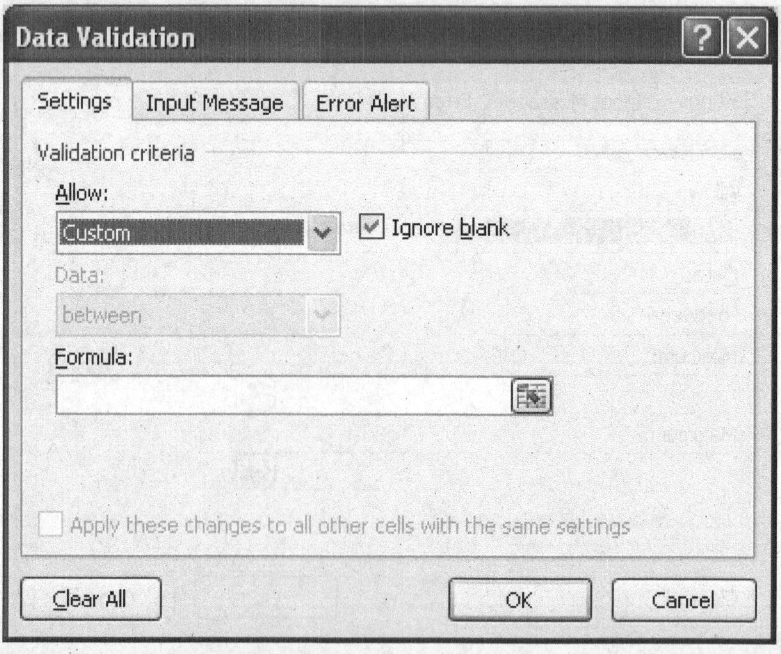

5. Specify how you want Microsoft Office Excel to respond when invalid data is entered.

   How?

   1. Click the Error Alert tab, and make sure that the Show error alert after invalid data is entered check box is selected.
   2. Select one of the following options for the Style box:
      - To display an information message that does not prevent entry of invalid data, select Information.
      - To display a warning message that does not prevent entry of invalid data, select Warning.
      - To prevent entry of invalid data, select Stop.
   3. Fill in the title and text for the message (up to 225 characters).

      If you don't enter a title or text, the title defaults to "Microsoft Excel" and the message to: "The value you entered is not valid. A user has restricted values that can be entered into this cell."

6. Test the data validation to make sure that it's working correctly.
7. Try entering both valid and invalid data in the cells to make sure that your settings are working as you intended and your messages are appearing when you expect.

   If you make changes to the validation in one cell, you can automatically apply your changes to all other cells that have the same settings.

Notes

- Apply protection, if needed If you are planning to protect the worksheet or workbook, protect

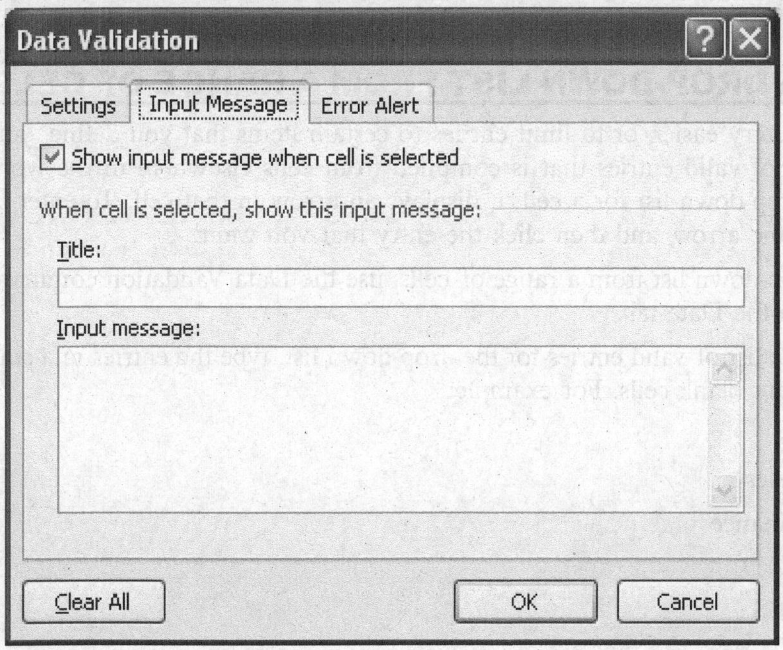

it after you have finished setting up validation. Make sure that you unlock any validated cells before protecting the worksheet, otherwise users won't be able to type in the cells.

- Share the workbook, if needed If you are planning to share the workbook, share it after you have finished setting up validation and protection. After you share a workbook, you won't be able to change the validation settings unless you stop sharing, but Excel will continue to validate the cells that you have designated while the workbook is shared.

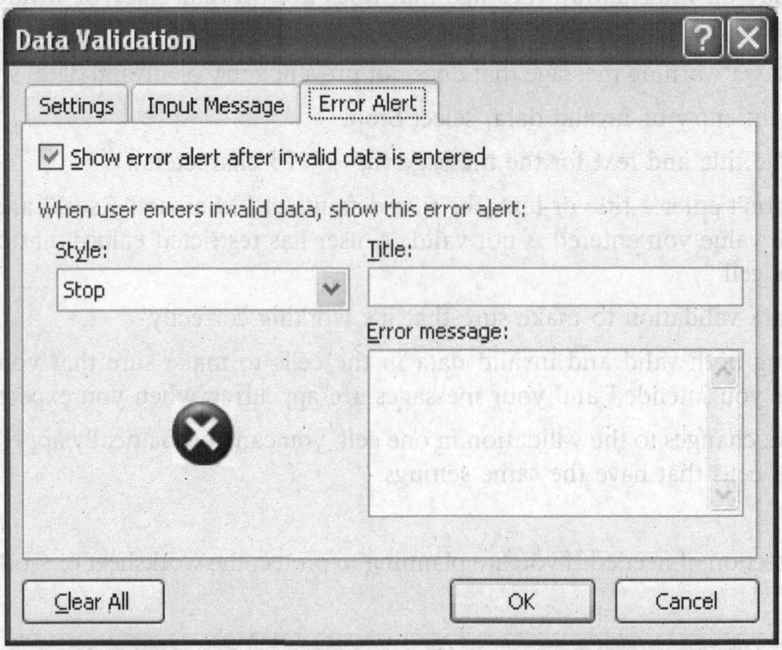

CREATE A DROP-DOWN LIST FROM A RANGE OF CELLS

To make data entry easier, or to limit entries to certain items that you define, you can create a drop-down list of valid entries that is compiled from cells elsewhere in the workbook. When you create a drop-down list for a cell, it displays an arrow in that cell. To enter information in that cell, click the arrow, and then click the entry that you want.

To create a drop-down list from a range of cells, use the Data Validation command in the Data Tools group on the Data tab.

1. To create a list of valid entries for the drop-down list, type the entries in a single column or row without blank cells. For example:

	A
1	Sales
2	Finance
3	R&D
4	MIS

You may want to sort the data in the order that you want it to appear in the drop-down list.

2. If you want to use another worksheet, type the list on that worksheet, and then define a name (name: A word or string of characters that represents a cell, range of cells, formula, or constant value. Use easy-to-understand names, such as Products, to refer to hard to understand ranges, such as Sales!C20:C30.) for the list.

How to define a name

1. Select the cell, range of cells, or nonadjacent selections (nonadjacent selection: A selection of two or more cells or ranges that don't touch each other. When plotting nonadjacent selections in a chart, make sure that the combined selections form a rectangular shape.) that you want to name.
2. Click the Name box at the left end of the formula bar (formula bar: A bar at the top of the Excel window that you use to enter or edit values or formulas in cells or charts. Displays the constant value or formula stored in the active cell.).
3. Type the name for the cells, for example, ValidDepts.
4. Press ENTER.

You cannot name a cell while you are changing the contents of the cell.

3. Select the cell where you want the drop-down list.
4. On the Data tab, in the Data Tools group, click Data Validation.

The Data Validation dialog box is displayed.

5. Click the Settings tab.

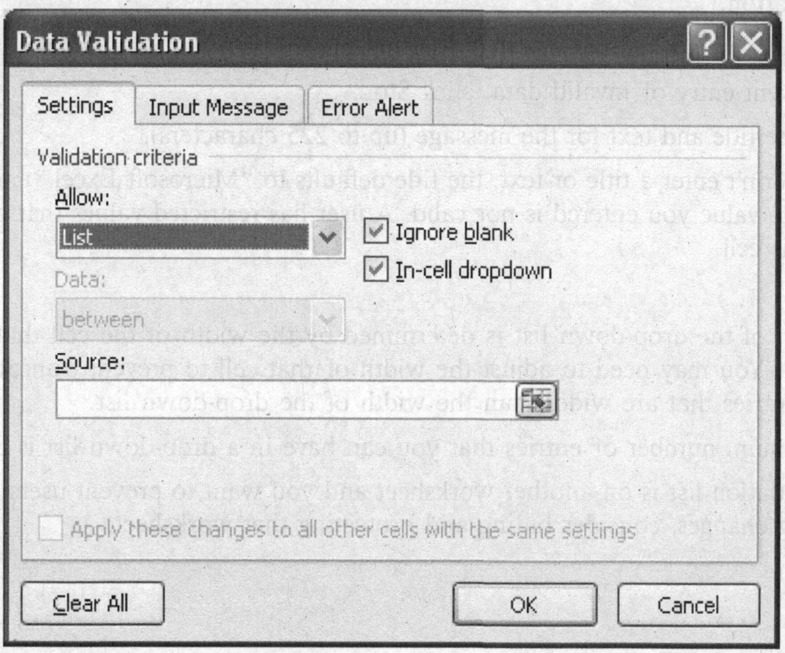

6. In the Allow box, click List.
7. To specify the location of the list of valid entries, do one of the following:
   - If the list is in the current worksheet, enter a reference to your list in the Source box.
   - If the list is on a different worksheet, enter the name that you defined for your list in the Source box.

   In both cases, make sure that the reference or name is preceded with an equal sign (=). For example, enter =ValidDepts.
8. Make sure that the In-cell drop-down check box is selected.
9. To specify whether the cell can be left blank, select or clear the Ignore blank check box.
10. Optionally, display an input message when the cell is clicked.

    How to display an input message
    1. Click the Input Message tab.
    2. Make sure that the Show input message when cell is selected check box is selected.
    3. Type the title and text for the message (up to 225 characters).
11. Specify how you want Microsoft Office Excel to respond when invalid data is entered.

    How to specify a response to invalid data
    1. Click the Error Alert tab, and make sure that the Show error alert after invalid data is entered check box is selected.
    2. Select one of the following options for the Style box:
       - To display an information message that does not prevent entry of invalid data, click Information.
       - To display a warning message that does not prevent entry of invalid data, click Warning.
       - To prevent entry of invalid data, click Stop.
    3. Type the title and text for the message (up to 225 characters).

       If you don't enter a title or text, the title defaults to "Microsoft Excel" and the message to: "The value you entered is not valid. A user has restricted values that can be entered into this cell."

Notes

- The width of the drop-down list is determined by the width of the cell that has the data validation. You may need to adjust the width of that cell to prevent truncating the width of valid entries that are wider than the width of the drop-down list.
- The maximum number of entries that you can have in a drop-down list is 32,767.
- If the validation list is on another worksheet and you want to prevent users from seeing it or making changes, consider hiding and protecting that worksheet.

CONNECT TO (IMPORT) EXTERNAL DATA

The main benefit of connecting to external data is that you can periodically analyze this data in Microsoft Office Excel without repeatedly copying the data, which is an operation that can be time-consuming and error-prone. After connecting to external data, you can also automatically refresh (or update) your Excel workbooks from the original data source whenever the data source is updated with new information.

Security Connections to external data may be disabled on your computer. To connect to data when you open a workbook, you must enable data connections by using the Trust Center bar, or by putting the workbook in a trusted location. For more information, see Create, remove, or change a trusted location for your files, Add, remove, or view a trusted publisher, and View my security settings in the Trust Center.

1. On the Data tab, in the Get External Data group, click Existing Connections.

   The Existing Connections dialog box is displayed.

2. In the Show drop-down list at the top of the dialog box, do one of the following:

   - To display all connections, click All Connections. This the default.
   - To display only the recently used list of connections, click Connections in this Workbook.

     This list is created from connections that you have already defined, that you have created by using the Select Data Source dialog box of the Data Connection Wizard, or that you have previously selected as a connection from this dialog box.

   - To display only the connections that are available on your computer, click Connection files on this computer.

     This list is created from the My Data Sources folder that is usually stored in the My Documents folder.

   - To display only the connections that are available from a connection file that is accessible from the network, click Connection files on the network.

     This list is created from an Excel Services Data Connection Library (DCL) on a Microsoft Office SharePoint Server 2010 site. A DCL is a document library in a Microsoft Office SharePoint Services 2010 site that contains a collection of Office Data Connection (ODC) files (.odc). Typically, a DCL is set up by a site administrator, who can also configure the SharePoint site to display ODC files from this DCL in the External Connections dialog box. For more information, see Office SharePoint Server 2010 Central Administration Help.

     If you don't see the connection that you want, you can create a connection by clicking Browse for More to display the Select Data Source dialog box, and then by clicking New Source to start the Data Connection Wizard.

     If you choose a connection from the Connection files on the network or Connection files on this computer categories, the connection file is copied into the workbook as a new workbook connection, and then it is used as the new connection information.

3. Select the connection that you want, and then click Open.

   The Import Data dialog box is displayed.

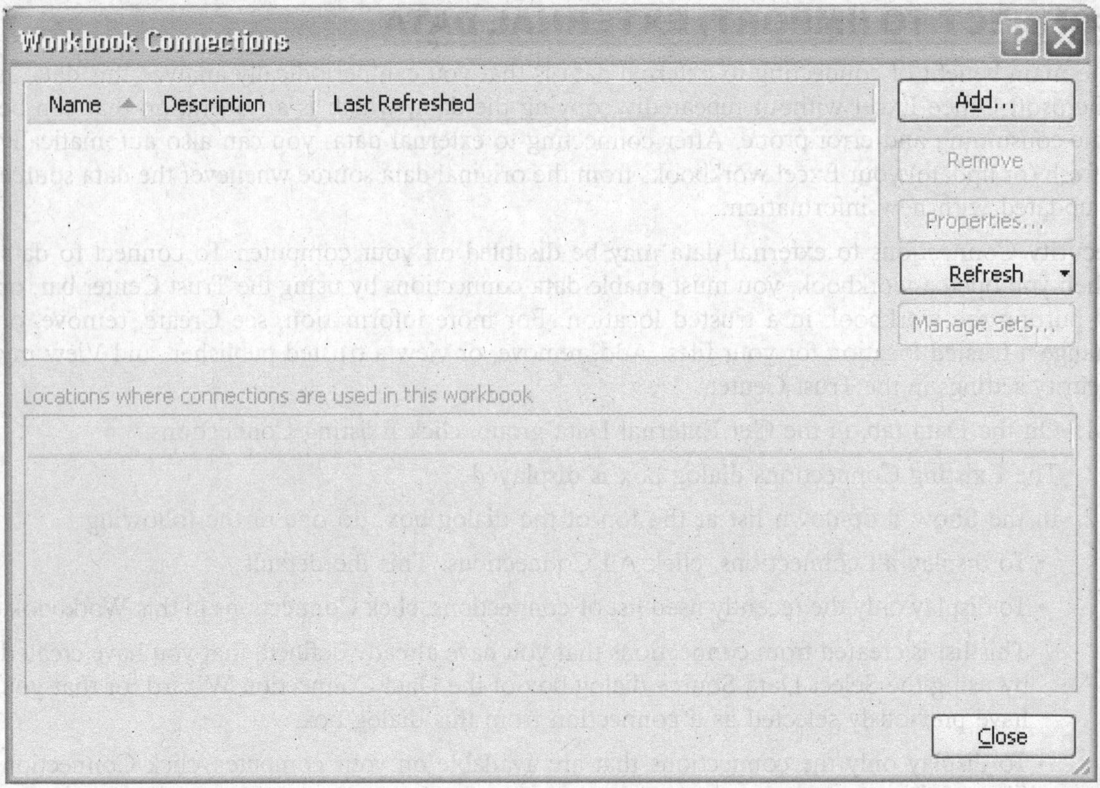

4. Under Select how you want to view this data in your workbook do one of the following:
   - To create a table for simple sorting and filtering, click Table.
   - To create a PivotTable report for summarizing large amounts of data by aggregating and subtotaling the data, click PivotTable Report.
   - To create a PivotTable report, and PivotChart report for visually summarizing data, click PivotChart and PivotTable Report.
   - To store the selected connection in the workbook for later use, click Only Create Connection.

   Use this option to store the selected connection in the workbook for later use. For example, if you are connecting to an Online Analytical Processing (OLAP) cube data source and you intend to convert PivotTable cells to worksheet formulas by using the Convert to Formulas command (On the Options tab, in the Tools group, click OLAP tools), you might use this option because you don't need to save the PivotTable report.

   These options are not available for all types of data connections, including text, Web Query, and XML.

5. Under Where do you want to put the data?, do one of the following:
   - To place the PivotTable or PivotChart report in an existing worksheet, select Existing worksheet, and then type the first cell in the range of cells where you want to locate the PivotTable report.

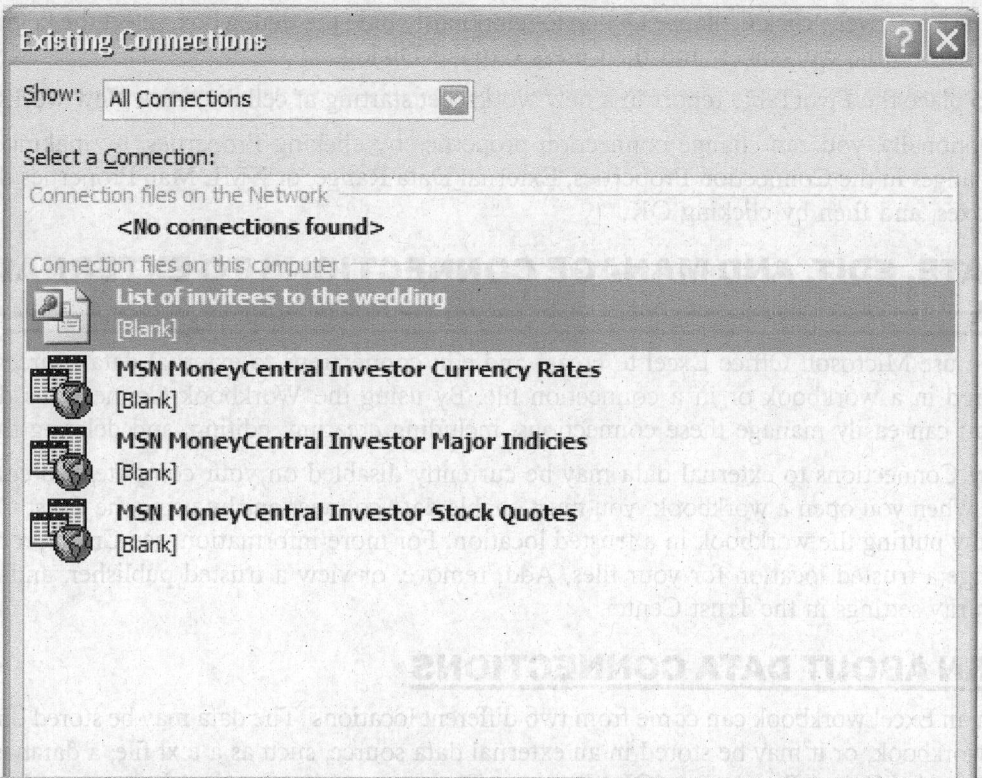
Existing Connections
Show:
All Connections
Select a Connection:
Connection files on the Network
<No connections found>
Connection files on this computer
List of invitees to the wedding
[Blank]
MSN MoneyCentral Investor Currency Rates
[Blank]
MSN MoneyCentral Investor Major Indicies
[Blank]
MSN MoneyCentral Investor Stock Quotes
[Blank]

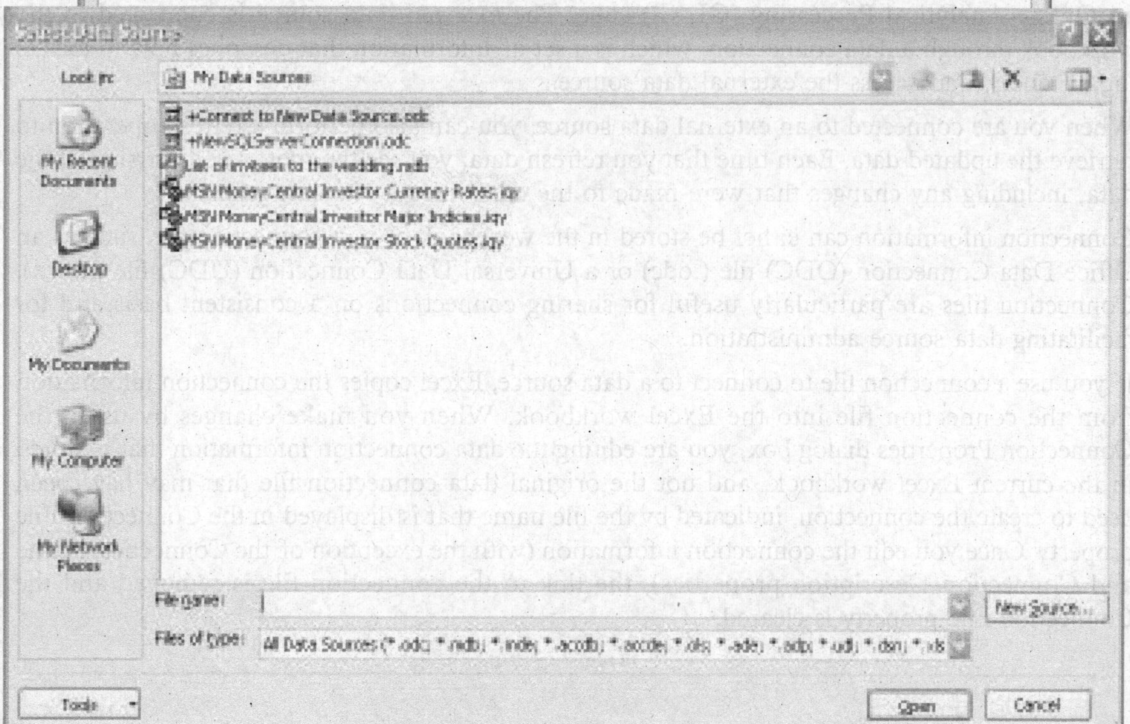
Select Data Source
Look in:
My Data Sources
+Connect to New Data Source.odc
+NewSQLServerConnection.odc
List of invitees to the wedding.odc
MSN MoneyCentral Investor Currency Rates.iqy
MSN MoneyCentral Investor Major Indicies.iqy
MSN MoneyCentral Investor Stock Quotes.iqy
My Recent Documents
Desktop
My Documents
My Computer
My Network Places
File name:
New Source...
Files of type:
Tools
Open
Cancel

Alternatively, click Collapse Dialog to temporarily hide the dialog box, select the beginning cell on the worksheet, and then press Expand Dialog.

6. To place the PivotTable report in a new worksheet starting at cell A1, click New worksheet.
7. Optionally, you can change connection properties by clicking Properties, by making your changes in the Connection Properties, External Data Range, or XML Map Properties dialog boxes, and then by clicking OK.

CREATE, EDIT, AND MANAGE CONNECTIONS TO EXTERNAL DATA

You can use Microsoft Office Excel to create and edit connections to external data sources that are stored in a workbook or in a connection file. By using the Workbook Connections dialog box, you can easily manage these connections, including creating, editing, and deleting them.

Security Connections to external data may be currently disabled on your computer. To connect to data when you open a workbook, you must enable data connections by using the Trust Center bar, or by putting the workbook in a trusted location. For more information, see Create, remove, or change a trusted location for your files, Add, remove, or view a trusted publisher, and View my security settings in the Trust Center.

LEARN ABOUT DATA CONNECTIONS

Data in an Excel workbook can come from two different locations. The data may be stored directly in the workbook, or it may be stored in an external data source, such as a text file, a database, or an Online Analytical Processing (OLAP) cube. The external data source is connected to the workbook through a data connection, which is a set of information that describes how to locate, log in, query, and access the external data source.

When you are connected to an external data source, you can also perform a refresh operation to retrieve the updated data. Each time that you refresh data, you see the most recent version of the data, including any changes that were made to the data since it was last refreshed.

Connection information can either be stored in the workbook or in a connection file, such as an Office Data Connection (ODC) file (.odc) or a Universal Data Connection (UDC) file (.udcx). Connection files are particularly useful for sharing connections on a consistent basis and for facilitating data source administration.

If you use a connection file to connect to a data source, Excel copies the connection information from the connection file into the Excel workbook. When you make changes by using the Connection Properties dialog box, you are editing the data connection information that is stored in the current Excel workbook, and not the original data connection file that may have been used to create the connection, indicated by the file name that is displayed in the Connection File property. Once you edit the connection information (with the exception of the Connection Name and Connection Description properties), the link to the connection file is removed and the Connection File property is cleared.

MANAGE CONNECTIONS BY USING THE WORKBOOK CONNECTIONS DIALOG BOX

The Workbook Connections dialog box helps you manage one or more connections to external data sources in your workbook. You can use this dialog box to do the following:

- Create, edit, refresh, and delete connections that are in use in the workbook.
- Verify where external data is coming from, because, for example, the connection was defined by another user.
- Show where each connection is used in the current workbook.
- Diagnose an error message about connections to external data.
- Redirect a connection to a different server or data source, or replace the connection file for an existing connection.
- Display the Existing Connections dialog box to create new connections.
- Display the Connection Properties dialog box to modify data connection properties, edit queries, and change parameters.
- Make it easy to create and share connection files with users.

To manage the connections in the current workbook, do one or more of the following:

Identify a connection

In the top portion of the dialog box, all connections in the workbook are displayed automatically with the following information:

Column	Comment
Name	The name of the connection, defined in the Connection Properties dialog box.
Description	An optional description of the connection, defined in the Connection Properties dialog box.
Last refreshed	The date and time that the connection was last successfully refreshed. If blank, then the connection has never been refreshed.

Add a connection

- Click Add to display the Existing Connections dialog box.

Display connection information

- Select a connection, and then click Properties to display the Connection Properties dialog box.

Refresh the external data

- Click the arrow next to Refresh, and then do one of the following:
- To refresh specific connections, select one or more connections, and then click Refresh.
- To refresh all connections in the workbook, clear all connections, and then click Refresh All.

- To get status information about a refresh operation, select one or more connections, and then click Refresh Status.
- To stop the current refresh operation, click Cancel Refresh.

Remove one or more connections

- Select one or more connections to be removed from the workbook, and then click Remove.
- This button is disabled when the workbook is protected or an object, such as a PivotTable report, that uses the connection is protected.
- Removing a connection only removes the connection and does not remove any object or data from the workbook.

  Removing a connection breaks the connection to the data source and may cause unintended consequences, such as different formula results and possible problems with other Excel features.

Display the locations of one or more connections in the workbook

- Select one or more connections, and then under Locations where connections are used in this workbook, click the link Click here to see where the selected connections are used.

The following information is displayed.

Column	Comment
Sheet	The worksheet where the connection is used.
Name	The Excel query name.
Location	The reference to a cell, range, or object.
Value	The value of a cell, or blank for a range of cells.
Formula	The formula of a cell, or for a range of cells.

Selecting another connection at the top of the dialog box clears the display of the current information.

CREATE AN OFFICE DATA CONNECTION (ODC) FILE

By using the Connection Properties dialog box or the Data Connection Wizard, you can use Excel to create an Office Data Connection (ODC) file (.odc).

Do one of the following:

- Create a new connection to the data source. For more information, see the following help topics:
- Exchange (copy, import, export) data between Excel and Access
- Import or export text files
- Connect to (import) an OLAP database
- Use an existing connection.

Save the connection information to a connection file by clicking Export Connection File on the

Definition tab of the Connection Properties dialog box to display the File Save dialog box, and then save the current connection information to an ODC file.

IMPORT OR EXPORT TEXT FILES

There are two ways to import data from a text file by using Microsoft Office Excel: You can open the text file in Excel, or you can import the text file as an external data range (external data range: A range of data that is brought into a worksheet but that originates outside of Excel, such as in a database or text file. In Excel, you can format the data or use it in calculations as you would any other data.). To export data from Excel to a text file, use the Save As command.

There are two commonly used text file formats:

- Delimited text files (.txt), in which the TAB character (ASCII character code 009) usually separates each field of text.
- Comma separated values text files (.csv), in which the comma character (,) usually separates each field of text.

You can change the separator character that is used in both delimited and .csv text files. This may be necessary to make sure that the import or export operation works the way that you want it to.

Notes

- You can import or export up to 1,048,576 rows and 16,384 columns.
- Whether you are importing or exporting, you may want to learn more about Excel text converters.

CONNECTION PROPERTIES

Use the Connection Properties dialog box to control various settings for connections to external data sources, and to use, reuse, or switch connection files.

Security Connections to external data may be currently disabled on your computer. To connect to data when you open a workbook, you must enable data connections by using the Trust Center bar, or by putting the workbook in a trusted location. For more information, see Create, remove, or change a trusted location for your files, Add, remove, or view a trusted publisher, and View my security settings in the Trust Center.

Connection Name and Description Displays the connection name and optional description. To change the name and description, click the text in the box, and then edit the text. The connection name and description are displayed in the Workbook Connections dialog box. (On the Data tab, in the Connections group, click Connections.)

Note The connection name and description are stored in a Microsoft Office Excel workbook only, and they cannot be saved to a connection file.

Usage

The settings on the Usage tab control the way that the connection information is used in the workbook.

REFRESH CONTROL

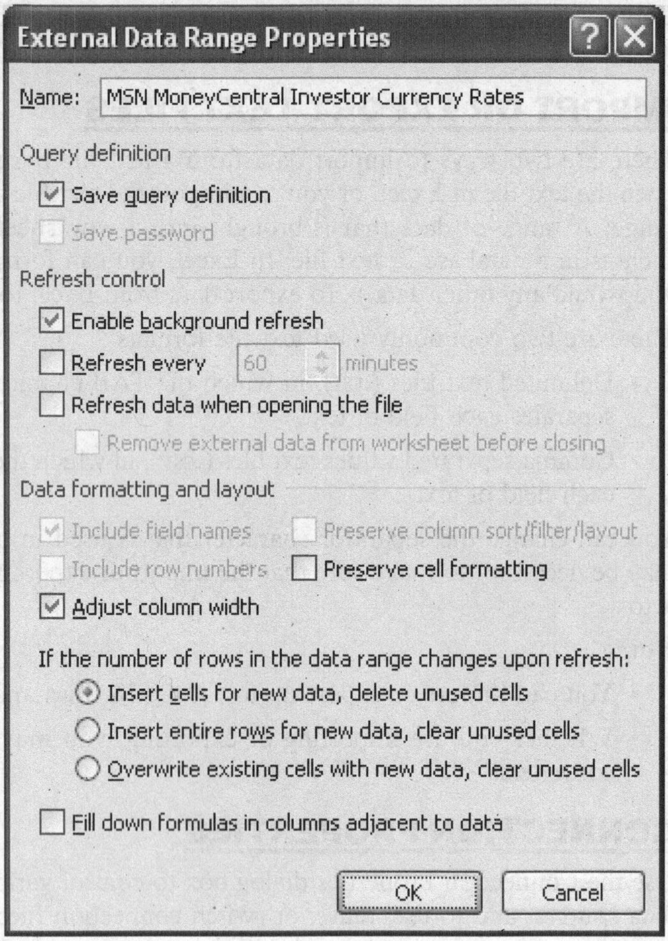

Enable background refresh

Select this check box to run the query in the background. Clear this check box to run the query while you wait. Running a query in the background enables you to use Excel while the query runs.

Refresh every n minutes

Select this check box to enable automatic external data refresh at regular time intervals, and then enter the number of minutes between each refresh operation. Clear this check box to disable automatic external data refresh.

Refresh data when opening the file

Select this check box to automatically refresh external data when you open the workbook. Clear this check box to immediately open the workbook without refreshing external data.

Remove data from the external data range before saving the workbook

Select this check box if you want to save the workbook with the query definition but without the external data. Clear this check box to save the query definition and data with the workbook. This check box becomes available only after you select the Refresh data when opening the file check box.

OLAP Server Formatting

Controls whether the following OLAP server formats are retrieved from the server and are displayed with the data.

Number Format

Select or clear this check box to enable or disable number formatting, such as currency, date, or time.

Font Style

Select or clear this check box to enable or disable font styles, such as bold, italic, underline, or strike-through.

Fill Color

Select or clear this check box to enable or disable fill colors.

Text Color

Select or clear this check box to enable or disable text colors.

OLAP Drill Through

Maximum number of records to retrieve Enter a number from 1 to 10,000 to specify the maximum number of records to retrieve when you expand a level of data in a hierarchy.

Language

Retrieve data and errors in the Office display language when available Select or clear this check box to enable or disable the retrieval of translated data and errors, if any, from the OLAP server.

Definition

The settings on the Definition tab control how the connection information is defined and the source of the connection information, either the workbook or a connection file.

Connection type

Displays the type of connection that is used, such as Office Data Connection or Microsoft Office Access Database.

Connection file

Displays the current connection file that is used to store the connection information and enables switching to a revised or new connection file. If this field is blank, a connection file was never used, or it was used and then modified so that the link to the connection file was broken.

To re-establish the link to the connection file, for example because it was updated and you want to use the new version, or to change the current connection and use a different connection file, click Browse, which displays the Select Data Source dialog box of the Data Connection Wizard. You can then select the revised connection file, a different connection file, or create a new connection file by clicking New Source.

Make sure that the new connection file is consistent with the object that has the data connection. You can change the connection, but you cannot switch connections between the following objects:

- An OLAP PivotTable or PivotChart report
- A non-OLAP PivotTable or PivotChart report
- An Excel table
- A text file
- An XML table
- A Web query to a Web page

Always use connection file Select this check box to ensure that the most up-to-date version of the connection file is always used whenever the data is displayed or refreshed. Clear this check box to use the connection information in the Excel workbook.

If the connection file is not available, Excel resorts to the connection information that is saved in the workbook. If you want to ensure that the most up-to-date version of the connection file is always used, make sure that the connection file is accessible and available.

Connection string

Displays the current connection information in the form of a connection string. Use a connection string to verify all of the connection information and to edit specific connection information that you cannot change through the Connection Properties dialog box.

Save password

Select this check box to save the username and password (password: A way to restrict access to a workbook, worksheet, or part of a worksheet. Excel passwords can be up to 255 letters, numbers, spaces, and symbols. You must type uppercase and lowercase letters correctly when you set and enter passwords.) in the connection file. The saved password is not encrypted. Clear this check box to log on to the data source, if a user name and password are required, the first time that you access it. This check box does not apply to data retrieved from a text file or a Web query.

Security

Avoid saving logon information when connecting to data sources. This information may be stored as plain text, and a malicious user could access the information to compromise the security of the data source.

Command type Select one of the following command types:

- SQL
- Table
- Default

Command text

Displays the name of the command type. To change the command text, click the text in the box and then edit the text.

Excel Services

Authentication settings Click this button to display the Excel Services Authentication Settings dialog box and to choose a method of authentication when you access the data source that is connected to a workbook and that is displayed in Excel Services. Select one of the following options to log on to the data source:

- Windows Authentication Select this option to use the Windows user name and password of the current user. This is the most secure method, but it can impact performance when there are many users.
- SSO Select this option to use Single Sign On, and then enter the appropriate identification string in the SSO ID text box. A site administrator can configure a SharePoint site to use a Single Sign On database where a user user name and password can be stored. This method can be the most efficient when there are many users.
- None Select this option to save the username and password in the connection file.

Security

Avoid saving logon information when connecting to data sources. This information may be stored as plain text, and a malicious user could access the information to compromise the security of the data source.

The authentication setting is only used by Excel Services, and not by Microsoft Office Excel. If you want to ensure that the same data is accessed whether you open the workbook in Excel or Excel Services, make sure that the authentication setting in Excel is the same.

Edit Query

Click this button to change the query that is used to retrieve data from the data source. Depending on the type of data source, displays one of the following:

- The Data Connection Wizard for an Office Data Connection (ODC) file (.odc) OLEDB connection.
- Microsoft Query for an ODBC connection.
- The Edit Web Query dialog box for a Web page.
- The Text Import Wizard for a text file.

You cannot edit the query if the connection information is currently linked to a connection file.

Parameters

Click this button to display the Parameters dialog box and to edit Parameter information for a Microsoft Query or Web Query connection.

Export Connection File

Click this button to display the File Save dialog box and to save the current connection information to a connection file.

Always Use Connection File

Avoid saving logon information command text command type Connection Description Connection file Connection Name connection properties connection string CONNECTION TYPE Data connection wizard default definition edit query Enable background refresh Excel Services: Authentication settings excel table Export Connection File External Data Sources fill color font style language Manage Connections dialog box Microsoft Query for an ODBC connection. non-OLAP PivotTable or PivotChart report number format OLAP Drill Through OLAP PivotTable or PivotChart report OLAP Server Formatting parameters refresh control Refresh data when opening the file Refresh every n minutes Remove external data from query table before saving worksheet save password security Single Sign On sql SSO switch connection files. table text color text file The Edit Web Query dialog box for a Web page. The Text Import Wizard for a text file. Trust Center bar trusted location usage web query windows authentication xl XML table.

Review Questions

1. How would you create a hyperlink?
2. How would you change the appearance of Hyperlink Text?
3. Describe the process of deleting a hyperlink.
4. Describe the method of creating a drop-down list from a range of cells.
5. Describe the method of connecting to an External Data.
6. How would you create, edit and manage connections to external data?
7. Describe the method of managing connections by using the Workbook Connections dialog box.

8

Functions in Microsoft Excel 2010

INTRODUCTION

Functions play important part in Microsoft Excel 2010 since they can be called upon to perform from anywhere in the worksheet.

DATABASE FUNCTIONS

Common Variables	
Database	Indicates the range of cells that make up the database list. The range of cells is considered a database list when the first row contains the labels for the columns and the columns contain the fields of data. The database table can be referenced as a range of cells or as a named range.
Field	Indicates the column within the database table that is used by the function. The column reference can either refer to the column name specified in double quotes.
Criteria	Indicates a reference to the range of cells that contains the conditions that need to be met before the function can be applied. Only the cells within the list that match the specified criteria are used by the function.

Function	DAVERAGE
Syntax	**=DAVERAGE(Database, Field, Criteria)**
Description	Returns the average of selected database entries.
Function	DCOUNT
Syntax	**=DCOUNT(Database, Field, Criteria)**
Description	Counts the cells that contain numbers in a particular field of records that match specified criteria in a database.
Function	DCOUNTA

Syntax	**=DCOUNTA(Database, Field, Criteria)**
Description	Counts non blank cells in a particular field of records that match specified criteria in a database.
Function	DGET
Syntax	**=DGET(Database, Field, Criteria)**
Description	Extracts a single record from a database that matches the specified criteria.
Function	DMAX
Syntax	**=DMAX(Database, Field, Criteria)**
Description	Returns the maximum value from selected database entries.
Function	DMIN
Syntax	**=DMIN(Database, Field, Criteria)**
Description	Returns the minimum value from selected database entries.
Function	DPRODUCT
Syntax	**=DPRODUCT(Database, Field, Criteria)**
Description	Multiplies the values in a particular field of records that match the criteria in a database.
Function	DSTDEV
Syntax	**=DSTDEV(Database, Field, Criteria)**
Description	Estimates the standard deviation based on a sample of selected database entries.
Function	DSTDEVP
Syntax	**=DMIN(Database, Field, Criteria)**
Description	Calculates the standard deviation based on the entire population of selected database entries.
Function	DSUM
Syntax	**=DSUM(Database, Field, Criteria)**
Description	Sums the values in a particular field for all records that match the specified criteria.
Function	DVAR
Syntax	**=DVAR(Database, Field, Criteria)**
Description	Estimates variance based on a sample from selected database entries.
Function	DVARP
Syntax	**=DVARP(Database, Field, Criteria)**
Description	Calculates variance based on the entire population of selected database entries.

Date and Time Functions

Common Variables	
Start_Date	This date must be prior to the date specified at the End_Date argument, or Excel returns an error value. You can use a cell reference that contains a date or even a calculated date from a function.
End_Date	This date must be after the date specified at the Start_Date argument, or again the Excel will return an error. You can use a cell reference that contains a date or even a calculated date from a function.
Serial_Number	This argument specifies a valid date or time value. The argument can be an actual date, a cell reference or the result of another function.

Function	DATE
Syntax	**=DATE(Year, March, Day)**
Description	Returns the serial number of a particular date.
Function	DATEVALUE
Syntax	**=DATEVALUE(Date_Text)**
Description	Converts a date in the form of text to a serial number.
Function	DAY
Syntax	**=DAY(Serial_Number)**
Description	Converts a serial number to a day of the month.
Function	DAYS360
Syntax	**=DAYS360(Start_Date, End_Date, Method)**
Description	Calculates the number of days between two dates based on a 360-day year.
Function	HOUR
Syntax	**=HOUR(Serial_Number)**
Description	Converts a serial number to an hour.
Function	MINUTE
Syntax	**=MINUTE(Serial_Number)**
Description	Converts a serial number to a minute.
Function	MONTH
Syntax	**=MONTH(Serial_Number)**
Description	Converts a serial number to a month.
Function	NOW
Syntax	**=NOW()**
Description	Returns the serial number of the current date and time.

Function SECOND

Syntax **=SECOND(Serial_Number)**

Description Converts a serial number to a second.

Function TIME

Syntax **=TIME(Hour, Minute, Seconds)**

Description Returns the serial number of a particular time.

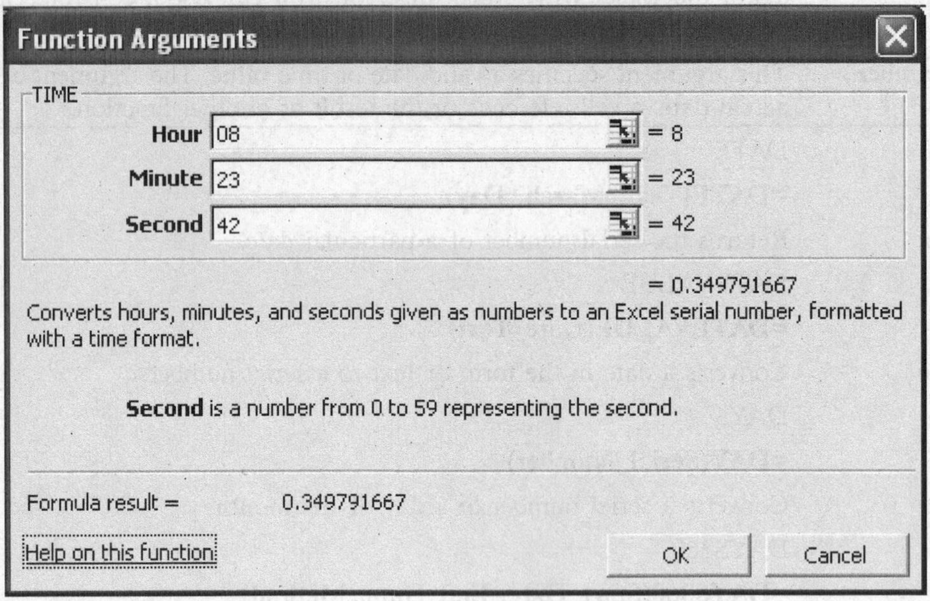

Function TIMEVALUE

Syntax **=TIMEVALUE(Time_Text)**

Description Converts a time in the form of text to a serial number.

Function TODAY

Syntax **=TODAY()**

Description Returns the serial number of today's date.

Function WEEKDAY

Syntax **=WEEKDAY(Serial_Number, Return_Type)**

Description Converts a serial number to a number that represents a day of the week.

Function YEAR

Syntax **=YEAR(Serial_Number)**

Description Converts a serial number to a year.

Financial Functions

Common Variables	
Basis	This argument must be an integer value between 0 and 4 that indicates the way the days in a month and year are counted.
Frequency	This argument must be an integer value of 1, 2, or 4, indicating the number of times per year that interest is paid on the security. A value of 1 indicates payments made annually, 2 specifies payment made half-yearly and 4 specifies quarterly.
FV	Indicates the future value of the investment. If you take out a loan, the future value will be 0 when you make the last payment.
Issue	Indicates the date the security was issued. The date specified must be prior to the date specified for Settlement. The argument can be an actual date, a cell reference or the results of another function.
Maturity	Indicates the date when the security expires. This is the date when the initial value of the security is repaid.
Nper	Specifies an integer value that indicates the total number of payments.
PR	Indicates the face value of the security. This the value for which the security was purchased.
PV	Indicates the present value of the investment. If you have a loan, this is the loan value without interest payments.
Redemption	It specifies the value of the security when it matures.
Salvage	It indicates the amount you could sell the asset for at the end of its useful life.
Settlement	It indicates the date when the payment was actually made to purchase the security.
Type	It specifies either 0 or 1 as a value for this argument to indicate when the payment is made. If the payment is made at the beginning of the period, specify a 0, otherwise specify 1 for the end of the period.

Function DB

Syntax **=DB(Cost, Salvage, Life, Period, Month)**

where the terms are:

Cost A numeric value that indicates the total amount paid to acquire the asset.

Life An integer value that indicates the number of periods that the asset will be depreciated over.

Period An integer value that indicates the period that you want to calculate the depreciation for, such as 2 for the second year's depreciation amount.

Month An optional value that indicates the number of months in the first year of depreciation.

Description Returns the depreciation of an asset for a specified period using the fixed-declining balance method.

Function DDB

Syntax **=DDB(Cost, Salvage, Life, Period, Factor)**

where the terms are:

Cost A numeric value that indicates the total amount paid to acquire the asset.

Life An integer value that indicates the number of periods that the asset will be depreciated over.

Period An integer value that indicates the period that you want to calculate the depreciation for, such as 2 for the second year's depreciation amount.

Factor By default, the function uses a Factor value of 2 for double declining balance depreciation.

Description Returns the depreciation of an asset for a specified period using the double-declining balance method or some other method you specify.

Function FV

Syntax **=FV(Rate, Nper, Pmt, PV, Type)**

where the terms are:

Rate Indicates the interest rate used to calculate the rate for each period.

Pmt Indicates payment that is made for each period.

Description Returns the future value of an investment.

Function IPMT

Syntax **=IPMT(Rate, Per, Nper, PV, Fv, Type)**

where the terms are:

Rate Indicates the interest rate used to calculate the rate for each period.

Per An integer value between 1 and the value specified for the Nper argument indicating the period that you want to calculate the interest payment for.

Description Returns the interest payment for an investment for a given period.

Function IRR

Syntax **=IRR(Value, Guess)**

where the terms are:

Value Contain a series of numbers that you want used to determine the internal rate of return.

Guess This is an optional argument that can be used to indicate your guess as to the rate of return.

Description Returns the internal rate of return for a series of cash flows.

Function ISPMT

Syntax **=ISPMT(Rate, Nper, PV, Start_Period, End_Period, Type)**

where the terms are:

Rate The Rate argument indicates the interest rate used to calculate the rate for each period.

Per This argument needs to be a number between 1 and the value specified for the Nper argument indicating the period that you want to calculate the interest payment for.

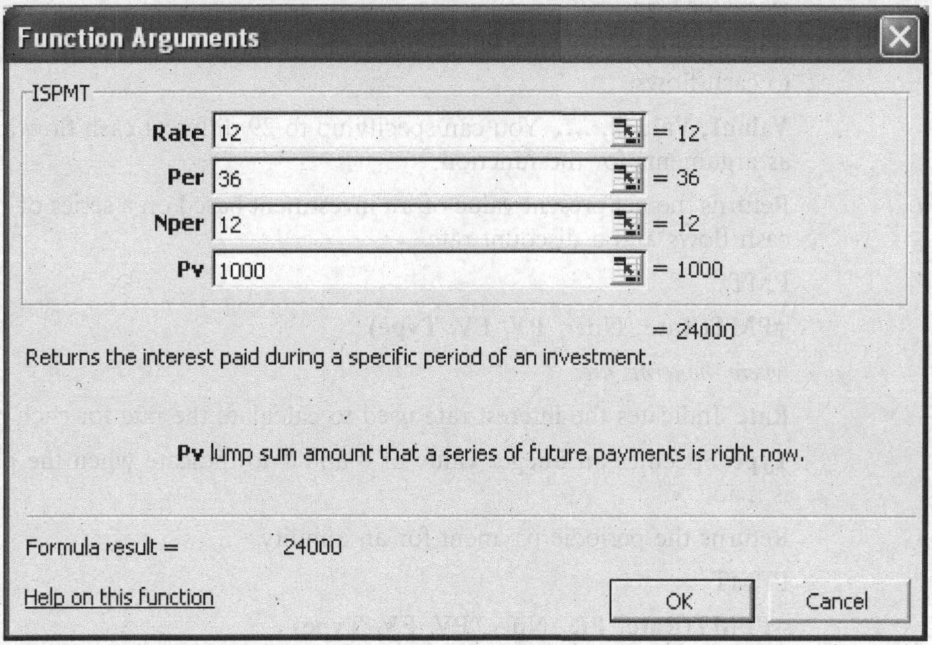

Description Returns the straight-loan payment interest.

Function MIRR

Syntax **=MIRR(Values, Finance_Rate, Reinvest_Rate)**

where the terms are:

Values Contains a series of numbers that you want used to determine the internal rate of return.

Finance_Rate Specifies a numeric value that represents the interest rate that is paid on the initial investment.

Reinvest_Rate Specifies a numeric value that represents the interest rate that is paid for investing the cash flows from the initial investment.

Description Returns the internal rate of return where positive and negative cash flows are financed at different rates.

Function NPER

Syntax **=NPER(Rate, Pmt, PV, FV, Type)**

where the terms are:

Rate Indicates the interest rate for each period.

Pmt Indicates payment that is made for each period.

Description Returns the number of periods for an investment.

Function NPV

Syntax **=NPV(Rate, Value1, Value2, ...)**

where the terms are:

Rate Specifies a decimal value that indicates the discount rate that is applied to cash flows.

Value1, Value2, ... You can specify up to 29 different cash flow amounts as arguments for the function.

Description Returns the net present value of an investment based on a series of periodic cash flows and a discount rate.

Function PMT

Syntax **=PMT(Rate, Nper, PV, FV, Type)**

where the terms are:

Rate Indicates the interest rate used to calculate the rate for each period.

Type Specifies an integer value of 0 and 1 to indicate when the payment is made.

Description Returns the periodic payment for an annuity.

Function PPMT

Syntax **=PPMT(Rate, PR, Nper, PV, FV, Type)**

where the terms are:

Rate Indicates the interest rate used to calculate the rate for each period.

Per Specifies an integer value between 1 and the value specified for the Nper argument indicating the period that you want to calculate the principal payment for.

Description Returns the payment on the principal for an investment for a given period.

Function PV

Syntax **=PV(Rate, Nper, Pmt, Fv, Type)**

Description Returns the present value of an investment.

Function	RATE
Syntax	**=RATE(Nper, Pmt, PV, FV, Type, Guess)** *where the terms are:* **Pmt** Indicates payment that is made for each period. **PV** Indicates the present value of the annuity. **FV** Indicates the future value of the annuity. **Guess** This is an optional argument that can be used to indicate your guess as to the interest rate for the annuity.
Description	Returns the interest rate per period of an annuity.
Function	SLN
Syntax	**=SLN(Cost, Salvage, Life)**
Description	Returns the straight-line depreciation of an asset for one period.
Function	SYD
Syntax	**=SYD(Cost, Salvage, Life, Per)** *where the terms are:* **Cost** Indicates the total amount paid to acquire the asset. **Life** An integer value that indicates the number of periods that the asset will be depreciated over. **Per** An integer value that indicates the period that you want to calculate the depreciation for.
Description	Returns the sum-of-years digits depreciation of an asset for a specified period.
Function	VDB
Syntax	**=VDB(Cost, Salvage, Life, Start_Period, End_Period, Factor, No_Switch)** *where the terms are:* **Cost** Indicates the total amount paid to acquire the asset. **Life** An integer value that indicates the a number of periods that the asset will be depreciated over. **Start_Period** An integer value that represents the starting of the period of time that you want to calculate the depreciation amount. **End_Period** An integer value that represents the end of the period of time that you want to calculate the depreciation amount. **Factor** If omitted, VDB uses a Factor value of 2 for double declining balance depreciation. **No_Switch** If specified, this argument must have a value of either true or false indicating the depreciation method that should be used when the value of the depreciation amount is larger than the declining balance amount.

False If you omit a value for the No_Switch argument, this the value that Excel uses.

True If you specify a value of true, Excel does not modify the depreciation method.

Description Returns the depreciation of an asset for a specified or partial period using a declining balance method.

Information Functions

Common Variables	
Number	References a numeric value. If the number is not an integer it is truncated by the function.
Value	It refers to any valid value in Excel.

Function CELL

Syntax **=CELL(Info_Type, Reference)**

where the terms are:

Info_Type Specifies one of the following text values that indicates the type of information that should be returned about the specified cell.

Address Returns the cell reference of the first cell in the range of cells specified in references.

Col Returns the column number of the reference.

Color Returns a value of 1 if negative values display in colour. Otherwise returns a value of 0.

Contents Returns the contents of the upper-left cell in the range of cells specified in references.

Filename If the file containing the reference has been saved, the filename is returned; otherwise the function returns empty text.

Format Returns a text value that identifies the type of formatting applied to the cell.

Prefix Returns a specific character indicating alignment of the text in the cell.

Protect Returns 0 if the cell is not locked, and 1 if the cell is locked.

Row Returns the row number of the reference.

Type Returns a value of b if the cell is blank, 1 if the cell contains a text label and v is the cell contains anything else.

Width Returns an integer value that specifies the column width of the cell.

Reference Indicates a reference to the cell you want to return information for.

Description	Returns information about the formatting, location, or contents of a cell.
Function	ERRORTYPE
Syntax	**=ERRORTYPE(Error_Val)** *where the terms are:* **Error_Val** This required argument indicates an error value or a reference to a cell you want checked for an error value.
Description	Returns a number corresponding to an error type.
Function	INFO
Syntax	**=INFO(Type_Text)** *where the terms are:* **Info_Type** This required argument specifies one the following text values that indicates the type of information that should be returned about the operating system. **directory** Returns the path of the current directory or folder. **memavail** Returns a numeric value that indicates the amount of memory available in bytes. **memused** Returns a numeric value that indicates the amount of memory currently being used. **numfile** Returns an integer value that specifies the number of active worksheets. **origin** Returns a reference to the top-left visible cell based upon he current scrolling position. **osversion** Returns a text value that identifies the current operating system version. **recalc** Returns a value of Automatic or Manual to indicate the current recalculation mode. **release** Returns a value that specifies the current version of Excel. **system** Returns a text value that specifies the current operating environment. **totmen** Returns a numeric value in bytes that specifies the total amount of available memory.
Description	Returns information about the current operating environment.
Function	ISBLANK
Syntax	**=ISBLANK(Value)**
Description	Returns TRUE if the value is blank.
Function	ISERR
Syntax	**=ISERR(Value)**
Description	Returns TRUE if the value is any error value expect #N/A.

Function	ISERROR
Syntax	**=ISERROR(Value)**
Description	Returns TRUE if the value is any error value.
Function	ISEVEN
Function	ISLOGICAL
Syntax	**=ISLOGICAL(Value)**
Description	Returns TRUE if the value is a logical value.
Function	ISNA
Syntax	**=ISNA(Value)**
Description	Returns TRUE if the value is the #N/A error value.
Function	ISNONTEXT
Syntax	**=ISNONTEXT(Value)**
Description	Returns TRUE if the value is non text.
Function	ISNUMBER
Syntax	**=ISNUMBER(Value)**
Description	Returns TRUE if the value is a number.
Function	ISREF
Syntax	**=ISREF(Value)**
Description	Returns TRUE if the value is reference.
Function	ISTEXT
Syntax	**=ISTEXT(Value)**
Description	Returns TRUE if the value is text.
Function	N
Syntax	**=N(Value)**
Description	Returns a value converted to a number.
Function	NA
Syntax	**=NA()**
Description	Returns the error value #N/A.
Function	TYPE
Syntax	**=TYPE(Value)**
Description	Returns a number indicating the data type of a value.

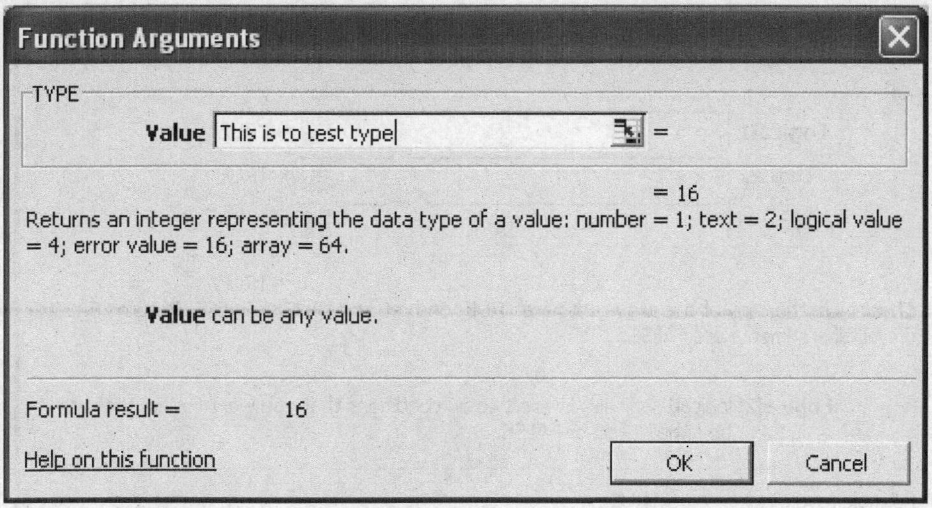

Logical Functions

Common Variables	
Logical_Text	Indicates a logical expression that can be evaluated to return a value of true or false. This expression can use any operators and functions available within Excel.
Value_If_False	Indicates the value that is returned by the function if the expression specified by Logical_Test evaluates to false. If this value is a text string, make sure you enclose it is double quotes.
Value_If_True	Indicates the value that is returned by the function if the expression specified by Logical_Test evaluates to true. If this value is a text string, make sure you enclose it in double quotes.

Function	AND
Syntax	**=AND(Logical1, Logical2, ...)**
Description	Returns TRUE if all its arguments are TRUE.
Function	FALSE
Syntax	**=FALSE()**
Description	Returns the logical value FALSE.
Function	IF
Syntax	**=IF(Logical_Test, Value_If_True, Value_If_False)**
Description	Specifies a logical test to perform.
Function	NOT
Syntax	**=NOT(Logical)**
Description	Reverses the logic of its argument.

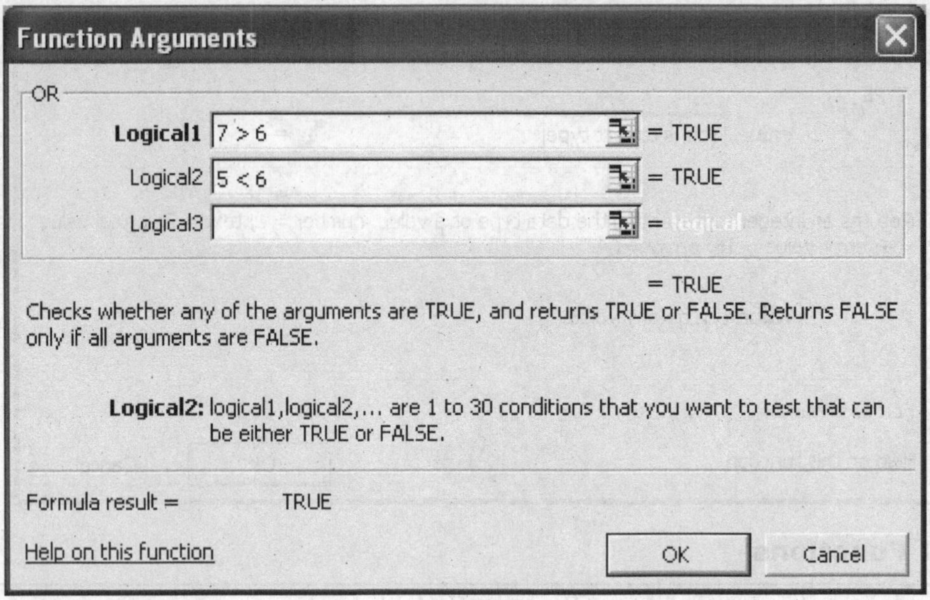

Function	OR
Syntax	**=OR(Logical1, Logical2, ...)**
Description	Returns TRUE if any argument is TRUE.
Function	TRUE
Syntax	**=TRUE()**
Description	Returns the logical value TRUE.

Lookup and Reference Functions

Common Variables	
Array	Indicates a range of cells.
Column_Num	A positive integer value used to reference a specific column. If the argument specifies a decimal value the decimal portion of the number is truncated.
Range_Lookup	An optional argument that specifies a logical value of true or false indicating the type of match you want the function to make. If this argument is omitted or contains a value of true an approximate match to the value specified for the Lookup_Value argument is specified.
Reference	A reference to a specific cell or a range or cells. You can specify multiple references by placing them in parentheses and separating each range with a comma.
Row_Num	A positive integer value used to reference a specific row. If the argument specifies a decimal value that decimal portion of the number is truncated.
Table_Array	Specifies the range of the table that contains the data that you want to locate.

Function	ADDRESS
Syntax	**=ADDRESS(Row_Num, Column_Num, Abs_Num, Sheet_Text)**

where the terms are:

Abs_Num This optional argument specifies an integer value of 1, 2, 3, or 4 indicating the type of cell reference to return.

1 Absolute reference. If the contents of the cell are cut or copied the address does not change.

2 Absolute reference for row but relative reference for column.

3 Absolute reference for column but relative reference for row.

4 Relative reference for both row and column.

A1 This optional argument specifies a logical value of true or false that indicates the style used to represent the cell address.

Sheet_Text This optional argument is used to specify the name of a sheet that you want to reference.

Description	Returns the number of areas in a reference.
Function	AREAS
Syntax	**=AREAS(Reference)**
Description	Returns the number of areas within a reference.
Function	CHOOSE
Syntax	**=CHOOSE(Index_Num, Value1, Value2, ...)**

where the terms are:

Index_Num An integer value between 1 and 29 that specifies the Value argument to select.

Value1, Value2, ... You can specify up to 29 different arguments that you want to check that can reference either a single cell or an array of values.

Description	Chooses a value from a list of values.
Function	COLUMN
Syntax	**=COLUMN(Reference)**
Description	Returns the column number of a reference.
Function	COLUMNS
Syntax	**=COLUMNS(Array)**
Description	Returns the number of columns in a reference.
Function	GETPIVOTDATA
Syntax	**=GETPIVOTDATA(Pivot_Data, Name)**

where the terms are:

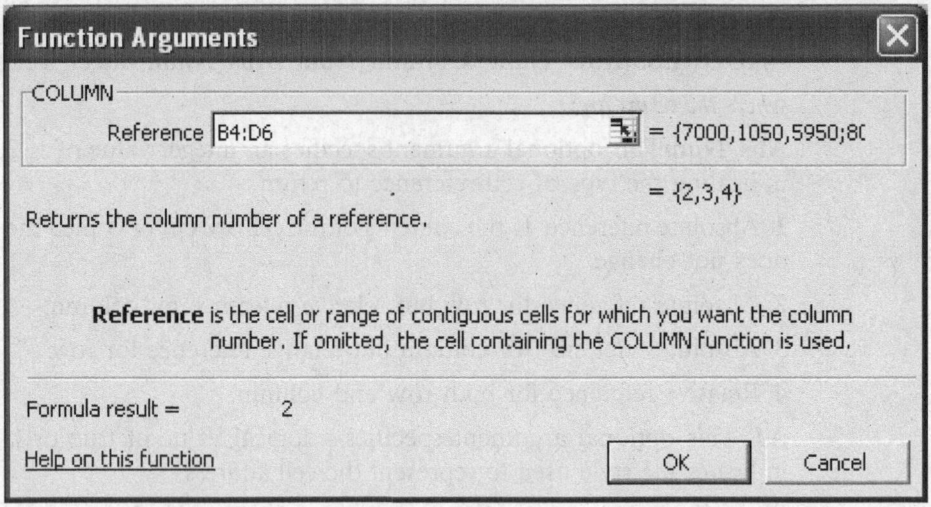

Pivot_Table A reference to the pivot table that contains the desired data.

Name A text string enclosed in double quotes that describes the data that you want to return from the table.

Description Returns data stored in a PivotTable.

Function HLOOKUP

Syntax **=HLOOKUP(Lookup_Value, Table_Array, Row_Index, Row_Index_Num, Range_Lookup)**

where the terms are:

Lookup_Value Specifies the value that should be located in the first row of the table.

Row_Index_Num An integer value that specifies the row in the table that you want to return.

Description Looks in the top row of an array and returns the value of a cell in the same column, in the row that you specify.

Function HYPERLINK

Syntax **=HYPERLINK(Link_Location, Friendly_Name)**

where the terms are:

Link_Location Indicates the path- and filename of a document to which you want to link.

Friendly_Name Indicates the text that you want to have displayed in the cell to represent the link.

Description Creates a shortcut or jump that opens a document stored on a network server, an intranet, or the internet.

Function INDEX

Syntax	**=INDEX(Array, Row_Num, Column_Num)**
	where the terms are:
	Area_Num An optional argument that indicates an integer value that specifies the range within the Reference argument that you want to return a value.
Description	Uses an index to choose a value from a reference or array.
Function	INDIRECT
Syntax	**=INDIRECT(Ref_Text, A1)**
	where the terms are:
	Ref_Text References another cell or a named range.
	A1 A logical value that specifies the type of reference specified by the cell that is referenced by the Ref_Text argument.
Description	Returns a reference indicated by a text value.
Function	LOOKUP
Syntax	**=LOOKUP(Lookup_Value, Lookup_Vector, Result_Vector)**
	where the terms are:
	Lookup_Value Indicates the value that you want to locate in a row or column range specified by Lookup_Vector.
	Lookup_Vector Indicates the range of cells that you want to search for the value specified for the Lookup_Value argument.
	Result_Vector Must indicate a row or column of the same size as the range specified for the Lookup_Vector argument that contains the values to be returned.
Description	Looks up values in a one-row or one-column vector or array.
Function	MATCH
Syntax	**=MATCH(Lookup_Value, Lookup_Array, Match_Type)**
	where the terms are:
	Lookup_Value Indicates the value you want to use to find the value in the array.
	Lookup_Array Indicates a contiguous range of cells that you want to search for the specified value.
	Match_Type An optional value of –1, 0, or 1 that indicates the type of match that should be made.
Description	Looks up values in a reference or array and returns its relative position in the array.
Function	OFFSET
Syntax	**=OFFSET(Reference, Rows, Cols, Height, Width)**

where the terms are:

Rows An integer value that indicates the number of rows you want to move from the base value specified by the Reference argument.

Cols An integer value that indicates the number of columns you want to move from the base value specified by the Reference argument.

Height Indicates the number of rows you want in the returned reference.

Width Indicates the number of columns you want in the returned reference.

Description Returns a reference offset from a given reference.

Function ROW

Syntax **=ROW(Reference)**

Description Returns the row number of a reference.

Function ROWS

Syntax **=ROWS(Array)**

Description Returns the number of rows in a reference.

Function TRANSPOSE

Syntax **=TRANSPOSE(Array)**

Description Returns the transpose of an array.

Function VLOOKUP

Syntax **=VLOOKUP(Lookup_Value, Table_Array, Col_Index_Num, Range_Lookup)**

where the terms are:

Lookup_Value Specifies the value that should be located in the first column of the table.

Col_Index_Num An integer value that specifies the column in the table that you want to return.

Description Looks in the first column of an array and moves across the row to return the value of a cell in the column you specify.

Math and Trigonometric Functions

Common Variables	
Array	An array is essentially just a listing of data that is stored in rows and columns.
Exponent	An exponent indicates the power to which a number should be raised.
Factorial	A factorial is the product of multiplying the numbers starting at 1, up to and including the factorial number.
Hyperolic	These functions are designed to work with a plane curve that is generated by plotting a series of values.

Matrix A matrix is an array of elements that has rows and columns.

Pi Pi is a constant used with calculations that relate to circular objects. It is typically represented by the symbol π.

Product This is a mathematical term that refers to the result of multiplying a series of values together.

Radians These are common method for measuring angles.

Square Determining the square of a number is essentially just taking the number and multiplying it by itself.

Function ABS

Syntax **=ABS(Number)**

where the terms are:

Number This argument is required, and must have a value that can equal any numeric value.

Description Returns the absolute value of a number.

Function ACOS

Syntax **=ACOS(Number)**

where the terms are:

Number This required argument must specify a number between –1 and 1 that indicates the cosine value.

Description Returns the arccosine of a number.

Function ACOSH

Syntax **=ACOSH(Number)**

where the terms are:

Number This required argument must specify a numeric value that is larger than 1.

Description Returns the inverse hyperbolic cosine of a number.

Function ASIN

Syntax **=ASIN(Number)**

where the terms are:

Number This required argument must specify a number between –1 and 1 that indicates the sine value.

Description Returns the arcsine of a number.

Function ASINH

Syntax **=ASINH(Number)**

where the terms are:

Number This required argument must specify a numeric value.

Description	Returns the inverse hyperbolic sine of a number.
Function	ATAN
Syntax	**=ATAN(Number)** *where the terms are:* **Number** This required argument must specify a numeric value that indicates the tangent value.
Description	Returns the arctangent of a number.
Function	ATAN2
Syntax	**=ATAN2(X_Num, Y_Num)** *where the terms are:* **X_Num** Specifies a numeric value that represents the x-coordinate of the point. **Y_Num** Specifies a numeric value that represents the y-coordinate of the point.
Description	Returns the arctangent from x- and y- coordinates.
Function	ATANH
Syntax	**=ATANH(Number)** *where the terms are:* **Number** This required argument must specify a number between –1 and 1.
Description	Returns the inverse hyperbolic tangent of a number.
Function	CEILING
Syntax	**=CEILING(Number, Significance)** *where the terms are:* **Number** Indicates a numeric value. **Significance** A numeric value that indicates the value that you want the number to be rounded up to.
Description	Rounds a number up to the nearest integer or to the nearest multiple of significance.
Function	COMBIN
Syntax	**=COMBIN(Number, Number_Chosen)** *where the terms are:* **Number** An integer value that indicates the number of items that you want to combine. **Number_Chosen** An integer value that indicates he number of items that you want to place in each group.
Description	Returns the number of combinations for a given number of objects.

Function	COS
Syntax	**=COS(Number)**
	where the terms are:
	Number This required argument must specify the radian measurement of the angle for which you want to determine the cosine.
Description	Returns the cosine of a number.
Function	COSH
Syntax	**=COSH(Number)**
	where the terms are:
	Number This required argument must specify a numeric value.
Description	Returns the hyperbolic cosine of a number.
Function	DEGREES
Syntax	**=DEGREES(Angle)**
	where the terms are:
	Angle This required argument indicates a radians value that you want to convert to degrees.
Description	Converts radians to degrees.
Function	EVEN
Syntax	**=EVEN(Number)**
	where the terms are:
	Number This required argument must be a numeric value that you want to round.
Description	Rounds a number up to the nearest even integer.
Function	EXP
Syntax	**=EXP(Number)**
	where the terms are:
	Number This required argument must be numeric value that indicates the power you want to raise natural logarithm to.
Description	Returns e raised to the power of a given number.
Function	FACT
Syntax	**=FACT(Number)**
	where the terms are:
	Number This required argument must be positive numeric value that indicates factorial you want to calculate.
Description	Returns the factorial of a number.

Function FLOOR

Syntax **=FLOOR(Number, Significance)**

where the terms are:

Number This argument must be a numeric value.

Significance This argument must be a numeric value that indicates the multiple value that you want the number to be round to.

Description Rounds a number down, toward zero.

Function INT

Syntax **=INT(Number)**

where the terms are:

Number This required argument specifies the numeric value that you want to round down to the closest integer value.

Description Rounds a number down to the nearest integer.

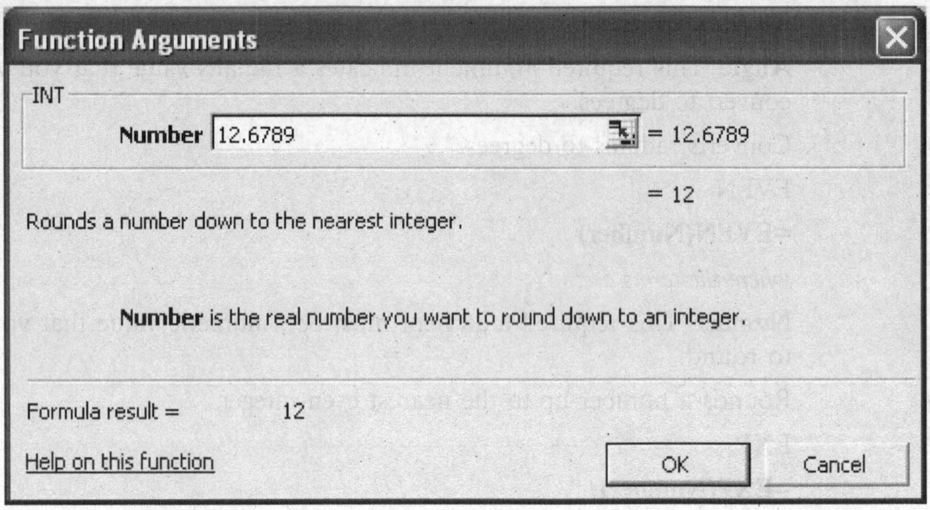

Function LN

Syntax **=LN(Number)**

where the terms are:

Number This required argument indicates the positive numeric value that you want to find the natural logarithm for.

Description Returns the natural logarithm of a number.

Function LOG

Syntax **=LOG(Number, Base)**

where the terms are:

Number Indicates the positive numeric value for which you want to determine the logarithm.

Base This optional argument specifies the base you want to use for the logarithm.

Description Returns the logarithm of a number to a specified base.

Function LOG10

Syntax **=LOG10(Number)**

where the terms are:

Number This required argument indicates the positive numeric value for which you want to determine the logarithm.

Description Returns the base-10 logarithm of a number.

Function MDETERM

Syntax **=MDETERM(Array)**

where the terms are:

Array This required argument must specify an array that has an equal number of rows and columns.

Description Returns the matrix determinant of an array.

Function MINVERSE

Syntax **=MINVERSE(Array)**

where the terms are:

Array This required argument must specify an array with equal rows and columns.

Description Returns the matrix inverse of an array.

Function MMULT

Syntax **=MMULT(Array1, Array2)**

where the terms are:

Array1, Array2, ... Specifies an array that contains only numeric values.

Description Returns the matrix product of two arrays.

Function MOD

Syntax **=MOD(Number, Divisor)**

where the terms are:

Number Indicates a numeric value.

Divisor Indicates a numeric value that you want to divide into the value of the Number argument.

Description Returns the remainder from division.

Function ODD

Syntax **=ODD(Number)**

where the terms are:

Number This required argument must be a numeric value that you want to round.

Description Rounds a number up to the nearest odd integer.

Function PI

Syntax **=PI()**

Description Returns the value of p (pi) to 15 digits.

Function POWER

Syntax **=POWER(Number, Power)**

where the terms are:

Number Specifies a numeric value that you want to raise to the value of the Power argument.

Power Specifies a numeric value that to use as the exponent in the equation.

Description Returns the result of a number raised to a power.

Function PRODUCT

Syntax **=PRODUCT(Number1, Number2, ...)**

where the terms are:

Number1, Number2, ... You must specify between 1 and 30 numeric values that you want to multiply.

Description Multiplies its arguments.

Function RADIANS

Syntax **=RADIANS(Angle)**

where the terms are:

Angle This argument indicates a degrees value that you want to convert to radians.

Description Converts degrees to radians.

Function RAND

Syntax **=RAND()**

Description Returns a random number between 0 and 1.

Function ROMAN

Syntax **=ROMAN(Number, From)**

where the terms are:

Number Indicates the numeric value that you want to convert to a Roman numeral.

Form An optional value that indicates how concise you want to express the numeric value.

Description Converts an arabic numeral to roman, as text.

Function ROUND

Syntax **=ROUND(Number, Num_Digits)**

where the terms are:

Number Specifies a numeric value that you want to round.

Num_Digits An integer value that specifies the number of decimal places that you want to round the numeric value specified for the Number argument to.

Description Rounds a number to a specified number of digits.

Function ROUNDDOWN

Syntax **=ROUNDDOWN(Number, Num_Digits)**

where the terms are:

Number Specifies a numeric value that you want to round.

Num_Digits An integer value that specifies the number of decimal places that you want to round the numeric value specified for the Number argument to.

Description Rounds a number down, toward zero.

Function ROUNDUP

Syntax **=ROUNDUP(Number, Num_Digits)**

where the terms are:

Number Specifies a numeric value that you want to round.

Num_Digits An integer value that specifies the number of decimal places that you want to round the numeric value specified for the Number argument to.

Description Rounds a number up, away from zero.

Function SIGN

Syntax **=SIGN(Number)**

where the terms are:

Number This required argument must specify a numeric value.

Description Returns the sign of a number.

Function SIN

Syntax **=SIN(Number)**

where the terms are:

Number This required argument specifies the radian measurement of the angle for which you want to determine the sine.

Description Returns the sine of the given angle.

Function SINH

Syntax **=SINH(Number)**

where the terms are:

Number This required argument must specify a numeric value.

Description Returns the hyperbolic sine of a number.

Function SQRT

Syntax **=SQRT(Number)**

where the terms are:

Number This required argument specifies a positive number for which you want to find the square root.

Description Returns a positive square root.

Function SUBTOTAL

Syntax **=SUBTOTAL(Function_Num, Ref1, Ref2, ...)**

where the terms are:

Function_Num An integer value between 1 and 11 that specifies the function that you want to sum the list of values, as given below.

1 AVERAGE

2 COUNT

3 COUNTA

4 MAX

5 MIN

6 PRODUCT

7 STDEV

8 STDEVP

9 SUM

10 VAR

11 VARP

Ref1, Ref22, ... There must be between 1 and 29 numeric values specified as argument for this function.

Description Returns a subtotal in a list or database.

Function SUM

Syntax **=SUM(Number1, Number2, ...)**

where the terms are:

Number1, Number2, ... There must be between 1 and 30 different numeric arguments specified for this function.

Description Adds its arguments.

Function SUMIF

Syntax **=SUMIF(Range, Criteria, Sum_Range)**

where the terms are:

Range Specifies the cell or range of cells that you want to evaluate.

Criteria Specifies the criteria that must be met by the cells specified for the Range argument.

Sum_Range Indicates the cells that should be summed if criteria specified in the Range and Criteria arguments are met.

Description Adds the cells specified by a given criteria.

Function SUMPRODUCT

Syntax **=SUMPRODUCT(Array1, Array2, ...)**

where the terms are:

Array1, Array2, ... Each Array argument must specify an array with the same dimension.

Description Returns the sum of the products of corresponding array components.

Function SUMSQ

Syntax **=SUMSQ(Number1, Number2, ...)**

where the terms are:

Number1, Number2, ... You must specify between 1 and 30 different numeric arguments for this function.

Description Returns the sum of the squares of the arguments.

Function SUMX2MY2

Syntax **=SUMX2MY2(Array_X, Array_Y)**

where the terms are:

Array_X, Array_Y, ... Both arguments must specify arrays of numeric values.

Description Returns the sum of the difference of squares of corresponding values in two arrays.

Function SUMX2PY2

Syntax **=SUMX2PY2(Array_X, Array_Y)**

where the terms are:

Array_X, Array_Y Both arguments must specify arrays of numeric data.

Description	Returns the sum of the sum of squares of corresponding values in two arrays.
Function	SUMXMY2
Syntax	**=SUMXMY2(Array_X, Array_Y)**
	where the terms are:
	Array_X, Array_Y Both arguments must specify arrays of numeric values.
Description	Returns the sum of squares of differences of corresponding values in two arrays.
Function	TAN
Syntax	**=TAN(Number)**
	where the terms are:
	Number This required argument must specify the radian measurement of the angle for which you want to determine the tangent.
Description	Returns the tangent of a number.
Function	TANH
Syntax	**=TANH(Number)**
	where the terms are:
	Number This required argument must specify a numeric value.
Description	Returns the hyperbolic tangent of a number.
Function	TRUNC
Syntax	**=TRUNC(Number, Num_Digits)**
	where the terms are:
	Number This required argument specifies the numeric value that you want to truncate.
	Num_Digits This argument is optional.
Description	Truncates a number to an integer.

Statistical Functions

Common Variables	
Alpha	A positive numeric value that indicates the shape of the distribution.
Array1, Array2	Each array must indicate an equal-sized series of numeric values. If one array is larger than the other an error will be returned.
Beta	A positive numeric value that indicates the shape of the distribution.
Const	Indicates a logical value of true or false that specifies whether there is a constant coefficient in the least squares linear regression equation. If the value is false the line is forced to pass through the origin.

Cumulative	This argument must be a logical value of true or false that indicates actual form of the function. If this argument is true, the function returns the cumulative distribution function. If the value of this argument is false, the function returns the probability mass function.
Degrees_Freedom	It specifies a numeric value between 1 and 1,000,000,000 that indicates the degrees of freedom to allow for the distribution.
Known_Ys	Indicates a series of data point values for the y axis.
Known-Xs	Indicates a series of data point values for the x-axis.
Number1, Number2,	Each number argument must specify at least numeric value.
Probability	Specifies a decimal value between 0 and 1 that indicates the probability associated with the distribution.
Range	Specifies the cell or range of cells that you want to evaluate.
Value1, Value2, ...	You can specify up to 30 different arguments that you want to check for numeric values.

Function	AVEDEV
Syntax	**=AVEDEV(Number1, Number2, ...)**
Description	Returns the average of the absolute deviations of data points from their mean.
Function	AVERAGE
Syntax	**=AVERAGE(Number1, Number2, ...)**
Description	Returns the average of its arguments.
Function	AVERAGEA
Syntax	**=AVERAGEA(Number1, Number2, ...)**
Description	Returns the average of its arguments, including numbers, text, and logical values.
Function	BETADIST
Syntax	**=BETADIS(X, Alpha, Beta, A, B)**
Description	Returns the cumulative beta probability density function.
Function	BETAINV
Syntax	**=BETAINV(Probability, Alpha, Beta, A, B)**
Description	Returns the inverse of the cumulative beta probability density function.
Function	BINOMDIST
Syntax	**=BINOMDIST(Number_s, Trials, Probability_s, Cumulative)**
Description	Returns the individual term binomial distribution probability.
Function	CHIDIST
Syntax	**=CHIDIST(X, Degrees_Freedom)**

Description	Returns the one-tailed probability of the chi-squared distribution.
Function	CHIINV
Syntax	**=CHIINV(Probability, Degrees_Freedom)**
Description	Returns the inverse of the one-tailed probability of the chi-squared distribution.
Function	CHITEST
Syntax	**=CHITEST(Actual_Range, Expected_Range)**
Description	Returns the test for independence.
Function	CONFIDENCE
Syntax	**=CONFIDENCE(Alpha, Standard_Dev, Size)**
Description	Returns the confidence interval for a population mean.
Function	CORREL
Syntax	**=CORREL(Array1, Array2,)**
Description	Returns the correlation coefficient between two data sets.
Function	COUNT
Syntax	**=COUNT(Value1, Value2, ...)**
Description	Counts how many numbers are in the list of arguments.
Function	COUNTA
Syntax	**=COUNTA(Value1, Value2)**
Description	Counts how many values are in the list of arguments.
Function	COUNTBLANK
Syntax	**=COUNTBLANK(Range)**
Description	Counts the number of blank cells within a range.
Function	COUNTIF
Syntax	**=COUNTIF(Range, Criteria)**
Description	Counts the number of non blank cells within a range that meet the given criteria.
Function	COVAR
Syntax	**=COVAR(Array1, Array2)**
Description	Returns covariance, the average of the products of paired deviations.
Function	CRITBINOM
Syntax	**=CRITBINOM(Trials, Probability_s, Alpha)**
Description	Returns the smallest value for which the cumulative binomial distribution is less than or equal to a criterion value.

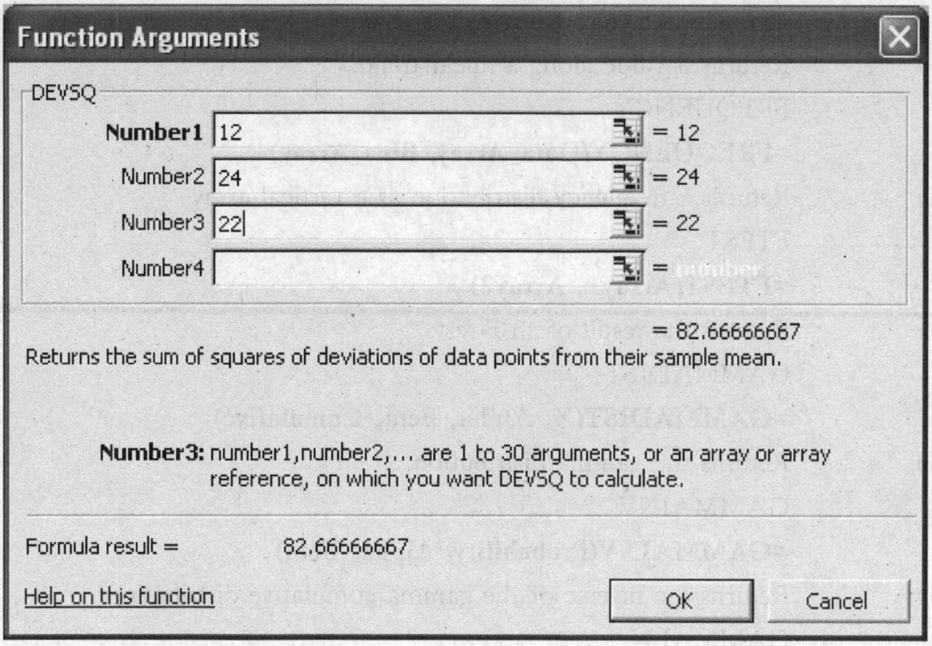

Function DEVSQ
Syntax **=DEVSQ(Number1, Number2, ...)**
Description Returns the sum of squared of deviations.

Function EXPONDIST
Syntax **=EXPONDIST(X, Lambda, Cumulative)**
Description Returns the exponential distribution.

Function FDIST
Syntax **=FDIST(X, Degrees_Freedom1, Degrees_Freedom2)**
Description Returns the F probability distribution.

Function FINV
Syntax **=FINV(Probability, Degrees_Freedom1, Degrees_Freedom2)**
Description Returns the inverse of the F probability distribution.

Function FISHER
Syntax **=FISHER(x)**
Description Returns the Fisher transformation.

Function FISHERINV
Syntax **=FISHERINV(x)**
Description Returns the inverse of the Fisher transformation.

Function FORECAST

Syntax	**=FORECAST(X, Known_Y's, Known_X's)**
Description	Returns a value along a linear trend.
Function	FREQUENCY
Syntax	**=FREQUENCY(Data_Array, Bins_Array)**
Description	Returns a frequency distribution as a vertical array.
Function	FTEST
Syntax	**=FTEST(Array1, Array2)**
Description	Returns the result of an F-test.
Function	GAMMADIST
Syntax	**=GAMMADIST(X, Alpha, Beta, Cumulative)**
Description	Returns the gamma distribution.
Function	GAMMAINV
Syntax	**=GAMMAINV(Probability, Alpha, Beta)**
Description	Returns the inverse of the gamma cumulative distribution.
Function	GAMMALN
Syntax	**=GAMMALN(x)**
Description	Returns the natural logarithm of the gamma function, G(x).
Function	GEOMEAN
Syntax	**=GEOMEAN(Number1, Number2, ...)**
Description	Returns the geometric mean.
Function	GROWTH
Syntax	**=GROWTH(Known_Y's, Known_X's, New_X's, Const)**
Description	Returns values along an exponential trend.
Function	HARMEAN
Syntax	**=HARMEAN(Number1, Number2, ...)**
Description	Returns the harmonic mean.
Function	HYPGEOMDIST
Syntax	**=HYPGEOMDIST(Sample_S, Number_Sample, Population_S, Number_Population)**
Description	Returns the hypergeometric distribution.
Function	INTERCEPT
Syntax	**=INTERCEPT(Known_Y's, Known_X's)**
Description	Returns the intercept of the linear regression line.
Function	KURT

Syntax	**=KURT(Number1, Number2, ...)**
Description	Returns the kurtosis of a data set.
Function	LARGE
Syntax	**=LARGE(Array, K)**
Description	Returns the kth largest value in a data set.
Function	LINEST
Syntax	**=LINEST(Known_Y's, Known_X's, Const, Stats)**
Description	Returns the parameters of a linear trend.
Function	LOGEST
Syntax	**=LOGEST(Known_Y's, Known_X's, Const, Stats)**
Description	Returns the parameters of an exponential trend.
Function	LOGINV
Syntax	**=LOGINV(Probability, Mean, Standard_Dev)**
Description	Returns the inverse of the lognormal distribution.
Function	LOGNORMDIST
Syntax	**=LOGNORMDIST(X, Mean, Standard_Dev)**
Description	Returns the cumulative lognormal distribution.
Function	MAX
Syntax	**=MAX(Number1, Number2, ...)**
Description	Returns the maximum value in a list of arguments.
Function	MAXA
Syntax	**=MAXA(Value1, Value2, ...)**
Description	Returns the maximum value in a list of arguments, including numbers, text, and logical values.
Function	MEDIAN
Syntax	**=MEDIAN(Number1, Number2, ...)**
Description	Returns the median of the given numbers.
Function	MIN
Syntax	**=MIN(Number1, Number2, ...)**
Description	Returns the minimum value in a list of arguments.
Function	MINA
Syntax	**=MINA(Values1, Values2, ...)**
Description	Returns the smallest value in a list of arguments, including numbers, text, and logical values.

Function	MODE
Syntax	**=MODE(Number1, Number2, ...)**
Description	Returns the most common value in a data set.
Function	NEGBINOMDIST
Syntax	**=MEDIAN(Number_f, Number_s, Probability_s)**
Description	Returns the negative binomial distribution.
Function	NORMDIST
Syntax	**=NORMDIST(X, Mean, Standard_Dev, Cumulative)**
Description	Returns the normal cumulative distribution.
Function	NORMSINV
Syntax	**=NORMSINV(Probability, Mean, Standard_Dev)**
Description	Returns the inverse of the standard normal cumulative distribution.
Function	PEARSON
Syntax	**=PEARSON(Array1, Array2)**
Description	Returns the Pearson product moment correlation coefficient.
Function	PERCENTILE
Syntax	**=PERCENTILE(Array, K)**
Description	Returns the kth percentile of values in a range.
Function	PERCENTRANK
Syntax	**=PERCENTRANK(Number, Ref, Significance)**
Description	Returns the percentage rank of a value in a data set.
Function	PERMUT
Syntax	**=PERMUT(Number, Number_Chosen)**
Description	Returns the number of permutations for a given number of objects.
Function	POISSON
Syntax	**=POISSON(X, Mean, Cumulative)**
Description	Returns the Poisson distribution.
Function	PROB
Syntax	**=PROB(X_Range, Prob_Range, Lower_Limit, Upper_Limit)**
Description	Returns the probability that values in a range are between two limits.
Function	QUARTILE
Syntax	**=QUARTILE(Array, Quart)**
Description	Returns the quartile of a data set.
Function	RANK

Syntax	**=RANK(Number, Ref, Order)**
Description	Returns the rank of a number in a list of numbers.
Function	RSQ
Syntax	**=RSQ(Known_Y's, Known-X's)**
Description	Returns the square of the Pearson product moment correlation coefficient.
Function	SKEW
Syntax	**=SKEW(Number1, Number2, ...)**
Description	Returns the skewness of a distribution.
Function	SLOPE
Syntax	**=SLOPE(Known_Y's, Known-X's)**
Description	Returns the slope of the linear regression line.
Function	SMALL
Syntax	**=SMALL(Array, K)**
Description	Returns the kth smallest value in a data set.
Function	STANDARDIZE
Syntax	**=STANDARDIZE(X, Mean, Standar_Dev)**
Description	Returns a normalized value.
Function	STDEV
Syntax	**=STDEV(Number1, Number2, ...)**
Description	Estimates standard deviation based on a sample.
Function	STDEVA
Syntax	**=STDEVA(Value1, Value2, ...)**
Description	Estimates standard deviation based on a sample, including numbers, text, and logical values.
Function	STDEVP
Syntax	**=STDEVP(Number1, Number2, ...)**
Description	Calculates standard deviation based on the entire population.
Function	STDEVPA
Syntax	**=STDEVPA(Value1, Value2, ...)**
Description	Calculates standard deviation based on the entire population, including numbers, text, and logical values.
Function	STEYX
Syntax	**=STEYX(Known_Y's, Known_X's)**
Description	Returns the standard error of the predicted y- value for each x in the regression.

Function	TDIST
Syntax	**=TDIST(X, Degrees_Freedom, Tails)**
Description	Returns the Student's t-distribution.
Function	TINV
Syntax	**=TINV(Probability, Degrees_Freedom)**
Description	Returns the inverse of the Student's t-distribution.
Function	TREND
Syntax	**=TREND(Known_Y's, Known_X's, New_X's, Const)**
Description	Returns values along a linear trend.
Function	TRIMMEAN
Syntax	**=TRIMEAN(Array, Percent)**
Description	Returns the mean of the interior of a data set.
Function	TTEST
Syntax	**=TTEST(Array1, Array2, Tails, Type)**
Description	Returns the probability associated with a Student's t-test.
Function	VAR
Syntax	**=VAR(Number1, Number2, ...)**
Description	Estimates variance based on a sample.
Function	VARA
Syntax	**=VARA(Value1, Value2, ...)**
Description	Estimates variance based on a sample, including numbers, text, and logical values.
Function	VARP
Syntax	**=VARP(Number1, Number2, ...)**
Description	Calculates variance based on the entire population.
Function	VARPA
Syntax	**=VARPA(Value1, Value2, ...)**
Description	Calculates variance based on the entire population, including numbers, text, and logical values.
Function	WEIBULL
Syntax	**=WEIBULL(X, Alpha, Beta, Cumulative)**
Description	Returns the Weibull distribution.
Function	ZTEST
Syntax	**=ZTEST(Array, X, Sigma)**
Description	Returns the two-tailed P-value of a z-test.

Text Functions

Common Variables	
Decimals	An integer value that indicates the number of decimal places that you want to round the number to. If this argument is omitted the function rounds the numeric value to two decimal places.
New_Text	Indicates the text string that you want to use to replace the specified characters specified by the Old_Text argument.
Number	Indicates a numeric value.
Num_Chars	Specifies an integer value that indicates the number of characters you want to return from the string. If this argument is omitted, the function returns the first character in the string.
Old_Text	Indicates the text string that contains the characters you want to replace.
Start_Num	Specifies an integer value that indicates the first character in the string when you want to start.
Text	This required argument must specify the desired text. This is a reference to specific cells or a string of values.

Function	CHAR
Syntax	**=CHAR(Number)**
Description	Returns the character specified by the code number.
Function	CLEAN
Syntax	**=CLEAN(Text)**
Description	Removes all nonprintable characters from text.
Function	CODE
Syntax	**=CODE(Text)**
Description	Returns a numeric code for the first character in a text string.
Function	CONCATENATE
Syntax	**=CONCATENATE(Text1, Text2, ...)**
Description	Joins several text items into one text item.
Function	DOLLAR
Syntax	**=DOLLAR(Number, Decimals)**
Description	Converts a number to text, using currency format.
Function	EXACT
Syntax	**=EXACT(Text1, Text2)**
Description	Checks to see if two text values are identical.
Function	FIND

Syntax	**=FIND(Find_Text, Within_Text, Start_Num)**
Description	Finds one text value within another (case-sensitive).
Function	FIXED
Syntax	**=FIXED(Numbers, Decimals, No_Commas)**
Description	Formats a number as text values are identical.
Function	LEFT
Syntax	**=LEFT(Text, Num_Chars)**
Description	Returns the leftmost characters from a text value.

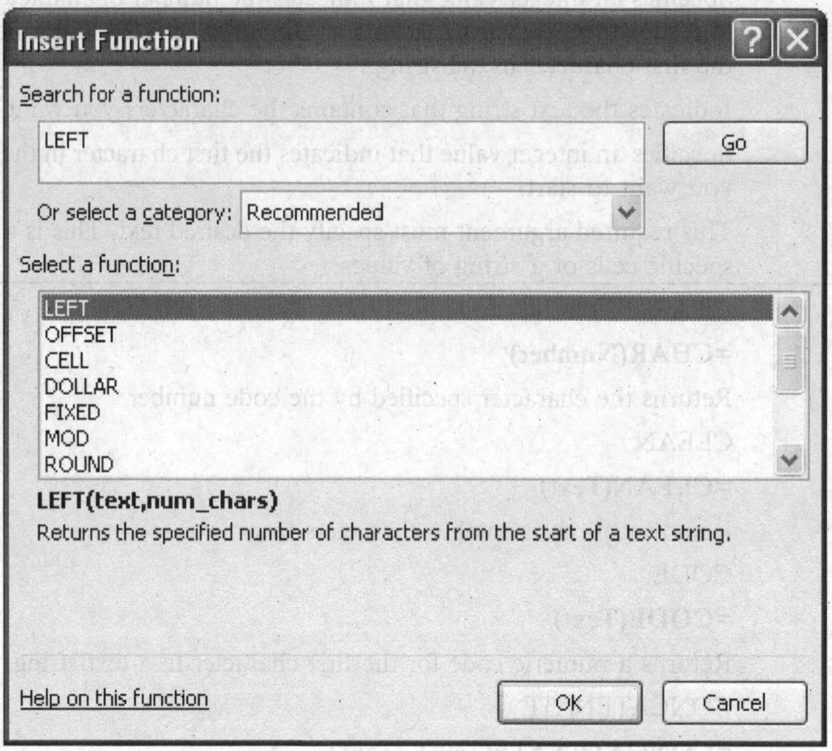

Function	LEN
Syntax	**=LEN(Text)**
Description	Returns the number of characters in a text string.
Function	LOWER
Syntax	**=LOWER(Text)**
Description	Converts text to lowercase.
Function	MID
Syntax	**=MID(Text, Start_Num, Num_Chars)**

Description	Returns a specific number of characters from a text string starting at the position you specify.
Function	PROPER
Syntax	**=PROPER(Text)**
Description	Capitalizes the first letter in each word of a text value.
Function	REPLACE
Syntax	**=REPLACE(Old_Text, Start_Num, New_Text)**
Description	Replaces characters within text.
Function	REPT
Syntax	**=REPT(Text, Number_Times)**
Description	Repeats text a given number of times.
Function	RIGHT
Syntax	**=RIGHT(Text, Num_Chars)**
Description	Returns the rightmost characters from a text value.
Function	SEARCH
Syntax	**=SEARCH(Find_Text, Within_Text, Start_Num)**
Description	Finds one text value within another (not case-sensitive).
Function	SUBSTITUTE
Syntax	**=SUBSTITUTE(Text, Old_Text, New_Text, Instance_Num)**
Description	Substitutes new text for old text in a text string.
Function	T
Syntax	**=T(Value)**
Description	Converts its arguments to text.
Function	TEXT
Syntax	**=TEXT(Value, Format_Text)**
Description	Formats a number and converts it to text.
Function	TRIM
Syntax	**=TRIM(Text)**
Description	Removes spaces from text.
Function	UPPER
Syntax	**=UPPER(Text)**
Description	Converts text to uppercase.
Function	VALUE
Syntax	**=VALUE(Text)**
Description	Converts a text argument to a number.

Review Questions

1. Describe the various functions available under the

Database Functions	Date and Time Functions
Financial Functions	Information Functions
Logical Functions	Lookup and Reference Functions
Math and Trignometric Functions	Statistical Functions
Text Functions.	

9

Keyboard Shortcuts of Microsoft Excel 2010

CTRL COMBINATION SHORTCUT KEYS

Key	Description
Ctrl+Shift+(	Unhides any hidden rows within the selection.
Ctrl+Shift+)	Unhides any hidden columns within the selection.
Ctrl+Shift+&	Applies the outline border to the selected cells.
Ctrl+SHIFT_	Removes the outline border from the selected cells.
Ctrl+Shift+~	Applies the General number format.
Ctrl+Shift+$	Applies the Currency format with two decimal places (negative numbers in parentheses).
Ctrl+Shift+%	Applies the Percentage format with no decimal places.
Ctrl+Shift+^	Applies the Exponential number format with two decimal places.
Ctrl+Shift+#	Applies the Date format with the day, month, and year.
Ctrl+Shift+@	Applies the Time format with the hour and minute, and AM or PM.
Ctrl+Shift+!	Applies the Number format with two decimal places, thousands separator, and minus sign (-) for negative values.
Ctrl+Shift+*	Selects the current region around the active cell (the data area enclosed by blank rows and blank columns). In a PivotTable, it selects the entire PivotTable report.
Ctrl+Shift+:	Enters the current time.
Ctrl+Shift+"	Copies the value from the cell above the active cell into the cell or the Formula Bar.
Ctrl+Shift+Plus (+)	Displays the Insert dialog box to insert blank cells.
Ctrl+Minus (-)	Displays the Delete dialog box to delete the selected cells.

Ctrl+;	Enters the current date.
Ctrl+‘	Alternates between displaying cell values and displaying formulas in the worksheet.
Ctrl+’	Copies a formula from the cell above the active cell into the cell or the Formula Bar.
Ctrl+1	Displays the Format Cells dialog box.
Ctrl+2	Applies or removes bold formatting.
Ctrl+3	Applies or removes italic formatting.
Ctrl+4	Applies or removes underlining.
Ctrl+5	Applies or removes strikethrough.
Ctrl+6	Alternates between hiding objects, displaying objects, and displaying placeholders for objects.
Ctrl+8	Displays or hides the outline symbols.
Ctrl+9	Hides the selected rows.
Ctrl+0	Hides the selected columns.
Ctrl+A	Selects the entire worksheet. If the worksheet contains data, Ctrl+A selects the current region. Pressing Ctrl+A a second time selects the current region and its summary rows. Pressing Ctrl+A a third time selects the entire worksheet.When the insertion point is to the right of a function name in a formula, displays the Function Arguments dialog box.Ctrl+Shift+A inserts the argument names and parentheses when the insertion point is to the right of a function name in a formula.
Ctrl+B	Applies or removes bold formatting.
Ctrl+C	Copies the selected cells. Ctrl+C followed by another Ctrl+C displays the Clipboard.
Ctrl+D	Uses the Fill Down command to copy the contents and format of the topmost cell of a selected range into the cells below.
Ctrl+F	Displays the Find and Replace dialog box, with the Find tab selected. Shift+F5 also displays this tab, while Shift+F4 repeats the last Find action.Ctrl+Shift+F opens the Format Cells dialog box with the Font tab selected.
Ctrl+G	Displays the Go To dialog box. F5 also displays this dialog box.
Ctrl+H	Displays the Find and Replace dialog box, with the Replace tab selected.
Ctrl+I	Applies or removes italic formatting.
Ctrl+K	Displays the Insert Hyperlink dialog box for new hyperlinks or the Edit Hyperlink dialog box for selected existing hyperlinks.
Ctrl+N	Creates a new, blank workbook.

Ctrl+O	Displays the Open dialog box to open or find a file. Ctrl+Shift+O selects all cells that contain comments.
Ctrl+P	Displays the Print dialog box. Ctrl+Shift+P opens the Format Cells dialog box with the Font tab selected.
Ctrl+R	Uses the Fill Right command to copy the contents and format of the leftmost cell of a selected range into the cells to the right.
Ctrl+S	Saves the active file with its current file name, location, and file format.
Ctrl+T	Displays the Create Table dialog box.
Ctrl+U	Applies or removes underlining. Ctrl+Shift+U switches between expanding and collapsing of the formula bar.
Ctrl+V	Inserts the contents of the Clipboard at the insertion point and replaces any selection. Available only after you have cut or copied an object, text, or cell contents.
Ctrl+W	Closes the selected workbook window.
Ctrl+X	Cuts the selected cells.
Ctrl+Y	Repeats the last command or action, if possible.
Ctrl+Z	Uses the Undo command to reverse the last command or to delete the last entry that you typed. Ctrl+Shift+Z uses the Undo or Redo command to reverse or restore the last automatic correction when AutoCorrect Smart Tags are displayed.

FUNCTION KEYS

Key	Description
F1	Displays the Microsoft Office Excel Help task pane. Ctrl+F1 displays or hides the ribbon. Alt+F1 creates a chart of the data in the current range. Alt+Shift+F1 inserts a new worksheet.
F2	Edits the active cell and positions the insertion point at the end of the cell contents. It also moves the insertion point into the Formula Bar when editing in a cell is turned off. Shift+F2 adds or edits a cell comment.Ctrl+F2 displays the Print Preview window.
F3	Displays the Paste Name dialog box. Shift+F3 displays the Insert Function dialog box.
F4	Repeats the last command or action, if possible. Ctrl+F4 closes the selected workbook window.
F5	Displays the Go To dialog box. Ctrl+F5 restores the window size of the selected workbook window.
F6	Switches between the worksheet, ribbon, task pane, and Zoom controls. In a worksheet that has been split (View menu, Manage This Window, Freeze Panes, Split Window command), F6 includes the split panes when switching between panes and the ribbon area. Shift+F6 switches between the worksheet, Zoom controls, task pane, and ribbon. Ctrl+F6 switches to the next workbook window when more than one workbook window is open.

F7 Displays the Spelling dialog box to check spelling in the active worksheet or selected range. Ctrl+F7 performs the Move command on the workbook window when it is not maximized. Use the arrow keys to move the window, and when finished press Enter, or Esc to cancel.

F8 Turns extend mode on or off. In extend mode, Extended Selection appears in the status line, and the arrow keys extend the selection. Shift+F8 enables you to add a nonadjacent cell or range to a selection of cells by using the arrow keys. Ctrl+F8 performs the Size command (on the Control menu for the workbook window) when a workbook is not maximized. Alt+F8 displays the Macro dialog box to create, run, edit, or delete a macro.

F9 Calculates all worksheets in all open workbooks. Shift+F9 calculates the active worksheet. Ctrl+Alt+F9 calculates all worksheets in all open workbooks, regardless of whether they have changed since the last calculation. Ctrl+Alt+Shift+F9 rechecks dependent formulas, and then calculates all cells in all open workbooks, including cells not marked as needing to be calculated. Ctrl+F9 minimizes a workbook window to an icon.

F10 Turns key tips on or off. Shift+F10 displays the shortcut menu for a selected item. Alt+Shift+F10 displays the menu or message for a smart tag. If more than one smart tag is present, it switches to the next smart tag and displays its menu or message. Ctrl+F10 maximizes or restores the selected workbook window.

F11 Creates a chart of the data in the current range. Shift+F11 inserts a new worksheet. Alt+F11 opens the Microsoft Visual Basic Editor, in which you can create a macro by using Visual Basic for Applications (VBA).

F12 Displays the Save As dialog box.

OTHER USEFUL SHORTCUT KEYS

Key	Description
Arrow Keys	Move one cell up, down, left, or right in a worksheet. Ctrl+ARROW KEY moves to the edge of the current data region (data region: A range of cells that contains data and that is bounded by empty cells or datasheet borders.) in a worksheet. Shift+ARROW KEY extends the selection of cells by one cell. Ctrl+Shift+ARROW KEY extends the selection of cells to the last nonblank cell in the same column or row as the active cell, or if the next cell is blank, extends the selection to the next nonblank cell. Left Arrow or Right Arrow selects the tab to the left or right when the ribbon is selected. When a submenu is open or selected, these arrow keys switch between the main menu and the submenu. When a ribbon tab is selected, these keys navigate the tab buttons. Down Arrow or Up Arrow selects the next or previous command when a menu or submenu is open. When a ribbon tab is selected, these keys navigate up or down the tab group.In a dialog box, arrow keys move between options in an open drop-down list, or between options in a group of options. Down Arrow or Alt+Down Arrow opens a selected drop-down list.
Backspace	Deletes one character to the left in the Formula Bar. Also clears the content of the active cell. In cell editing mode, it deletes the character to the left of the insertion point.

Delete	Removes the cell contents (data and formulas) from selected cells without affecting cell formats or comments. In cell editing mode, it deletes the character to the right of the insertion point.
End	Moves to the cell in the lower-right corner of the window when SCROLL LOCK is turned on. Also selects the last command on the menu when a menu or submenu is visible. Ctrl+End moves to the last cell on a worksheet, in the lowest used row of the rightmost used column. If the cursor is in the formula bar, Ctrl+End moves the cursor to the end of the text. Ctrl+Shift+End extends the selection of cells to the last used cell on the worksheet (lower-right corner). If the cursor is in the formula bar, Ctrl+Shift+End selects all text in the formula bar from the cursor position to the end—this does not affect the height of the formula bar.
Enter	Completes a cell entry from the cell or the Formula Bar, and selects the cell below (by default). In a data form, it moves to the first field in the next record. Opens a selected menu (press F10 to activate the menu bar) or performs the action for a selected command. In a dialog box, it performs the action for the default command button in the dialog box (the button with the bold outline, often the OK button). Alt+Enter starts a new line in the same cell. Ctrl+Enter fills the selected cell range with the current entry. Shift+Enter completes a cell entry and selects the cell above.
Esc	Cancels an entry in the cell or Formula Bar. Closes an open menu or submenu, dialog box, or message window.It also closes full screen mode when this mode has been applied, and returns to normal screen mode to display the Ribbon and status bar again.
Home	Moves to the beginning of a row in a worksheet. Moves to the cell in the upper-left corner of the window when SCROLL LOCK is turned on. Selects the first command on the menu when a menu or submenu is visible. Ctrl+Home moves to the beginning of a worksheet. Ctrl+Shift+Home extends the selection of cells to the beginning of the worksheet.
Page Down	Moves one screen down in a worksheet. Alt+Page Down moves one screen to the right in a worksheet. Ctrl+Page Down moves to the next sheet in a workbook. Ctrl+Shift+Page Down selects the current and next sheet in a workbook.

KEYBOARD SHORTCUTS FOR USING THE HELP WINDOW

The Help window provides access to all Office Help content. The Help window displays topics and other Help content.

To do this	Press
Open the Help window.	F1
Close the Help window.	Alt+F4

Switch between the Help window and the active program.	Alt+Tab
Go back to Program Name Home.	Alt+Home
Select the next item in the Help window.	Tab
Select the previous item in the Help window.	Shift+Tab
Perform the action for the selected item.	Enter
In the Browse Program Name Help section of the Help window, select the next or previous item.	Tab or Shift+Tab
In the Browse Program Name Help section of the Help window, expand or collapse the selected item.	Enter
Select the next hidden text or hyperlink, including Show All or Hide All at the top of a Help topic.	Tab
Select the previous hidden text or hyperlink.	Shift+Tab
Perform the action for the selected Show All, Hide All, hidden text, or hyperlink.	Enter
Move to the previous Help topic (Back button).	Alt+Left Arrow or Backspace
Move to the next Help topic (Forward button).	Alt+Right Arrow
Scroll small amounts up or down within the current Help topic.	Up Arrow, Down Arrow
Scroll larger amounts up or down within the current Help topic.	Page Up, Page Down
Change whether the Help window appears connected to (tiled) or separate from (untiled) the active program.	Alt+U
Display a menu of commands for the Help window. This requires that the Help window is the active focus. (Click in the Help window.)	Shift+F10
Stop the last action (Stop button).	Esc
Refresh the window (Refresh button).	F5
Print the current Help topic. Note If the cursor is not in the current Help topic, press F6 and then press Ctrl+P.	Ctrl+P
Change the connection state.	F6, and then click Down Arrow
Type text in the Type words to search for box.	F6, and then click Down Arrow
Switch among areas in the Help window; for example, switch between the toolbar, Type words to search for box, and Search list.	F6
In a Table of Contents in tree view, select the next or previous item.	Up Arrow, Down Arrow
In a Table of Contents in tree view, expand or collapse the selected item.	Left Arrow, Right Arrow

KEYBOARD SHORTCUTS FOR MICROSOFT OFFICE BASICS

Display and use windows

To do this	Press
Switch to the next window.	Alt+Tab

Switch to the previous window.	Alt+Shift+Tab
Close the active window.	Ctrl+W or Ctrl+F4
Restore the size of the active window after you maximize it.	Ctrl+F5
Move to a task pane from another pane in the program window (clockwise direction). You may need to press F6 more than once. Note If pressing F6 doesn't display the task pane that you want, try pressing Alt to place focus on the menu bar or the Ribbon, and then press Ctrl+Tab to move to the task pane.	F6
Move to a pane from another pane in the program window (counterclockwise direction).	Shift+F6
When more than one window is open, switch to the next window.	Ctrl+F6
Switch to the previous window.	Ctrl+Shift+F6
When a document window is not maximized, perform the Move command (on the Control menu for the window). Use the arrow keys to move the window, and, when finished, press Esc.	Ctrl+F7
When a document window is not maximized, perform the Size command (on the Control menu for the window). Press the arrow keys to resize the window, and, when finished, press Esc.	Ctrl+F8
Minimize a window to an icon (works for only some Microsoft Office programs).	Ctrl+F9
Maximize or restore a selected window.	Ctrl+F10
Copy a picture of the screen to the Clipboard.	Print Screen
Copy a picture of the selected window to the Clipboard.	Alt+Print Screen

Change or Resize the Font

To do this	Press
Change the font.	Ctrl+Shift+F
Change the font size.	Ctrl+Shift+P
Increase the font size of the selected text.	Ctrl+Shift+>
Decrease the font size of the selected text.	Ctrl+Shift+<

Move around in text or cells

To do this	Press
Move one character to the left.	Left Arrow
Move one character to the right.	Right Arrow
Move one line up.	Up Arrow
Move one line down.	Down Arrow
Move one word to the left.	Ctrl+Left Arrow

Move one word to the right.	Ctrl+Right Arrow
Move to the end of a line.	End
Move to the beginning of a line.	Home
Move up one paragraph.	Ctrl+Up Arrow
Move down one paragraph.	Ctrl+Down Arrow
Move to the end of a text box.	Ctrl+End
Move to the beginning of a text box.	Ctrl+Home
In Microsoft Office PowerPoint, move to the next title or body text placeholder. If it is the last placeholder on a slide, this will insert a new slide with the same slide layout as the original slide.	Ctrl+Enter
Repeat the last Find action.	Shift+F4

Move around in and work in tables

To do this	Press
Move to the next cell.	Tab
Move to the preceding cell.	Shift+Tab
Move to the next row.	Down Arrow
Move to the preceding row.	Up Arrow
Insert a tab in a cell.	Ctrl+Tab
Start a new paragraph.	Enter
Add a new row at the bottom of the table.	Tab at the end of the last row

Access and use task panes

To do this	Press
Move to a task pane from another pane in the program window. (You may need to press F6 more than once.) Note If pressing F6 doesn't display the task pane that you want, try pressing Alt to place focus on the menu bar, and then press Ctrl+Tab to move to the task pane.	F6
When a menu or toolbar is active, move to a task pane. (You may need to press Ctrl+Tab more than once.)	Ctrl+Tab
When a task pane is active, select the next or previous option in the task pane.	Tab or Shift+Tab
Display the full set of commands on the task pane menu.	Ctrl+Down Arrow
Move among choices on a selected submenu; move among certain options in a group of options in a dialog box.	Down Arrow or Up Arrow
Open the selected menu, or perform the action assigned to the selected button.	Spacebar or Enter

Open a shortcut menu; open a drop-down menu for the selected gallery item. Shift+F10

When a menu or submenu is visible, select the first or last command on the menu or submenu. Home or End

Scroll up or down in the selected gallery list. Page Up or Page Down

Move to the top or bottom of the selected gallery list. Ctrl+Home or Ctrl+End

Open the Research task pane. Note This keyboard shortcut does not work in Microsoft Office PowerPoint or Microsoft Office SharePoint Designer. Alt+Click

Access and use smart tags

To do this	Press
Display the menu or message for a smart tag. If more than one smart tag is present, switch to the next smart tag and display its menu or message.	Alt+Shift+F10
Select the next item on a smart tag menu.	Down Arrow
Select the previous item on a smart tag menu.	Up Arrow
Perform the action for the selected item on a smart tag menu.	Enter
Close the smart tag menu or message.	Esc

Press Ctrl+Tab repeatedly to select the toolbar or task pane that you want.

Do one of the following:

Resize a toolbar

On the toolbar, press Ctrl+Spacebar to display the Toolbar Options menu.

Click the Size command, and then press Enter.

Use the arrow keys to resize the toolbar. Press Ctrl+ the arrow keys to resize one pixel at a time.

Move a toolbar

On the toolbar, press Ctrl+Spacebar to display the Toolbar Options menu.

Click the Move command, and then press Enter.

Use the arrow keys to position the toolbar. Press Ctrl+ the arrow keys to move one pixel at a time. To undock the toolbar, press Down Arrow repeatedly. To dock the toolbar vertically on the left or right side, press Left Arrow or Right Arrow when the toolbar is all the way to the left side or right side.

Resize a task pane

In the task pane, press Ctrl+Spacebar to display a menu of additional commands.

Use the Down Arrow key to select the Size command, and then press Enter.

Use the arrow keys to resize the task pane. Use Ctrl+ the arrow keys to resize one pixel at a time.

Move a task pane

In the task pane, press Ctrl+Spacebar to display a menu of additional commands.

Use the Down Arrow key to select the Move command, and then press Enter.

Use the arrow keys to position the task pane. Use Ctrl+ the arrow keys to move one pixel at a time.

When you finish moving or resizing, press Esc.

Use dialog boxes

To do this	Press
Move to the next option or option group.	Tab
Move to the previous option or option group.	Shift+Tab
Switch to the next tab in a dialog box.	Ctrl+Tab
Switch to the previous tab in a dialog box.	Ctrl+Shift+Tab
Move between options in an open drop-down list, or between options in a group of options.	Arrow keys
Perform the action assigned to the selected button; select or clear the selected check box.	Spacebar
Open the list if it is closed and move to that option in the list.	First letter of an option in a drop-down list
Select an option; select or clear a check box.	Alt+ the letter underlined in an option
Open a selected drop-down list.	Alt+Down Arrow
Close a selected drop-down list; cancel a command and close a dialog box.	Esc
Perform the action assigned to a default button in a dialog box.	Enter

Use edit boxes within dialog boxes

An edit box is a blank box in which you type or paste an entry, such as your user name or the path to a folder.

To do this	Press
Move to the beginning of the entry.	Home
Move to the end of the entry.	End
Move one character to the left or right.	Left Arrow or Right Arrow
Move one word to the left.	Ctrl+Left Arrow
Move one word to the right.	Ctrl+Right Arrow
Select or cancel selection one character to the left.	Shift+Left Arrow
Select or cancel selection one character to the right.	Shift+Right Arrow
Select or cancel selection one word to the left.	Ctrl+Shift+Left Arrow

Select or cancel selection one word to the right.	Ctrl+Shift+Right Arrow
Select from the insertion point to the beginning of the entry.	Shift+Home
Select from the insertion point to the end of the entry.	Shift+End

Use the Open and Save As dialog boxes

To do this	Press
Go to the previous folder.	Alt+1
Up One Level button: open the folder up one level above the open folder.	Alt+2
Search the Web button: close the dialog box and open your Web search page.	Alt+3
Delete button: delete the selected folder or file.	Alt+3
Create New Folder button: create a new folder.	Alt+4
Views button: switch among available folder views.	Alt+5
Tools button: show the Tools menu.	Alt+L
Display a shortcut menu for a selected item, such as a folder or file.	Shift+F10
Move between options or areas in the dialog box.	Tab
Open the Look in list.	F4 or Alt+I
Refresh the file list.	F5

Keyboard shortcuts for SmartArt graphics

The keyboard shortcuts described in this Help topic refer to the U.S. keyboard layout. Keys on other layouts might not correspond exactly to the keys on a U.S. keyboard.

To print this topic, press Tab to select Show All, press Enter, and then press Ctrl+P.

Insert a SmartArt graphic in a 2010 Microsoft Office system document

In the Microsoft Office program where you want to insert the graphic, press Alt, then N, and then M to open the SmartArt Graphic dialog box.

Press Up Arrow or Down Arrow to select the type of graphic that you want.

Press Tab to move to the Layout task pane.

Press the arrow keys to select the layout that you want.

Press Enter to insert the selected layout.

Work with shapes in a SmartArt graphic

To do this	Press
Select the next element in a SmartArt graphic.	Tab
Select the previous element in a SmartArt graphic.	Shift+Tab
Select all shapes.	Ctrl+A
Remove focus from the selected shape.	Esc

Nudge the selected shape up.	Up Arrow
Nudge the selected shape down.	Down Arrow
Nudge the selected shape left.	Left Arrow
Nudge the selected shape right.	Right Arrow
Edit text in the selected shape.	Enter or F2
Delete the selected shape.	Delete or Backspace
Cut the selected shape.	Ctrl+X or Shift+Delete
Copy the selected shape.	Ctrl+C
Paste the contents of the Clipboard.	Ctrl+V
Undo the last action.	Ctrl+Z

Move and resize shapes in a SmartArt graphic

To do this	Press
Enlarge the selected shape horizontally.	Shift+Right Arrow
Reduce the selected shape horizontally.	Shift+Left Arrow
Enlarge the selected shape vertically.	Shift+Up Arrow
Reduce the selected shape vertically.	Shift+Down Arrow
Rotate the selected shape to the right.	Alt+Right Arrow
Rotate the selected shape to the left.	Alt+Left Arrow

Work with text in a SmartArt graphic

To do this	Press
Move one character to the left.	Left Arrow
Move one character to the right.	Right Arrow
Move up one line.	Up Arrow
Move down one line.	Down Arrow
Move one word to the left.	Ctrl+Left Arrow
Move one word to the right.	Ctrl+Right Arrow
Move one paragraph up.	Ctrl+Up Arrow
Move one paragraph down.	Ctrl+Down Arrow
Move to the end of a line.	End
Move to the beginning of a line.	Home
Move to the end of a text box.	Ctrl+End
Move to the beginning of a text box.	Ctrl+Home

Cut selected text.	Ctrl+X
Copy selected text.	Ctrl+C
Paste selected text.	Ctrl+V
Undo the last action.	Ctrl+Z
Delete one character to the left.	Backspace
Delete one word to the left.	Ctrl+Backspace
Delete one character to the right.	Delete
Delete one word to the right.	Ctrl+Delete
Promote the selected text.	Alt+Shift+Right Arrow
Demote the selected text.	Alt+Shift+Left Arrow
Check the spelling (not available in Microsoft Office Word 2010).	F7

Apply character formatting

To do this	Press
Open the Font dialog box.	Ctrl+Shift+F or Ctrl+Shift+P
Increase the font size of the selected text.	Ctrl+Shift+>
Decrease the font size of the selected text.	Ctrl+Shift+<
Switch the case of selected text (lower case, Title Case, Upper Case).	Shift+F3
Apply bold formatting to the selected text.	Ctrl+B
Apply an underline to the selected text (not available in Office Word 2010).	Ctrl+U
Apply italic formatting to the selected text.	Ctrl+I
Apply subscript formatting to the selected text.	Ctrl+Equal Sign
Apply superscript formatting to the selected text.	Ctrl+Shift+Plus Sign
Adjust the superscript/subscript offset up.	Ctrl+Alt+Shift+>
Adjust the superscript/subscript offset down.	Ctrl+Alt+Shift+<
Remove all character formatting from the selected text.	Ctrl+Spacebar

Copy text formatting

To do this	Press
Copy formatting from the selected text.	Ctrl+Shift+C
Paste formatting to the selected text.	Ctrl+Shift+V

Apply paragraph formatting

To do this	Press
Center a paragraph.	Ctrl+E

Justify a paragraph.	Ctrl+J
Left align a paragraph.	Ctrl+L
Right align a paragraph.	Ctrl+R
Demote a bullet point.	Tab or Alt+Shift+Right Arrow
Promote a bullet point.	Shift+Tab or Alt+Shift+Left Arrow

Use the Text pane

To do this	Press
Merge two lines of text.	Delete at the end of the first line of text
Display the shortcut menu.	Shift+F10
Switch between the Text pane and the drawing canvas.	Ctrl+Shift+F2
Close the Text pane.	Alt+F4
Switch the focus from the Text pane to the border of the SmartArt graphic.	Esc
Open the SmartArt graphics Help topic.	Ctrl+Shift+F1